MEMOIR OF MY YOUTH IN CUBA

ATLANTIC CROSSINGS

Rafe Blaufarb, Series Editor

Gabriel Paquette, Area Editor

MEMOIR OF MY YOUTH IN CUBA

A Soldier in the Spanish Army during the Separatist War, 1895–1898

Josep Conangla
Edited by Joaquín Roy
Translated by D. J. Walker

The University of Alabama Press
Tuscaloosa

The University of Alabama Press
Tuscaloosa, Alabama 35487-0380
uapress.ua.edu

Typeface: Adobe Caslon Pro

Manufactured in the United States of America
Cover image: Portrait of Josep Conangla; courtesy of the Conangla family
Cover design: David Nees

∞

Cataloging-in-Publication data is available from the Library of Congress.
ISBN: 978-0-8173-5892-1
E-ISBN: 978-0-8173-9076-1

In Memoriam
Christopher Schmidt-Nowara (1966–2015)
— D. J. Walker

In memory of Domingo Cabrerizo Frías,
my maternal grandfather,
who also endured this Cuban experience.
—Joaquín Roy

Contents

Illustrations

Translator's Note

The translator has added the illustrations, bracketed explanations within the text, bracketed notes, and the index.

Acknowledgments

Portions of this introduction reproduce in Spanish a part of my book originally published in Catalan on the Catalan presence in Cuba, titled *Catalunya a Cuba* (Barcelona: Editorial Barcino/Fundació Jaume I, 1988, 196 pp.), the introduction to my edition of *La Constitució de L'Havana i altres escrits* (Barcelona: Edicions de La Magrana/Diputació de Barcelona, 1986, 329 pp.), and successive variants of a study concerning the relationship between the poetry of Josep Conangla and his memoir on the War in Cuba, published in the *Revista de Catalunya*, No. 19 (May 1988), pp. 151–63; *Actes del Colloqui d'Estudis Catalans a Nord-America* (Barcelona: North American Catalan Society/Publications de l'Abadia de Montserrat, 1988), pp. 201–18; *III. Jornades d'Estudis Catalano-Americans* (Barcelona: Generalitat de Catalunya, 1990), pp. 197–208; and *Revista Iberoamericana*, Nos. 146–47 (January–June 1989), pp. 129–59. I want to express my gratitude to all the members of the Conangla family—Jordi Carulla, Josep María Fradera, Ramón Goicoechea, Josep Gomis, Pere Grases, Albert Manent, Ambler H. Moss, and Enric Ucelay de Cal—for their support in the preparation of this edition as well as for their constant support in respect to the abovementioned publications. I am grateful for the contributions of Rodrigo Garza, José María Hernández, and Kevin Taracido during the process of annotating the text of this *Memoir*, and later for the corrections of Guillermo Cabrera Leiva and Manuel Mariñas.

This English translation is based on Josep Conangla y Fontanilles's *Memorias de mi juventud en Cuba. Un soldado español en la guerra separatista (1895–1898)* (Barcelona: Ediciones Península, 1998). The original manuscript, along with most other works by Conangla, is permanently deposited at the National Archives of Catalonia (Carrer Jaume I, 33–51, 08195, Sant Cugat del Vallès, Barcelona, Spain, ancsala@gencat.cat, phone [34] 93 589 77 88).

Joaquín Roy

MEMOIR OF MY YOUTH IN CUBA

Introduction

A Biographical Sketch of Josep Conangla i Fontanilles

Joaquín Roy

Appointment with the Disaster of 1898

Josep Conangla arrived in Cuba for the first time as a recruit toward the end of 1895. A fortunate survivor of the war, he was repatriated to Spain in December 1898, but in 1905 he immigrated to Cuba, where he resided until his death in 1964. These two biographical details were shared by thousands of Spaniards who found themselves obliged by the war, by economic or political necessities, or by preference, to move to the island during the last century. Conangla's biography is emblematic of the two nations.

The event that marked Conangla's life took place on February 24, 1895, when the definitive Cuban War of Independence began, a conflict that led the Spanish government to send thousands of recruits to Cuba who were untrained, poorly equipped, demoralized, and poorly led. All of them were victims of Spain's blindness as a colonial power unable to accept the irremissible end of empire, an outcome obscured since 1824 by the illusion of a political bond with Cuba, Puerto Rico, and the Philippines.

Even today the numbers are hard to pin down. In his masterful and lucid book[1] on relations between Spain and Cuba, Moreno Fraginals, basing himself on the synthesis and interpretation of diverse sources, calculated that between 1895 and 1898, 220,285 soldiers were transported to the island in addition to the troops mobilized within Cuba. Dramatically and accurately, he called this army the largest to cross the Atlantic before the US mobilization brought about by World War II. Conangla was to be one of the last of 112,921 soldiers and officers transported to Cuba in 1895 alone. In 1896, more than 80,000 arrived on the island. Moreno reckons that between 1887 and 1899, 345,698 commanders, officers and soldiers were sent to Cuba (to take part in the successive conflicts), but only 146,683 are confirmed to have returned to Spain. The Cuban historian reasonably concludes that the difference (an elevated figure of 200,000) cannot correspond to the number of dead, disappeared, or deserters.[2] Rather, he suspects that thousands of soldiers went into hiding to avoid repatriation, and that they gladly preferred to stay in a country they did not consider hostile.[3] In addition, Moreno Fraginals calls attention to the global panorama of the "assimilation" of Spanish soldiers in Cuba, which is even more spectacular. In the thirty years spanning 1868 to 1898 (the War of Thirty Years), almost half a million civilians and more than half a million soldiers arrived in Cuba. If repatriations and deaths are added up, the conclusion is that Cuba received 700,000 Spanish immigrants, precisely in the bloodiest period of the wars of independence.

As for the economic sector, from May 4, 1895, to June 30, 1898, an impoverished Spain spent almost 2 billion pesetas[4] on that war adventure. Thus was Canovas's promise of remaining in Cuba "down to the last man and the last *peseta*" fulfilled.

Josep Conangla arrived in Cuba for the first time in 1895 as a Spanish soldier. Fortunate, in contrast to many less fortunate soldiers, he survived yellow fever, he was allowed to serve as a bureaucrat exempted from combat because of his elevated cultural level, and at the end of the war, he was repatriated to Spain. But the island had marked him emotionally, and a few years later he returned to Cuba to adopt it as his new country. There he built a solid body of work, encompassing journalism and essays; in addition, he transformed himself into the protagonist and symbol of Catalan nationalism. Among his unedited works, the chronicle of the experiences he lived through during the war stands out.

On December 27, 1958, in Havana, Conangla, elderly by now—stooped, his vision dimmed—put his signature to one volume of his projected memoir. After decades of residence in Cuba, he had already satisfied the great debt to his adopted country, yet he decided to leave proof of his sincere affection for Cuba by transcribing his recollections in what apparently was to be the first volume of his intended autobiography, titled *Memoir of My Youth in Cuba during the Separatist War (1895–1898)*.[5]

He gathered together his recollected experiences of sixty years earlier as a member of the Spanish expeditionary force in that disastrous war. At nearly the same moment, a former Cuban sergeant by the name of Fulgencio Batista was readying a plane in order to flee to the Dominican Republic. He was abandoning the presidency of the Republic just as the followers of Fidel Castro began their triumphal entrance into the Cuban capital. In this way a crucial new stage in Cuban history and inter-American relations began, besides leading to obvious consequences in the future relationship between Cuba and Spain. From then on, nothing would be the same.

There are numerous clues for understanding Conangla's ideological evolution buried in the pages of his text, which remained unedited until now. The myopia of the Spanish government is evident in its failure to understand the inevitable end of the remains of the colonial empire, the rot in the governmental power base, and the impotence of the progressive and nationalist Catalan sectors in opposing the state of national disaster. Conangla saw his life as a student and journalist in Catalonia cut off in 1895 when he was conscripted to go to Cuba, and this event marked him for life. When he returned to Spain after the 1898 defeat, he had already decided to return to Cuba, this time voluntarily and perhaps definitively. Possessed of a nearly unequaled intellectual sensibility, young Conangla preferred to declare himself a tabula rasa and begin a new life in Havana rather than remain in Spain immobilized by the increasing frustration that threatened the intellectual and political milieus of Barcelona at the turn of the century.

Josep Conangla i Fontanilles was born on September 15, 1875, in Montblanc, in the region of the Conca de Barberà, in the province of Tarragona. His house was located in the place known as *cal fuster coix* on the street where the chapel of Santa Tecla was situated. His father was Antoni Conangla i Balcells (1824–1895), a native of Santa Coloma de Queralt, and a practicing notary and lawyer in the region. He was a man of exquisite culture and strong character, who taught Josep his first letters and instilled in him the conscience of a Spartan. "Always act honorably, my son . . . !"[6] was the advice that Conangla transcribes in a margin of his memoir as the only message he received when he went to Cuba for the first time as a recruit in the 1895–1898 war. His father died while Conangla was serving in Cuba. The official denial of permission to go to Montblanc on this occasion marked Conangla for life. His mother was Dolors Fontanilles i Voltas (1847–1913).

Building upon the foundation his father had provided, Conangla continued his studies in the Colegio Provincial and in the Instituto de Segunda Enseñanza de Tarragona (1885–1890), where he earned his baccalaureate in *Letras y Ciencias*. Then, in Barcelona, he prepared to begin the course of *Filosofía y Letras*, and he even managed to complete two years in the Facultad de Derecho in 1891–1893. Logically, his professional career was to be focused on law, probably alternating a practice with his incipient political activity and the cultivation of literature. But this plan was cut short when he was called up.

At the end of 1894, it seemed that Conangla had evaded military service thanks to the high number he obtained in the lottery. He did not have to make use of the insurance policy that his father—in accord with the common practice at the time—had purchased for him in case he might be called up. But on February 24 of the following year, the so-called *Grito de Baire* was proclaimed. At this signal, the Revolución Libertadora abandoned the superficial truce guaranteed by the *Paz de Zanjón* (February 11, 1878) that had ended the Ten Years War.

This conflict had begun on October 10, 1868, with the *Grito de Yara*, a proclamation of independence issued by Carlos Manuel de Céspedes at *La Demajagua*, his sugar plantation in Oriente Province. After he freed his slaves and incorporated them into the liberation army, he denounced arbitrary government, unjust taxes, corruption, the exclusion of Cubans from administrative positions, and the absence of freedom of religion and association. Under the civil leadership of Céspedes, military operations for the independence movement were directed by the Dominican, Máximo Gómez, who organized the rebel forces to wage guerrilla warfare. In 1871, the independence fighters had been confined to Oriente Province. Gómez suggested an offensive in the western part of the island, an operation supported by the mulatto leader Antonio Maceo ("The Bronze Titan"). His impressive military victories had converted Maceo into a hero with great prestige. He became the focus of envy on the part of more moderate elements in the rebellion, who feared that Maceo would try to imitate the example of Haiti and proclaim a republic headed by himself.[7]

Gómez's plans were abandoned. Céspedes was removed from office in 1873. He took refuge in Oriente Province and fell in combat before the Spanish forces on February 27, 1874. Gómez continued the fight, but petty internal quarrels and the lack of support by exiles in the United States led to his resignation in 1876. The war officially ended two years later. Yet, while the greater part of the military leadership accepted this compromise, Maceo directly rejected Arsenio Martínez Campos's peace proposal and decided to continue the fight with the *Protesta de Baraguá*. Backed by the Cuban leadership, he decided that he would go abroad to collect funds. With authorization provided by Martínez Campos, Maceo left Cuba on the cruiser *Fernando el Católico* en route to Jamaica, and from there he sailed to New York on May 30, 1879. The so-called *Guerra Chiquita* (1879–1880) was launched in Santiago de Cuba on the twenty-sixth of August. In Kingston, its supreme commander, Calixto García, explained to Maceo that in order to prevent the appearance of racial conflict in the war of independence, it was best that he not become the head of the military sector. Nevertheless, with the aid of his brother Marcos and several friends, Maceo prepared an expedition that was to join the rebels. On August 3, shortly after landing, Calixto García was taken prisoner.

Tired of fighting, many Cubans, whether moderate or radical in their ideas for attaining independence, resolved to bet on the new formula of autonomy that revitalized solutions proposed in the first half of the nineteenth century. Autonomy was to serve as an alternative to drastic calls for annexation (converting Cuba into a part of the United States) or to a weak policy for reform without specific solutions. Members of the new *Partido*

Liberal Autonomista sought to achieve the highest possible level of political and economic liberalization, while maintaining basic ties to Spain. This plan did not achieve its goal, and the indecision of autonomist leaders left the way clear for Cuban sectors demanding independence to take the lead in deciding the future of the island. The leader who began to stand out in this connection was José Martí (1853–1895), who, after years of exile, prison, and disagreements with Gómez and Maceo, founded the *Partido Revolucionario Cubano* in the United States and from that country proclaimed his plans for independence. But at the outset of hostilities, Martí died in combat and leadership passed to Maceo and Gómez.

The new insurrection was to dispel once and for all the mirage that was all that remained of the Spanish Empire, and it provoked the North American intervention in 1898. Conangla and thousands of men classified in the *excedente de cupo* [men exempted from military service because they obtained a high number in the lottery] were called up to take the place in the Peninsula of men who had been sent with urgency to Cuba. From his initial destination of Vilafranca del Penedès, he was later transferred to Cartagena and incorporated into the *Regimiento de Infantería España número 46*. Five months later, the order came down to organize an expeditionary battalion to be sent to Cuba.

His state of mind is reflected in the first pages of his *Memoir*. After dashed hopes—based as much on pacifist sentiment as on strong patriotism, in accord with one's ideology—that the war would end soon, the order to embark for Conangla and thousands of recruits was like a hammer blow. Conangla transformed the memory of that traumatic journey into the theme of his best lyric and prose essay pages. In the text of his *Memoir*, the experience serves as a prologue to the narration of events in Cuba. He retained the last images of Cartagena in his mind and depicted them in a passage dedicated to the day of departure. Attentive readers of his poems would have noted that the version of events in poetry was present in his best collections, *Elegía de la guerra*[8] and *El meu pare y Eternal*.[9] One of them, translated by the author and inserted into his *Memoir*, reflects that moment:

I have the unforgettable picture
forever vivid in my mind:
the disorderly multitudes
that were circling the port.
. . .
Everything came to an end.
Hoarse cries

shouted out frenetically.
Then, only silhouettes
increasingly dim,

of a fluttering of handkerchiefs
moving in the distance.[10]

On December 11, 1895, the steamship *San Francisco* finally arrived in the Bay of Cienfuegos. There began a cruel experience for Conangla, who, in the port of Tunas de Zaza, confirmed the harsh reality of Cuba. These first impressions remained fixed in his mind. Bogus patriotism and the repressive politics of reconcentration could not prevent malaria, colonial myopia, guerrilla actions, and the final blow from the United States from coming together to produce the disaster of 1898.

A Modernist Poet

In Barcelona in 1904, Joan Maragall answered a letter from young Conangla, back from Cuba following the 1898 disaster. Conangla had asked him for a few words to use as a prologue to his poetic work. The leader of Catalan modernism clearly saw that the sentiments of the repatriated recruit (who recounted his passage through the war in poetry) needed a very different mode of expression in order to convey the events that underlay the images: "Many things that you have felt are too wounding to express with the holy serenity of poetry . . . and others that you have felt too much with your head prevent them from emerging with the spontaneity of song."[11]

Sixty years later the once young poet, now elderly, would build the bridge that Maragall had suggested, that is, the transition between urgent, intimate experiences (in his poems) and critical reflection on his recollections (in his essays). His *Memoir*, unedited until now, more than a chronicle of the war, is an amplification and commentary on the historical context of the poems. The inclusion of some poems (originally written and published in Catalan) round out its testimonial value while casting a new light on the author's poetic esthetic.

Conangla was admired for his work on nationalism but was not well known for his poetry. The preservation of his unedited *Memoir* on the Cuban War sheds necessary light on his first poems, collected in *Elegía, El meu pare*, and *Eternal*. The remainder of his poetry is dispersed in dozens of newspapers and magazines in Cuba and Spain.

Elegía is his most consistent and compact poetic work, as much for its monographic theme, its autobiographical aspect, the sincerity and rigor of its language, as for its color and sonority—all within the most mature modernist tradition. The provisional title was *Odes del cor*. The subtitle of its first and only edition is *Impressions de la Guerra de Cuba*. It is divided into three parts: "Impresiones," "Recuerdos," and "Reflexiones." Some of the poems it contained were published in contemporary magazines. The complete book of poetry was presented to the public complemented by a few words from Francesc Pi i Sunyer, president of "Catalunya Federal," on May 20, 1904.

If Latin American literary modernism is often circumscribed by the appearance of *Azul* (1888) and the death of Rubén Darío (1906)—although these limits are arbitrary—Catalan literary modernism[12] for practical reasons is also limited by the *Exposición Universal* of Barcelona in 1888 and the death of Joan Maragall in 1911, or it may be said to extend from 1881 up to the consecration of *noucentism*[13] in 1906. Modernism in Latin America and in Catalonia was related, but it was the product of two distinct societies. In Catalonia there were not only esthetic, but also ideological underpinnings. Like the assumptions underlying Castilian modernism, *modernisme* shared a universe tangential to the ideology of regeneration in 1898.[14] It was a reaction against the literature of the Restoration and against naturalism. It rejected everything old and obsessively defended the active role of the young. Its greatest support came from the Barcelona bourgeoisie, but it began as a movement of artistic ferment and it identified with the Catalan nationalism that precisely at that time gathered new impetus (for some critics, a foundational impetus).[15] *Modernisme* was diffused through magazines such as *L'Avenç*[16] and *Joventut*,[17] with a great variety of criteria regarding esthetic assumptions. It recognized Joan Maragall and Santiago Rusiñol as leaders and substituted the *Festes Modernistes* for the traditional *Juegos Florales*. Josep Conangla was formed in this environment.

Despite its limited circulation, *Elegía* was well received in the culture and literature pages of the daily newspapers and magazines of the time.[18] The critics and poets Carles Rahola and Antoni Rovira i Virgili discovered affinities with the work of Emili Guanyabens[19] and Ignasi Iglesias[20] (in addition to Maragall).[21] Rovira drew attention to the evolution of Conangla's poetry found within the book itself: "Compare the verses that form the principal body of the book written in Cuba six years ago with the introduction and the 'Ofrenda' written a few months ago."[22] Bo y Singla wrote in *El Pacto*: "Other colonial wars have dispensed honors and wealth. Our friend has offered a bouquet of poems. He has not sung the honor of victory nor has he wept over defeats that were perhaps deserved."[23] Carles Rahola (using the pseudonym "Panida") affirmed in *El Autonomista* that: "[. . .] there is a love and hate that beat their wings unceasingly, leaving behind a luminous wake and a red trail: love of fraternity, love of kindness; hatred of war, of evil, of everything that signifies slavery, depression of the human personality, unhappiness; hatred of hatred."[24] The Galician poet Curros Enríquez in a note published in the prestigious *Diario de la Marina* wrote that: "[. . .] deep inspiration and a tender affection for all things Cuban pulsates in his work."[25] Antonio Andreu Cabestany urged him to: "[. . .] persevere, persevere, for the cause of justice and reason will gain much."[26] Joan Maragall in the above-mentioned letter[27] that served as an introduction to his book of poetry wrote: "I am not at all surprised at his decision to see the sequence of moments his spirit endured—that will surely remain as the most intense in his life—fixed in a book" (p. 6). In a few lines he summed up the content of the poems and intuited their origin: "The danger to one's own existence, the most blessed loving bonds painfully truncated, the sentiment felt toward one's country exalted by a forced removal from it, humanitarian instincts brutally contradicted, the flower of youth crushed, what then is there in you that does not suffer, that doesn't cry out, that doesn't weep, that doesn't hope?" (p. 6).

Witness to a War

This first volume of his *Memoir* (which was the last, since Conangla lacked the strength to organize the rest, which was barely sketched out in notes and clippings in folders) faithfully reflects his sentiments during the years he was destined to be in Cuba during the War of 1895 to 1898.

This edition of his recollections respects the original version with the exception of a few minor changes in punctuation to facilitate a smoother reading. The division of the text into chapters has also been respected essentially and altered minimally to make the reading more fluid. The titles of the fragments have either been transcribed or inferred. The divisions follow the logic of the author's itinerary in his successive posts on the island, posts that coincide with some of the vicissitudes of the conflict's evolution in its political and military aspects.

Chapter 1, titled "From Cartagena to Sancti Spíritus," encompasses his impressions from the beginning of his service as a recruit to mid-1896. After his stay in Cartagena, Conangla boarded the steamship *San Francisco* ("filthy, in poor repair and filled with misery"),[28] owned by the *Compañía Transatlántica*, and arrived in the Bay of Cienfuegos, Cuba, on December 11. Transferred to the tugboat *Antinógenes Menéndez*, he finally arrived in Tunas de Zaza, on the southern coast of the island, very close to the horrors of the war. His expeditionary unit was one of many others composed of untrained recruits. General Arsenio Martínez Campos, who had retired, had received an urgent reinforcement of 80,000 men. The rebels had begun the so-called invasion march and were crossing the province of Matanzas to enter into Havana Province, ending up on January 22, 1896, by taking Mantua, the westernmost point on the island. The independence forces were threatening the stability of the Cuban economy with their attacks on sugar plantations. During the first months of 1896, Maceo had managed to corner Spanish forces in the provinces of Pinar del Río and Havana. On February 10, General Valeriano Weyler arrived with an expeditionary force of more than 21,000 soldiers. These troops, added to the volunteers and the militia, increased the number of Spanish soldiers to more than 200,000, against 30,000 rebels. Those were the days of the suicidal policy that vowed the war against Cuba would continue "down to the last man and the last peseta."

Chapter 2 of the text, "The War in Aguacate," recounts Conangla's experiences in his new post while a revival of aggressive actions was taking place, owing in part, to a change with serious consequences in the Spanish military leadership. The more flexible Arsenio Martínez Campos had been replaced by the harsh Valeriano Weyler, who would then implement his plan of reconcentration. It aimed to isolate the guerrillas by depriving them of the support of the rural population, ordered to move to small urban nuclei.[29]

Chapter 3 of the text, "The Death of Maceo and the Transfer to Havana," is dedicated to the first part of 1897, which would culminate in July with Conangla's transfer to Havana. After Maceo's death on December 7, Gómez withdrew to the eastern provinces and from there proceeded to implement systematic tactics based on guerrilla warfare.

The second half of 1897 is reflected in chapter 4 of the *Memoir*, "In the Cuban Capital." Gómez had rejected all attempts at compromise aimed at converting Cuba into an autonomous province. After the assassination of Cánovas in 1897 and the transitional government of Marcelo Azcárraga, the formation of a liberal government under Práxedes Mateo Sagasta and the firing of Weyler (whose policy of reconcentration had not yielded the desired results), the global context—for a combination of factors—inexorably favored the intervention of the United States. In the first place, North American economic interests were seriously threatened by the continuation of the war. In the second place, the incipient North American ideology of "national security" demanded that the sea route to Central America be controlled. In the third place, Cuba had always been considered a prize that ought to end up being annexed to the United States—a sentiment that was exploited by the yellow press and the sectors of public opinion that pressured President William McKinley to intervene directly. At that time *anti-yanquismo* was born in Spain, which assimilated many of the anti-British prejudices dating from the era of confrontations between the English and the Spanish crowns.[30] In this respect, it would accord with the evolution of Latin American literary modernism (with the work of Martí, Darío, and above all, Rodó in his *Ariel*).

Chapter 5 of the *Memoir*, "The *Maine* and the Disaster," deals with the crucial months of 1898. The end of the war, the negotiations for peace, and the return to Spain comprise chapter 6, "Peace and the Return." An appendix consisting of documents added by the author himself ends the book.

The text faithfully reflects Conangla's impressions and sentiments *during* the years that the author served in Cuba. At eighty years of age, Conangla preserves its youthful tone as well as that appropriate to military documents. The narrative voice is not that of an old man, but rather that of an inexperienced recruit who reveals his honest reactions to the events that were unfolding around him. In short, in some pages more than in others, it seems that the writing was done much earlier than 1958, i.e., at the beginning of the twentieth century. Numerous fragments, instead of being composed in his house in the Havana neighborhood of the Vedado in the fifties, seem to be transcriptions of notes that Conangla may have taken on the ship that transported him back to Spain in 1898. Leaving aside a language evolved throughout decades of journalism, nationalist texts of different kinds, and language suitable for his historical essays, the *Memoir* seems to be a stenographic transcription of a historical consciousness. These pages present an archaizing prose, with some extremely long paragraphs—slightly modified in this edition—including an incomprehensible use of accentuation (normalized in this edition). It seems that Conangla transformed himself, erasing all his later experience as a mature, elderly man in order to write like that fearful recruit who left Montblanc in 1895, passed through Cartagena and Cádiz, and arrived in December of that year right in the midst of the Cuban countryside devastated by the horrors of the war.

A feature characteristic of the time stands out in all the fragments: the counterpoint between the harshness of the war—which Conangla did not experience in his own flesh—and the refuge provided by journalism and literary creation. In the countryside, in the *manigua*, and in the sordid world of the reconcentration decreed by Weyler, everything is bleeding, wounding, horrific. In newspaper offices, in literary gatherings, in the solitude of his office, all is peaceful. But it is a peace absent in the reality of those years. It is a peace anxiously sought after in conversations with the very few specific protagonists of his recollections—some military men whom he considered honorable and some Cuban families who merited his respect.

The text is a Manichean narration, featuring the good and the bad: the separatist (or silenced) Cuban people and the Spanish colonial authorities. In the middle are the Spanish people, who have been deceived and some (few) professional military men who try to comply with their duty; those who truly suffer the worst consequences are the Spanish recruits. Deriving from Conangla's prose essays against colonialism and the monarchy, the *Memoir* is a description and commentary on that period. They are not recollections of an active participant in the battle, but rather a testimonial offered from within, yet one that observes a certain distance; they are notes written by a recruit who did not want to be in that country, immersed in that absurd war. Conangla represents thousands of young men who lost their innocence, their health, and even their lives in the Cuban *manigua*. The *Memoir* sets a precedent for conscientious objection—with no practical mechanisms then to request it—before this objection was converted into routine guidelines in all succeeding wars. Conangla left Cartagena for Cuba, almost murmuring the words of a *habanera*: "Farewell for duty calls me, farewell for I am going to Havana, to fight, to fight for the nation. . . it is out of obligation."[31]

As far as its literary nature is concerned, the *Memoir* is a necessary gloss on his poetry, which is unknown and unnoticed in the nationalist tradition of Catalonia due to the fame accorded his separatist writings. It is isolated from the main current of Catalan poetry due to distance and to its appearance in limited editions that, in effect, were private. This poetry is divided into three poetic manners or attitudes: descriptive, meditative, and nostalgic. In the context of Hispanic literature, Conangla's poetry included in *Elegía* must be considered as fully modernist because of its language, images, and color. But it is not a question of a merely colorist poetry characteristic of the first period of the movement in Latin America; rather it is poetry that makes use of the best techniques of the "school" in order to be able to communicate everything that tormented him at the time. Regarding its content, it is located in the camp of the early members of the Generation of 1898, a dissident minority that gave voice to criticism through its investigation of the social and political cancer that produced the disaster: it is an impotent response to the bogus patriotism that had poisoned popular consciousness.[32]

From Poetry to Chronicle

Conangla strategically places his poems within the architecture of his *Memoir* in order to achieve a contrasting effect. The verses are the gloss on the text, which constitutes a narrative and is autobiographical; the poetry is the testimony of the *Memoir*, serving to explicate his sentiments precisely when the events are being narrated (or immediately afterward) or in order to portray the anguished nostalgia he felt for the land he left behind on the other side of the Atlantic. The reader views the most characteristic events of the period, at the same time that she is invited to ramble through the author's poetry. Essay and poem are united in this way. The narrative discourse culminates in the denunciation of the horrors of war. The anticlimax is the inclusion of the poems offered directly in his personal version in Castilian.

Antoni Rovira i Virgili commented on several poems[33] that Conangla inserted in *Elegía*: "The poet sees passing before his eyes, with a vision that is cinematic, animated pictures of his longed-for land."[34] The note is important for two reasons. In the first place, because at that time it was not yet commonplace to associate dramatic descriptions, full of movement and life, with the word *cinematic*, referring to what would later be recognized as the "seventh art," still in its infancy in 1904. Nevertheless, one must pay proper attention to this isolated comment upon reading different passages in the *Memoir*, beginning with the one dedicated to the embarkation in Cartagena in its double version as prose and as poetry. Rovira was on the right track since the depiction seems made for a documentary script, more specifically, a television script. Conangla assumes the same distance from events as the distance adopted by the cameraman working on television. But also, of course, intimate thoughts must be represented in the course of the narration. Only moments earlier, the recruit thinks that he is marching toward an unknown destiny, totally deprived of affection. This is how he expresses it in the *Memoir*, in the passage where he records a brief encounter with a girl in Cartagena: "Suddenly, a young unknown girl, who was sobbing, moved perhaps to pity by the obvious sadness on my face, approached and handed me a spikenard; and without being able to thank her because I was trembling with such deep emotions, I accepted the flower and carried it to my lips amidst copious tears."

In Cuba during the war, Conangla was able to take refuge in his office and in literary creation. Thus, the poem titled "Página de album" written in Sancti Spíritus, clearly expresses his pacifist ideas, his nationalist ideology, and his faith in his literary profession, sentiments shared with many other soldiers[35] who did not go to Cuba willingly. The poet and the essayist united with the cameraman:

A dreamer like me, you come from a land
where work is the creed of life.
I, too, came from there; and here, in the War,
the consolation of Art keeps us alive.
Soldiers of a country, not of its idea,
creative fever accompanies us in the Tropics;

and not the torch
held by others in the field of battle.

The first verse in the second strophe becomes the central, explicit theme ("out of obligation"), which is implicit throughout the book. It emerges as the title of another poem, "Soldado forzoso":

A soldier by force, not by conviction,
they brought me to a beautiful and rare world.

After his stay in Sancti Spíritus, Conangla undertook a spiritual journey and the *Memoir* reflects his state of mind as well as his identification with the Cuban landscape. "Naturaleza bella," "Aurora," and "Sensitiva" are the most representative poems.

At the end of May 1896, Conangla was transferred to Aguacate, a territory in the province of Havana, near the boundary with Matanzas. There he was inspired to write one of his most impressive poems, "En la nave del templo," based on the use of a church as a barracks—an encampment and depository for the horrors of the reconcentration. In another poem titled "La misa roja" ["The red mass"], Conangla, who was a liberal and a believer, once again denounced the identification between Church and State, whose complicity in this case led to a kind of Witches' Sabbath, thanks to the manipulation of the cult and its beliefs. It is one of his most graphic poems, replete with drama, color, auditory sensations, critical thought, and an outpouring of rage, along with a certain dose of repugnance at seeing himself forced to participate in a spectacle that he considered obscene. The catalyst for the poem was the celebration of a field mass, like those that were customarily held in Spanish military units throughout history. But on this occasion what would normally have been an event lacking any great transcendence became a drama since it took place in the midst of war, under the tropical sun of the month of May 1896, while all the participants (the vulnerable population, the sick, the wounded, the combat soldiers, and the desk job military) were suffering the consequences of the reconcentration.

The other notable example of this type of poem (which is at one and the same time a celebration of language and an expression of his thought) is "El incendio," in which he tries to reflect the harshness of life in a place struck tangentially by the war. The troops were near the Rosario plantation, one of the most important on the island. In October 1896, following an encounter between *mambises* and Spanish troops, a huge fire broke out in the countryside that threatened its inhabitants.

Later, in another counterpoint in his *Memoir* (just as in his body of poems), he flees the desolate inferno of the colonial war and returns in spirit to his country and to the memory of his father, who died when Conangla was at war. Ill in Aguacate with yellow fever (which killed more Spanish soldiers than did the actions of the separatists), he recuperated in the Havana hospital, *Las Ánimas*.[36] In this state, he composed the very poems that elicited Rovira i Virgili's reference to their cinematic character, "Soñando con mi tierra," "Recuerdos invernales," "La Retama," "Remembranza," and "Padre."

On December 7, 1896, Maceo fell in combat. As was to be expected, following the celebrations decreed by the Spanish authorities, the war entered a harsher phase. Conangla composed other, even more meditative poems. He included four compositions, "La tradición," "El filósofo," "El soldado," and "El poeta," under the general title of *Navidad*. The last poem is a reflection on his fleeting existence.

During his service as a hospital assistant, Conangla used his time to complete a series of locally inspired poems. "Aurora," "Un rayo de sol," "Tropical," "Insomnio," "La luciérnaga," and "Dolencia spiritual" are the most representative, while "Soldado de una nación" is the composition mentioned most often. "La guitarra" is a poem inspired by the gatherings soldiers enjoyed in their leisure time. The most gifted sang songs from their regions or improvised them on the spot.

Conangla was ultimately transferred to Puentes Grandes and Havana in June 1897. He followed the surrender of Cervera's fleet in the Bay of Santiago de Cuba from that posting. He made use of his time before embarking by composing more verses at his desk in the Castillo de La Fuerza, which would later serve as the occupation headquarters of the North American Armed Forces, and with the passage of time would be transformed into a library and national archive. Those poems would evolve into some of the best poems in *Elegía de la guerra*: "La Guerra y la paz," "Patrioterismo," and "Grito de paz." The first is a dreamlike comparison that recalls the structure of "La misa roja." "Patrioterismo" is a classic example of a denunciation of the manipulation of nationalistic ideals that led to the disaster of 1898. "Grito de paz" unites nostalgia for his native land, the remembrance of his father, and pacifist sentiments.

Repatriation to Spain and the Return to Cuba

Finally, close to embarking, when the return to Catalonia was only hours away, Conangla penned a farewell that would later become an "until later." The poems titled "Adiós a Cuba" and "A Cuba libre" are dedicated to what would become his adoptive country. Rovira i Virgili wrote about them: "He feels well-deserved sympathy for the Cuban insurrectionists, recognizing the legitimacy of the aspirations that led them to hoist the flag of combat. . . . The generosity of the poet, proclaiming the right of Cuba to be independent, in opposition to a dying bogus notion of an essential Spanishness, is one of the most engaging notes of *Elegía de la guerra*."[37]

He expresses his sentiments concerning the war in the first of these poems, along with his admiration for the Cuban landscape. In the *Memoir*, the crossing of the Atlantic[38] allowed him to comment on the preoccupations of the soldiers regarding an uncertain future—he recalls the songs of the repatriated soldiers, the card games, and the funerals at sea of the last soldiers ill with yellow fever.

In November 1898, the *Satrústegui* arrived in the Bay of Cádiz. In other Spanish ports thousands of repatriated soldiers disembarked in a pathetic state.[39] Conangla traversed all of the south and the Levant, leaving paragraphs in his *Memoir* that represent—in addition to a fine literary sensibility very much in consonance with the tone and content of Azorín's and Machado's writings on the disaster of 1898—his sincere fraternal sentiment for the lands and people of Spain: "I crossed over the dry plains of La Mancha, scenario of Cervantes's immortal conception. My vision was refreshed as I passed the cultivated, evocative fields of Elche and Alicante, dotted with date palms."

Once Conangla was demobilized, it took him only seven years to decide to immigrate to Cuba, where he remained until his death in 1965. In 1901, he married María Tomás i Guarro (also from Montblanc). In 1905, he decided to immigrate to Cuba, where he worked as a clerk in a business establishment in order to pay for the passages of his wife and two children, "Nena" and Amado. He revealed the reasons for his decision to immigrate once and for all to his friend Eduardo Benot in a letter of farewell:

> (. . .) to better my economic condition to the benefit, more than for my future, to that of my children (. . .) I am leaving this land because I am increasingly opposed to the disastrous institutions that misgovern it (. . .) the difficulty here in making enough money to cover the needs of a family through intellectual labor (. . .) it is desperate to have to focus one's attention and employ one's pen for ten hours on newspaper assignments and those of a commercial office without having four hours free, not even one, for the expansion of one's spirit (. . .) so as not to go on like this it is worth it to risk seeking a future in new lands where life and liberty are more generous and the economic situation is more favorable (. . .) it is worth something to ful-

> fill a dream; and mine consists in returning to Cuba (. . .) and to go where my will directs me as does my noble intention of identifying myself totally with that nascent democracy.[40]

He returned to Catalonia only three times after he was completely settled in Cuba. The first time was in 1913 due to his mother's death. The second was in 1920 when he took along his whole family for a prolonged stay of six months. The third and last was delayed until 1955, when he was accompanied by his eldest daughter—a kind of farewell to his native land.

In Cuba, he marked out a personal and ideological path with respect to the past, present, and future of Catalonia in the moments he could spare from the daily newspaper work that provided him with a living. He was the president of the *Centre Catalá* during two long periods, he directed the journal *La Nova Catalunya*, and contributed to the development of the Sociedad de Beneficia de Naturales de Cataluña. His moment of greatest triumph was the presentation, in his own hand, of the *Dictamen*, and his *Constitución Provisional de la República Catalana en la Asamblea Separatista de la Habana* in 1928.[41] The day when he fulfilled the request of Francesc Macía and personally handled over that precious document was one of the happiest of his life. Conangla's writings, which had appeared regularly until the final decade of the twenties, were later characterized by introspection and subtly lacked the explicit utopianism of his earlier work. In contrast, they dealt more and more with philosophical issues and the creation of documents with proposals for confederacy designed to provide political models for the political future of Catalonia.

He died in Havana on May 15, 1965, a few months before his ninetieth birthday. He is buried in the Colón Cemetery in Havana with a handful of soil from Catalonia taken to him by his daughter "Nena" in 1937. He guarded it as if it were a treasure, and his own granddaughter Marisela Alberti placed it in his hands. On September 10, 1971, the town of Montblanc paid him a well-deserved homage. Josep María Poblet read a masterful work of remembrance in the *Ayuntamiento*, and his son, Raúl Conangla, responded as the representative of the family, under the presidency of the mayor, Josep Gomis. Then, a commemorative stone was laid, giving his name to the pathway that begins at one of the portals in the city's medieval wall and leads toward the west. This act closed the circle that began on September 1895. Montblanc recovered its most illustrious citizen symbolically and posthumously.

His unpublished work or the work dispersed in a variety of places, however, is destined to follow a slow but steady process of publication and successive compilations. On December 28, 1958, as noted above, he signed the first volume of his *Memoir*, whose appearance was hindered by the rapid and drastic changes that were approaching in Cuba, for Fidel Castro was on the verge of entering Havana and toppling Batista. This *Memoir*, his most coherent and ambitious unpublished work, was reserved for the personal and bitter recollections of the war years. One hundred years after the events that led to his first journey to Cuba, the special relationship between Spaniards and Cubans is still in force despite the political changes in both countries—in both cases after such notable events as the Civil War and the dictatorship in Spain or the drastic change of regime in Cuba. One century later, it is hoped that editions such as this one will help in understanding this special relationship with greater clarity.

I
From Cartagena to Sancti Spíritus

(December 14, 1895, to June 5, 1896)

In late 1894, before I registered in the lists for the *quinta*[1] i.e., the annual drawing of names of those young men in each population who have reached the age of nineteen—a drawing conducted in order to determine the percentage of those who will be incorporated into obligatory military service (though redeemable with payment of 1,500 *pesetas*)—my father took out an insurance policy for 500 pesetas[2] from the house of Mompó Hermanos y Cía, of Valencia, in order to free me from military service in the unlucky event that I were to draw a low number. The drawing, however, was favorable, giving me a high number equivalent to being classified in the reserve forces, which, for the moment, exempted me from military service. And as a consequence, the insurance policy from the insurer referred to above did not apply.

However, on February 24, 1895, the *Grito de Baire*[3] sounded in Cuba, spreading the revolt for liberation throughout the island. The government of the disastrous Spanish monarchy immediately mobilized military contingents to send in successive expeditions against the Cuban patriots. By Royal Order the following April, the reserves from the previous drawing were called up and told to present themselves in their respective zones for enrollment in active service in order to cover the places that the first forces left vacant in the armed units of the Peninsula.

In the biographical evocation, *El meu pare, que en cel sía*,[4] I described the difficult circumstances and the sacrifices that my family, as well as I, had to confront, because of the demands and disruptions of my being called up. As the result of all those circumstances—reviewed in the biographical sketch referred to above—on July 5, 1895, I had to proceed to the Recruitment Zone of Vilafranca del Penedès[5] along with the other young men from Montblanc who were victims of the same fate.

Two days before I went to the Zone of Vilafranca, I visited the General of the Division in Barcelona, Don Lluís de Castellví,[6] to inform him of my situation. He was a native, like myself, of Montblanc,[7] and a friend of the family.

"You can choose," General Castellví said to me, "between the three contingents established in your zone: infantry, cavalry, and artillery."

"General," I asked, "would it be possible for me to remain in an infantry unit in Barcelona so that I could continue with my university studies?"

"No," he said, "Catalan reserves for the three categories have not been designated for Barcelona. The only contingent of infantry that you can choose is in Cartagena."[8]

"Well, in that case, I opt for Cartagena," I said to him.

Subsequently, thanks to a recommendation from General Castellví, not only I, but also other companions from Montblanc who had reported on July 5, 1895, to the Recruitment Zone of Vilafranca de Penedès, were assigned to the Regimiento de Infantería de España número 46, garrisoned in Cartagena. Along with other recruits we left for that city on a smoky and extremely uncomfortable train that traversed locales and landscapes in Tarragona, Valencia, Alicante, and Murcia, which at times were very attractive, but on the whole it was a tiring and disorienting trip until we reached Cartagena.

The occupants of each car on the train were organized into groups or sections. Due to my university affiliation, the captain in charge of the recruits named me the interim corporal of one of the groups. Based on the same qualification, but also because of the friendly recommendation that Lieutenant Juan Oller (a colleague of mine in high school in Tarragona) passed on to another lieutenant whose last name was Sierra, I was assigned to the offices of the regiment, a few days after arriving in Cartagena, and after receiving instruction in arms.

Within twenty days of joining the regiment in Cartagena, I felt ill. The upset caused by my change of life, due as much to the moral shocks of recent months as to the difficult adjustments to barracks discipline, led to a dangerous depression, which on doctor's orders, required me to enter the military hospital. But, thank God, I recovered due to proper medicines and two weeks of rest.

Learning of my promotion to colonel by a vote while I was still convalescing in the hospital also contributed to the restoration of my health. A colleague named Hermida, in charge of the small pedal press belonging to the regiment, communicated that agreeable surprise to me personally. Hermida handed me a printed Order of the Day in which my promotion was noted among those of others along with the no less surprising news that the distinctive honorific of *Don* had been placed before my name, an honor that was due me, according to what I was told, because I had graduated with a baccalaureate in Arts and Sciences and was beginning university studies.

Within five months of joining the Regimiento de Infantería de España número 46, the regiment received orders to organize an expeditionary battalion for Cuba. It is easy to imagine how that blow filled me with bitterness and how it caused my father and mother anguish as well, when they learned of the irreversible news. In the pages of the above-mentioned biographical sketch of my progenitor I expressed the intimate distress that I, along with my family members, suffered because of that tragic turn of events—tragic for me, as it had to be for so many other unfortunate youths and their relatives subjected to the same anxious concerns.

The illusion we had fostered—that the War with Cuba would end quickly—did not come true. The tenacious and heroic resistance mounted by Cuban patriots against the Spanish Army was increasingly vigorous. And the inevitable had to happen in view of the arrogance and stubbornness of the monarchist oligarchies of that politically absurd state. Instead of liberal measures to harmonize—if it were still possible—the just aspirations of the revolutionaries with the objectives of the vainglorious metropolis, nothing occurred to the absolutist rulers in Madrid in their fatal obsession with saving the monarchy other than to send successive waves of thousands of men, believing that they would be able to drown in blood the entirely legitimate aims of the insurrectionists.

The Spanish government poured more than two hundred thousand soldiers[9] into Cuba; with the most sarcastic disregard for the soldiers' lives since half of that number assuredly died in the island's *maniguas* [land covered with undergrowth], towns, and hospitals because of yellow fever—endemic at that time in the country to the further dishonor of the prevailing colonial madness—and because of dysentery brought on by bad food and military actions.

The strongest impressions Cartagena made on me, along with those of the anxious moments of the departure for Cuba, are fixed in three of my first books in Catalan: *El meu pare*, *Elegía de la guerra* and *Eternal.* As I described it in *Elegía*, embarking for Cuba in a disgusting, dirty, misery-filled steamship, the *San Francisco*, belonging to the *Compañia Transatlántica Española*,[10] alarmed me no end. The horrible uncertainty as to the future, doubt that I would be able to return to the bosom of my family, the moral aversion that was already intensifying in my conscience in regard to the political crimes of the Spanish State; all that accumulation of anguished sentiments, of fervent tears, disappointments, and mental distress, began to turn my hair gray and profoundly embitter my life.

The embarkation took place at noon on November 23, 1895, from the port of Cartagena, the hot, walled city of barracks, hospitals, shipyards, and arsenals; the frivolous, very Spanish city where at every step you see soldiers of all ranks, groups of soldiers and corporals, boastful sergeants, assistants and orderlies carrying large baskets; the city of the *Feria* and of the *Molinete*, of classic cafés and resale stores; of *churros* and prickly pears, fried fish, and *sandías sangrantes y tragantes* ["blood-red, mouthwatering watermelons"].

On that day, as throughout the year, Cartagena was impregnated with the strong scent of spikenard; an evocative scent that for the five months of my stay in the area around Cartagena acted as a balsam for the spiritual tribulations that I experienced when I was torn away from my native land. But I absorbed that penetrating scent along with more disturbing effects when my battalion, which was mustered forcibly, came down from its quarters in the heights of the city, and headed through the streets toward the dock, amid balcony hangings and decorative colored fringes, sounds of music played out of tune, stupid yells, clapping, and deafening shouts.

In those horrible moments of extremely cruel uncertainty, upset by tragic anguish, without familiar arms to seal a good-bye with an embrace, without friendly hands to shake, behold that suddenly, unexpectedly, a young unknown woman who was sobbing—perhaps because the obvious sadness on my face inspired pity—approached me and handed me a spikenard; and trembling from profound emotion that prevented me from expressing my gratitude, I accepted that flower and lifted it to my lips as I wept copious tears.

Moments later the embarkation began. I fixed the extremely vivid, exact, and sarcastic impression it made on me in one of the first pages of the book *Elegía de la guerra*, and I have reproduced it below, initially translated into Castilian from the original Catalan:

THE EMBARKATION

I hold the unforgettable picture[11]
always vivid in my mind:
the milling crowds
encircling the entire port.
Sobbing farewells,
embraces and sweet kisses
half-uttered words,
cries, moans and laments;
faints, nervous crises,
promises and vows;
trembling hands, in search
of other hands for support . . .

A multitude of men and women without measure;
and in sinister contrast.
the bloody *Marcha de Cádiz*,[12]
speeches of empty deception,
decorated cassocks
that did not leave the dock;
blasts from the filthy ship
already steaming in the port;
and the clatter of the chains
amidst inconsolable farewells!

Everything passed. Hoarse, frenetic
cries erupted.
Then, only the silhouettes
ever dimmer
of handkerchiefs waving,
fluttered in the distance!

On December 11, 1895, after eighteen days of smoke-filled navigation, the old transatlantic ship entered the splendid Bay of Cienfuegos.[13] We were captivated by the surprising calm of the tranquil waters of that spacious bay, the intense clarity of the blue firmament without clouds or even slight wisps of clouds, the gamut of green in the sun-drenched vegetation on the banks of the marvelous port. We were only distracted from admiring the scene before us when we heard the sharp blasts of several tugboats with flags flying that hastened to receive us and the hoarse braying of the sirens of the *San Francisco* itself mixing with the shouts, cheers, chatter, and uproar accompanying the military and maritime authorities and representatives from the garrison, along with the official commissions of *integrismo*[14] in Cienfuegos.

When the uproar occasioned by ultra-Spanish patriotism calmed down, we expected that we would be taken ashore in Cienfuegos. But only the battalion commanders disembarked; meanwhile some demonstrators from the noisy tugboats boarded the *San Francisco* to offer us tobacco and small red and yellow flags. Later, at midafternoon, the commanders of the expedition and we soldiers were transferred to a singular boat propelled by two big side wheels: the *Antinógenes Menéndez*, which in short order took us to Tunas de Zaza,[15] where we were made to camp in the outskirts of the village, near the railroad platform.

There we relieved ourselves of our rucksacks and had our first contacts with Cubans, especially with little boys from seven to ten who were selling a variety of sweets. The surprising and serene manner with which the child vendors proposed the purchase of those treats I found admirable. Some soldiers imprudently tried to make fun of the small vendors by deriding their wares or quibbling over the price despite their low cost. But the quick-witted kids with appropriate and precise explanations caught the attention and won the confidence of the recruits, who did not take long to give the small merchants their due respect, thanks to the readiness with which the kids offered and accredited their merchandise spread out on small boards, and for the reasons they gave to justify in technical terms the worth and irreducible prices of their articles.

The discovery of the mental and expressive capacity of those children confirmed my conviction that neither force of arms nor any recourse employed by tyranny would ever be able to quell the firm, independent decisions made by the Cuban people. A people such as this—I said to myself—whose children of seven to ten years of age already know how to conduct themselves with such positive revelations of will and character, as do these children of Tunas de Zaza, will inevitably know and be able, by means of well-justified ontological and patriotic reasoning, to free itself from any tyranny, the more so if it is a foreign tyranny.

Moreover, I asked myself: In the lands of the regressive Spanish state, would little boys the same age as the ones from Tunas de Zaza be able to conduct themselves with a governing serenity and capability equal to that of these children? And on reflection, the only answer I came up with, at least at that time, was: no.

At nightfall, after roll call, rations[16] of a sort were distributed to the soldiers, with abundant quantities of a wine with a very high alcoholic content, surely intentional, thanks to which a good number of drinkers, embracing their rucksacks on the floor of the railway station platform, went to sleep. And the next morning, almost at midday, they put us in several cars used to transport horses or cows to take us to Sancti Spíritus.[17] The engine was fueled not with coal but wood; and since there was not enough on board, the engineer had to stop twice to get more brush in the *manigua* on either side of the train. This posed a danger for the battalion and for a squad of *guerrilleros*[18] who accompanied us—the only ones who would have had to respond to any possible attack against the raw recruits, for as yet we did not have weapons, pending arrival at Sancti Spíritus.

When it grew dark, exhausted by the discomfort of the journey, and still under the influence of the soporific effects of that alcoholic brew in Tunas, we were made to get off the train on the outskirts of Sancti Spíritus. Each man of us with his bundle on his back was taken to several stables or long sheds where we were lodged temporarily. But those structures were not empty. There were horses and mules intermingled in them, stomping and neighing—animals destined for the commanders and officers and for the mule service assigned to the battalion, which, on the next, day, as we were told, was to go out on operations.

It was there in those sheds—stables, in effect—little more than a meter from the rumps of the noisy and pestilential horses where we were obliged to spread our mats on the hard ground, with the very high risk that, if we managed to get to sleep, we would be kicked or at the very least, become the victims of repugnant but inevitable and copious evacuations of the restless animals.

It was difficult for me to go to sleep as much because of the immediate dangers as because of the subjective enormity of suspicions and uncertainties that obsessed me. I fought against giving voice to my inner turmoil, which I had to repress in order not to reveal it to my companions in misfortune, who were, for the most part, as anguished and fearful as I. And I asked myself:

"My God, what will become of me in this unknown land where fate has brought me, spoiling the brightest illusions of my youth? Will I be fortunate enough to continue tomorrow in the battalion offices as I was promised? Will the war end soon, will I be able to go home, to Barcelona, to my studies and concerns, or will they be buried beforehand in this very cemetery of Sancti Spíritus, as were those of my uncle José María Fontanilles, a commanding military doctor, thirty years ago and a victim of yellow fever?"

The following day, after distributing Mauser[19] rifles and munitions to the soldiers, orders came down to prepare the battalion to leave Sancti Spíritus in order to relieve troops posted farther away, first of all in Fuerte Taguasco,[20] and to join other units in operations. Immediately, as well, the commanders and officers designated in Cartagena to run the battalion offices joined the respective *clases*[21] and soldiers from the original office with the object of accompanying us to the building that the military command had chosen in order to resume our sedentary tasks.

After we heard the reassuring confirmation of those respective officinesque assignments, it is not necessary to say what a sincere spiritual relief all of us office companions felt as we entered the building chosen for the representative and administrative seat of the battalion. After so many years I do not remember the name of the street, but I do have an exact recollection that those offices bordered the family residence of one of the most distinguished residents of the town, Señor Pina, the father or grandfather of the illustrious contemporary lawyer, Dr. Rogelio Pina. I well remember that when the latter was a boy of nine or ten years of age, we chatted often, he at the open window of his house and I from the sidewalk.

In those historic days, how could I suppose that twenty or twenty-five years later, in the time of the Cuban Republic, we would meet again, recognize each other and respect each other, not only in intellectual and intensely Cuban meetings in Havana, but also on an occasion that was very painful for me. We met on Fifth Avenue in New York on August 8, 1952, in the company of my adored twenty-year-old grandson Jorge, who died tragically four days later in Paris, the victim of a treacherous polio attack, which had been incubating from his last stay in Cuba.[22]

I spent five months and twenty-three days in Sancti Spíritus at my job as a clerk of the Batallón Expedicionario de España número 46. In just a few months, nonetheless, that illustrious city left impressions on my spirit of friendships, places, episodes, memories, and other unforgettable things. A good number of those impressions were attractive and stimulating; others, however, were horribly painful.

Among the agreeable impressions, I must evoke, first of all, the very noble, attentive, and cultivated figure of Dr. Francisco J. Rabell, a pharmacist, and one of the most illustrious directors of the *Partido Liberal Autonomista*[23] in Sancti Spíritus. The surname *Rabell* piqued my curiosity because it is widespread in Catalonia and also because it was the name of a great friend and federalist companion of mine who remained in Tarragona. For these reasons and because I wanted to become personally acquainted, if possible, with some of the town's intellectuals, I decided to enter Dr. Rabell's pharmacy with the pretext of buying some lozenges for my throat.

The pharmacist himself received me. He was a robust figure with a broad forehead, a noble and alert look, a thick mustache, and rounded beard. As he gave me the lozenges, I asked him whether he was the owner of the pharmacy. Smiling, he answered that he was. I explained then that he should not be surprised at the question for it sprang only from my curiosity to know if he or perhaps his father or grandfather was from Catalonia.

Touching on the possible Catalan origin of his surname and on my arrival in Cuba as a conscript, Dr. Rabell and I carried on a friendly conversation marked by evident mutual sympathy. In the course of our chat, encouraged by his exquisite civility, I was very pleased to have the chance to inform him of the unavoidable circumstances that brought me to Cuba. Clearly, I bore no prejudice against the Cuban people since my ideological preferences were honorably pacifist and were derived, in large part, from the teachings of Francesc Pi i Margall,[24] the venerable apostle of a federalist republic.

Dr. Rabell no doubt found my words sincere, for discreetly, but in essence unequivocally, he declared that he also felt deep admiration for the most distinguished and principled of the presidents who had served in the failed Spanish Republic of 1873. When I told him about my literary and journalistic vocation whose cultivation, along with my university studies, was suspended by the forced *quinta*, he invited me to visit him often so that he could provide me with select literary works as well as to allow me to collaborate in the journal *La Fraternidad*,[25] the organ of the prestigious Sociedad El Progreso.

Following that agreeable conversation with Dr. Rabell, I used to visit him two or three times a week. He always received me with pleasure and affectionate understanding, giving me also no less attractive opportunities to meet other inhabitants of the town in his pharmacy. Among those who frequently met with the helpful pharmacist were Castro Marín, Manuel Echemendía, and Marcelino Díaz de Villegas (secretary at the time of the *Ayuntamiento de Sancti Spíritus* and Secretary of the Treasury later; in the time of the Republic headed by General José Miguel Gómez).[26]

On one of those occasions Dr. Rabell introduced me to the very popular mayor of the town, Don Marcos García, an outstanding figure of Cuban patriotism before and later; as an active liberator in the War of 1868 up to the *Pacto del Zanjón*,[27] as governor of Las Villas during the semi-autonomous period, and as the exemplary and famous Corrections Judge of Havana during the first years of independence.

Following my acceptance of the gracious invitation to collaborate in *La Fraternidad*, I was very pleased to publish several articles in the prestigious town journal. I recall that I was inspired in one of those literary endeavors by the well-known legend of the Wandering Jew. And I was aided by the kind permission to use a *xilografia* or woodcut, the work of the Catalan draftsman Miguel Urrea, a companion of mine in the draft and also in my office. That artistic woodcut by Miguel Urrea in *La Fraternidad* inspired some verses in Catalan, included eight years later in *Elegía de la guerra*, translated initially into Castilian:

LEAF IN AN ALBUM

In the album of my friend Miguel Urrea[28]

A dreamer like me, you come from a land
where work is the credo of our lives.
I came from there also; and here, in the midst of War,
we are animated by the consolation of Art.
Soldiers from a country, not sharing its idea,

creative fever accompanies us
in the tropics, and not the torch
held by others in battle.
And since Catalonia tells us
that the pen and the pencil
are more glorious arms than the arms of death
wielded by this age athirst for victory,
let us continue to act as artists:
you with your drawings; I with my songs;
and thus, instead of warriors,
we shall be idealists of Progress and its charms.

How could I imagine forty-one years later, in 1937, in the course of time during republican independence, that that article of mine, illustrated with Miguel Urrea's woodcut, would be discovered by the illustrious historian from Sancti Spíritus, Don Manuel Martínez Moles,[29] chief of the civil prefecture that became part of the glorious Liberation Army and, later, senator of the Republic?

When Don Miguel came upon the article, he wrote to tell me about it with great pleasure in an affectionate letter that strengthened the bonds of intellectual fellowship we already shared in the governing *juntas* of the Escritores y Artistas Americanos, of the Instituto Nacional de Previsión y Reformas Sociales, and in simultaneous activities in other patriotic and cultural institutions such as the Sociedad Económica de Amigos del País of Havana, the Sociedad Geográfica de Cuba, and the Academia de la Historia.

Another unforgettable recollection from my stay in Sancti Spíritus had to do with a secret act I was able to carry out on behalf of a young man from the town who had been arrested as a suspected *mambí*.[30]

On the same street where the battalion offices were located, I went into a barber shop one afternoon to get my hair cut. When I was seated in the chair, the barber didn't dare speak to me, fearful, I surmised, of slipping up somehow in the presence of a man in a striped uniform.[31] But guessing what he feared, I led him to talk, bringing up banal topics that I skillfully used to sound him out in order to gain his confidence. And in this way, the discreet Figaro[32] was not long in realizing that despite my suspicious striped uniform, I was a conscript due to the unavoidable exigencies of the Spanish military service, but that I was devoid of any animosity toward the Cuban people since I was guided solely by my liberal sentiments as a native of Catalonia; and as a consequence, by my father's teachings and my own favored cultural studies.

These ingenuous words could have turned out to be imprudent on my part. But just as daring plain speaking of this kind had garnered me the confidence and friendship of Dr. Rabell, so my words calmed the very natural fears of the Creole barber, for with a kind of sob, revelatory of confidence and understanding and also of intimate anguish, he confided in me. In effect, as he told me—forgetting my hair for brief periods—he was experiencing, at that time, the misfortune of having a son of his in jail, on the pretext that one day recently, in the immediate limits of the town, a Spanish patrol arrested him and accused him of wanting to join up with the liberation forces.

"It was an arbitrary arrest," the anguished father told me, since his son's intention was simply to visit family friends who lived at the edge of the town, but near the exit post.

"What is the name and surname of your son?" I asked the afflicted father. He told me. And what an unexpected and sudden impression the answer provoked in me! Because days earlier, Lieutenant Resiles, one of the officers in the bureaucracy of the battalion (sub lieutenant in the reserve but promoted to effective lieutenant when he was incorporated into active duty) had appointed me as the secretary in the trial[33] against the barber's young son.

In order to avoid compromises that could prove prejudicial for the young prisoner and his father, I abstained out of discretion from revealing to the father that I was the secretary in charge of the judicial proceedings initiated against his son. I acted the more prudently since the military command of Sancti Spirítus had not yet designated a day and an hour for the judge and me to go to the jail with the object of filing charges and taking a deposition from the alleged *mambí*.

I tried to alleviate the distressing concerns of the unhappy father with the most pious notions I could muster. But since I wanted to use the most efficient means of discreetly helping the detained youth, I went immediately to Dr. Rabell's pharmacy and informed him of my conversation with the troubled father as well as the confidential information that I was the acting secretary in the pretrial investigation.

Dr. Rabell returned my confidence, telling me that he was already aware of that case, as well as other recent cases, the product, in the majority of cases, of systematic persecutions ordered by the General Command in the zone. He was hoping, nonetheless, that in response to urgent complaints lodged by Don Marcos García,[34] the civic-minded and energetic mayor of Sancti Spíritus, and telegraphed to the headquarters of the Captain-General's General Staff, the detained individuals, including the young man in question, would soon regain their freedom.

And that is what happened, for three or four days later, Lieutenant Resiles and other judges from the battalion office who were charged with investigations in similar cases received separate communications ordering them to suspend all procedures in the respective investigations and to send the summaries to the military command.

Consequently, numerous young men who were capriciously detained were freed through orders from the headquarters of the Captain-General's General Staff, and among those men freed from the obsessive persecutions was the son of the distressed father. He informed me of this development when I passed by the barber shop, although I had not told him about the spontaneous confidential mission to Dr. Rabell that I had initiated on behalf of his son.

On another occasion, due to a series of interconnected circumstances that appeared accidental, but were at bottom mysterious, I found myself involved in a very dangerous episode, from which I escaped unscathed solely—I have always believed this—through divine intervention.

In the middle of December 1895, we office workers in the offices of the battalion were taken unaware by the painful news that our doctor had died. When the expeditionary unit of the Regimiento de España número 46 was organized in Cartagena, that doctor, a charming man of twenty-seven and a recent graduate in medicine, solicited the position of first lieutenant for sanitation in the expedition. His petition was accepted and he was incorporated into the expeditionary forces as a credentialed doctor with the rank of first lieutenant.

One would imagine that such an energetic doctor would leave Cartagena with hopes or illusions of rapid promotion in the course of the war. But when he arrived in Sancti Spíritus he fell ill, and instead of going out on operations with the battalion he had to go to the hospital, where he died within a few days.

Given the unusual manner in which the young doctor enrolled in the expeditionary battalion, we scarcely had the opportunity to get to know him—we didn't even know his name. But when he met his lamentable end it became a question of the immediate removal of his body to the city cemetery. A captain in the office (whose surname was Ramírez, as I recall) gathered together the office workers under his command to tell us that the General Command of Sancti Spíritus was sending a squad of Civil Guards to take the cadaver of the medical officer to the necropolis. Ramírez also thought that our office, as a respectful homage and as representatives of the absent battalion, ought to send at least four office workers and a corporal to the burial, together with the captain whose proposal it was.

A family connection led me to participate in the transport of the recently deceased doctor to the cemetery. I wanted to visit the Sancti Spíritus cemetery where my uncle, José María Fontanilles y Voltas,[35] a military doctor and victim of yellow fever, was buried toward the end of the War of 68. This opportunity might let me discover whether there were still traces of the mausoleum with an inscription on a marble headstone, which, according to information sent to my grandfather Fontanilles, had been erected there.

Guided then by this sentimental motive and without suspecting that anything dangerous might come of it, I offered to participate as a corporal, a rank that the small detachment of office workers held as well, and who also wanted to join me on that mission. Among them was the orderly Antonio Gaya, a townsman of mine from Montblanc, the only person I had told about the likely gravesite of my uncle Fontanilles.

The following day at eight in the morning my four office mates and I left the office on the orders of the captain, Mausers hanging from our shoulders, on an ostensibly peaceful mission. But when we arrived at the cemetery, we were surprised to see that there was no squadron of Civil Guards, which we had been told would be there, nor did we see any sign of the scheduled burial. The office captain learned from a functionary at the cemetery that the medical officer's coffin had already been received, and that the Civil Guards, as soon as they fulfilled their duty, heard that an insurrectionist party beyond some nearby hills was prowling around, which led the squadron to set off quickly in that direction to fight the "band."

And, in fact, we could hear frequent gunfire, confirming what we were told at the entrance to the cemetery. Our captain, gripped by a violent warlike impulse, without calculating the deadly consequences his exaggerated reaction might entail for the four soldiers and for me (or perhaps calculating, tempted by ambition, that the sacrifice of all or of anyone of the five office workers could mean a promotion or a juicy Cruz de María Cristina),[36] turned to us and, pointing to the road to the hill, ordered in a fierce voice: "Hurry on up there, to the aid of the Civil Guard!"

The abrupt order terrified us, but we had to obey. And when the five of us set out, I thought fast about the best way to avoid the undoubted dangers of that forced incursion. Therefore, instead of continuing to head all together toward the ravine that the implacable captain pointed out to us, I shouted to my companions, turning away from our path: "Let's not go to the ravine! Let's go up the side of the hill like *guerrillas!*"

And that turned out to be a good move since as we advanced toward the gentle slope of the hill we saw two Civil Guards on horseback quickly heading toward us with a man laid across the back of a horse that we figured must have belonged to the dead or wounded man. We realized immediately that the two riders leading the body secured to the Creole horse belonged to the squadron of the Civil Guards. The two Guards also deduced from our striped uniforms the mission of the five fearful recruits who were surging up the small hill. They urged us to take the horse and the dead body to the entrance of the cemetery, as we did. The two Civil Guards also gave us the machete, some saddlebags, and the hat of the dead man—a *cabecilla* [rebel chieftain] named Cervantes, they told us.

We did all that as quickly as possible, certain that the handing over of the unfortunate insurgent patriot would appease the martial ardor of our captain and put an end to our anxious intervention in that risky undertaking. But the captain-spider in charge of the five ingenuous office workers, still eager to submit us to new, dangerous adventures, turned to me and ordered: "Go up there again and back up the Civil Guards!"

It is not necessary to describe the profound anger we felt at our combative captain's stubborn eagerness. Luckily, thank God, the second injudicious order given by that obese mandarin became moot when we saw something surprising that calmed us down—the riders of the Civil Guard were coming down the hill, their mission accomplished. Their chief told our captain that they had disbanded the "band" of the *cabecilla* Cervantes, who had been taken to the cemetery a dead man.

Consequently, the Civil Guard squad trotted off to their barracks and the captain, accompanied by us five weary office workers, who also began the return to our residence in Sancti Spíritus, luckily without having had to use our Mausers, but also without my being able to enter the cemetery, so that I would remain ignorant of the location of my uncle Fontanilles's sepulcher.

But the information about the supposed disbanding of the insurgent group was far from confirmed for, as we returned to Sancti Spíritus, we weren't long in learning that the body of the liberator Cervantes, taken by us to the cemetery, was retrieved by several valiant men belonging to his "band," who took it off to be buried in a place of their choosing.

The early death of the lieutenant doctor of our battalion and the fortuitous episode of the no less painful loss of the liberator, Cervantes, reverberated in our offices, and in my mind, especially, with a very painful impression, since the death of my compatriot, the orderly Antonio Gaya, followed from those events. The nervous strain of coming and going to the cemetery and, in particular, the overexertion of his weak heart caused by our being submitted to the unthinking order of our captain when he obliged us to go up the hill—all those imminent dangers, extreme fears, sudden emotions and trepidations, upset and exhausted the physical resistance of my esteemed fellow townsman from Montblanc, bringing on a grave cardiac crisis. Another office worker and I took him by coach to the hospital, where three days earlier the lieutenant doctor of the battalion had died.

Since Gaya had told me so earlier, I knew that some nuns—Sisters of Charity[37]—from the Peninsula were providing pious service in that hospital and that, among them, by a mysterious coincidence, was a first cousin of Gaya himself, also from Montblanc. I asked for her as soon as our dear companion entered the hospital and, in effect, when she was united with the young patient, the pious nun was deeply pained. She promised to take the best care possible of her cousin. His condition became so serious, however, that he died within two days according to what the director of the hospital told us in the battalion office.

But the transcendent consequences of the burial of the lieutenant doctor of the Batallón Expedicionario de España número 46 in Sancti Spíritus didn't end with the death of Antonio Gaya because thirty-five years later, twenty-five years after I had returned to independent Cuba out of my very free will and deeply felt desire to live there as my adoptive country, the recollection of those sad events lived through so intensely during the war of liberation still reverberated in my spirit with new and impressive surprises.

At the end of May 1930, I was once again in the midst of a maelstrom of different journalistic activities in Havana, especially due to my jobs as secretary of the editorial department and editorial contributor three times a week on *El Día*,[38] as well as the parliamentary chronicler and reviewer of the *Diario de Sesiones*[39] of the Chamber of Representatives. Among other publications on the newspaper exchange a copy of number 14 corresponding to the twenty-first of that month of the *Revista Política*[40] came into my hands. It was a weekly, recently founded by Dr. Santiago Rey, member of the glorious Liberation Army of Cuba, politician of the *Partido Liberal* at the time of Machado,[41] and a popular congressman in the Republic later on.

As I paged through that publication, I noted with surprise that among its sections, below the title "Recollections of War," there was a long article signed by Dr. Rey in which he described the episode of the death of a liberator named Cervantes and the removal of his body to the cemetery in Sancti Spíritus, a description very similar to my own in preceding pages of this *Memoir*, but amplified with interesting details regarding incidents that preceded and followed that episode.

Thanks to Santiago Rey's article, thirty-four years after the deeply felt death of the patriot Cervantes, and the eventful removal of his body to the cemetery in Sancti Spíritus, I was able to piece together the personal and combat characteristics of the unfortunate Cuban liberator and of other circumstances relevant to the places where that action took place. I shall sum up the most detailed revelations in Santiago Rey's article—which complement my own recollections—in the order in which they appear in the main text of the article published in the *Revista Política*.

The episode, according to Santiago Rey, began one morning in December 1895 or January 1896. "That morning at about nine or nine thirty, a group of insurrectionists, commanded by Lieutenant Juan Cervantes, from the Regimiento 'Honorato' and men from the squadron of then Commander Juan Agustín Sánchez, were camped in the shadow of the '*Mangos del Colector*,' in the fields near the town of Sancti Spíritus and right on the *Camino Real* to Havana.

"Juan Cervantes," Santiago Rey continued, "was brave to the point of rashness; charming, affectionate with his friends and companions, proud and decisive, with an exceptional 'practical' knowledge of all the broad terrain around Sancti Spíritus. He had been assigned the difficult and dangerous mission of placing a small escort of eight or ten well-armed men at the very gates to the city. They were supplied and equipped to undertake various missions to display the force and vigor of the revolution in that center of great importance, Sancti Spíritus, and to harass the Spanish troops and guerrillas from the moment they set foot outside the fortified city.

"The members of the insurgent group had left their horses secured at the edge of the stone barrier next to *Los Mangos* and the *Camino Real* and were resting under the canopy of trees. Then, one of the '*pacíficos*'[42] from Sancti Spíritus arrived and informed Lieutenant Cervantes that at that moment the burial of a commander or Spanish officer—since he was accompanied by many troops—was underway."

And Santiago Rey continued: "About a quarter of an hour after the *pacífico* made his report to Lieutenant Cervantes, we suddenly saw a man on horseback going up the hill. Another rider followed him and both men stayed there without moving. 'They look like Civil Guards,' said Lieutenant Cervantes. Two more riders joined the men after that, in the attitude of lookouts. The rebel lieutenant, convinced that the four riders on the hill were, in fact, Civil Guardsmen, made a quick decision: 'Yes, they are the Guards! Let's go after them!'

"But at that moment," Rey's narrative continued, "the Guards let loose a formidable volley that engulfed the vicinity in its noisy racket. Both sides fought without letup. Facing the *mambí* group, at about 150 or 200 meters on the slope of the hill and on the road through the fields to Sancti Spíritus, there were ten or twelve Guards on horseback, who were shooting at us constantly. And much farther away"—one reads in Rey's account—"there was a large infantry force formed in long lines, that was leveling heavy fire at us.

"As the group of insurrectionists advanced toward the hill and the fight began"—Rey's article goes on to say—"one of the guards dismounted and took careful aim at the Cubans. Within a few moments, Lieutenant Cervantes's horse fell along with the Lieutenant. The horse's wound was not serious and it got up right away, allowing Cervantes to mount it once again. But as fate would have it, when the lieutenant prepared to continue the fight with his machete, another bullet (this time in the middle of his forehead) killed him, leaving no time for him to utter a single word!"

Santiago Rey's very interesting narrative continued. In summary, the Civil Guard who dismounted was surely the man who first wounded the horse and then, having sharpened his aim, killed the lieutenant. In Rey's opinion, that Civil Guard, possibly a great shot, knew Juan Cervantes when the latter was an official hunter of bandits; he knew about his valor and, given how close they were, he was able to recognize him and even overhear Juan's intention to charge the Guards with his machete. For these reasons, the Guardsman was determined to take him down, as he did. It must have happened that way since it could not have been chance alone that first the horse and then the lieutenant himself were the targets of the Guards' only fire.

"When Juan Cervantes fell"—Rey continued— "'El Cubano,' a young man of about twenty-five, very brave and daring, and another man, dismounted to help him, assuming that he was only wounded. But when they were convinced that he was dead, they tried to place him on his horse. They didn't succeed since the horse was too agitated and because the Civil Guard, mounted again, set off at a gallop in pursuit of the *mambises*, while the volleys from the distant infantry also intensified. It was so extreme"—according to Rey—"that it seemed inconceivable that they wouldn't kill us all, for the buzzing of the bullets sounded like a stirred up beehive." The "*Cubano*" and the other man left the lieutenant's body on the ground, quickly mounted their horses, and the remaining men began the retreat, with the exception of Julio Acosta and the narrator.

In connection with the patriot, Julio Acosta, Rey wrote: "Before I explain the last part of that unfortunate episode in which the man who was one of the best hopes of the revolution lost his life, for Juan Cervantes had come to be a glorious chieftain and was prestigious on account of his valor and his great command of strategy, I want to describe the personality of Julio Acosta. He was at that time a man of about twenty-five to twenty-seven years of age, tall, muscular, white, resembling the descendants of Canary Islanders. He was not very expressive, a man of few words, but kind and a good companion. He was not boastful, nor did he brag about the proud attitude he displayed in the frequent almost daily exchanges of gunfire that we sustained. He was one of the eight or ten men who were with Juan Cervantes in the mission of *Los Mangos del Colector*."

Resuming his narrative on the death of Juan Cervantes, Rey explained that when the *Cubano* and the other *mambí* had dismounted to retrieve and help the fallen chief, they had to mount their horses again quickly and follow their companions in retreat because the Civil Guard was advancing toward the group at a gallop. Julio Acosta, however, kneeled down and tried to grab the body of Cervantes with his right hand, balancing it atop the latter's horse. At the same time he cried out to Rey: "Go on, Santiago, hurry, they're coming at you with machetes!"

And then Rey adds: "I don't know why I stayed with Acosta; perhaps because I was so upset I preferred to help in holding up and steadying the body, which was slipping off the horse. Since we couldn't do it, the body fell to the ground again." And then Acosta and Rey, in order to escape from the Guards, had to abandon the body and get away as fast as they could. "My horse," Rey adds, "flew rather than galloped, and after galloping pell-mell to flee the pursuers, I realized that Juan Acosta had disappeared and I believed then that the Civil Guards had killed him with a well-aimed bullet."

At the *Rincón de los Cuayos*, Rey was finally able to rejoin some of his companions. He told them about the death of Juan Cervantes and the possible fate of Julio Acosta, as well, although the latter, fortunately, was able to get away from his pursuers and join his companions later. When the men heard that Cervantes's body had already been taken to the depository of the Sancti Spíritus cemetery, the commander, Juan Agustín Sánchez, ordered all the men in the squadron (Santiago Rey among them) to go to the cemetery to retrieve the body of the ill-fated lieutenant and liberator, as was done moments later when the Civil Guards and we five harmless office workers were already on the way back to our quarters.

For some weeks after the episodes I have just referred to, public tranquility in Sancti Spíritus was disturbed only by false denunciations that malevolent agents of *integrismo* leveled against respectable elements in the city. These denunciations were refuted thanks to the swift actions of the civic-minded mayor, Don Marcos García, in cooperation with the local command, or by opportune telegraphic protests in defense of those unjustly accused. The protests were referred to the General Segundo Cabo [the seat of the Vice Governor of Cuba in Havana, named after its former vice governor], that is, to the commanding officers directly subordinate to the Captain-General while he was traveling through the interior of the island.

But when General Martínez Campos[43] resigned from the Gobierno Superior de Cuba and the implacable Weyler[44] succeeded him in February 1896, things changed very quickly. The situation throughout the island and in Sancti Spíritus became grave, given the pitiless repressive systems put in place by the ferocious Attila from the Balearic Islands.

During my frequent visits to Dr. Rabell I was able to evaluate with accuracy the intense worries that all the popular classes and especially the most legitimate representatives of the distinguished city shared from the beginning of that tragic period on account of the imminent dangerous circumstances it would lead to. And those preoccupations increased when General Pedro Pin took possession of the command of the zone, substituting for the gentlemanly General Aizpurua. The latter had comported himself in an understanding and humanitarian manner; but Pin, "a man lacking instruction and conscience," in the view of Marcos García, undertook the harshest persecutions against the Cuban population. He filled the jails with innocent people, making use of a pack of soulless minions in sadistic complicity with the directors of the *Casino Español*[45] in the commission of his brutal acts of vengeance. He converted Sancti Spíritus into a den of horrible suffering and despair.

How comforting to my afflicted spirit during those days were the frequent conversations I had with my affectionate friend. Because despite the age difference, the similarity of criteria and sentiments with regard to whatever matter we discussed—by preference the vexing realities of those times—the most sincere friendship and trust was established between us in the warmth of such spontaneous proofs of our kindred spirits.

In one of those opportunities we had to share our convictions and reciprocal condemnations of Weyler's iniquitous procedures throughout the island, along with the atrocities of Pin in the city and jurisdiction of Sancti Spíritus, Dr. Rabell showed that he was deeply preoccupied by the increasingly cruel virulence of Weyler's command in the city and the extensive zone around it, and the pleasure his representative took in implementing, broadening and exacerbating the atrocious measures of the Hispanic Caligula.

Dr. Rabell informed me of the total lack of scruples and human sympathy with which General Pin proceeded against unfortunate innocents, jailing some, mysteriously disappearing others, and relegating entire families to the most atrocious helplessness and misery. "Until now," Dr. Rabell told me, "the directors of the *Partido Liberal Autonomista* have been exempt from the vengeance that Pin wanted to unleash against us, too, but now we know through trustworthy sources that he wants to carry out his aims however he can. And, unfortunately, if this plan should be confirmed," Dr. Rabell added, "it occurred to me this morning to dedicate my portrait to you, as a testimony and souvenir of the sincere friendship you have inspired in me since I first met you."

As the reader of this *Memoir* may suppose, the delicate and spontaneous act with which Dr. Rabell wished to honor me awakened intense gratitude in my soul and the emotion I felt only intensified when I read the very generous dedication he wrote on the back of the photo and which reads as follows: "To my esteemed friend D. José Conangla Fontanilles, an inspired, fluent, passionate writer and a man with a generous soul. Francisco Rabell—April, 28–96.—Sancti Sptus."

A few days after the emotional conversation that I've just referred to, the sensational rumor spread publicly that General Pin had already ordered, as was feared, the proscription of the most important advocates of autonomy in the city, threatening them with removal as a group to Havana, but not to be held in the capital of the country, but rather to be deported immediately to one of the Spanish prisons in Ceuta, Chafarinas or Fernando Poo.[46]

I hastened to Dr. Rabell's pharmacy, concerned at such a serious piece of news, to find out whether the rumor was true or not. Unfortunately, it was true! In the early evening Dr. Rabell himself, in the back room, surrounded by some people I didn't know, received me looking very upset. He said to me with anguish: "Now you see, friend Conangla: our fears were not groundless. I am to leave without delay with the heartache of leaving my little son gravely ill!" And he added: "How is it possible that not even we autonomists can love Spain!"

Those who want to learn about the enormous atrocities committed by General Pin and his criminal assassins can refer to pages 25 to 52 of the interesting *Carta-Folleto* that Marcos García, the very popular mayor of Sancti Spíritus, wrote during that fatal period. It was sent three years later to Don José María Gálvez,[47] president of the autonomous cabinet during the last stages of Spanish dominion in Cuba.[48] In those pages the author describes with vigorous strokes, equivalent to a masterful watercolor, the atrocities that Weyler's satrap committed in the vicinity of the terrorized city at that time. Not even the most prestigious representatives of the *Partido Liberal Autonomista* could free themselves from such iniquitous outrages.

Thanks to the urgent, civic negotiations that Marcos García mobilized by means of a forceful telegraphic appeal to General Ochanda, head of the Captain-General's General Staff (whom he knew from the time of the *Pacto de Zanjón*), the illustrious inhabitants of the city, although they could not evade their shameful removal to the capital, were spared nonetheless, from the threatened confinement in Spanish prisons in Africa. Dr. Rabell and several others remained in Havana, others immigrated to the United States and one or another, in angry disappointment with pacifism, joined the ranks of the liberators.

One of the last acts of ferocity committed by Pin's hired killers, which I witnessed in its horrific, hair-raising effects, left an indelible impression of fright and pity. I can do no less than include my recollection in this *Memoir*. It was as follows: "A few days after the forced exodus of the representatives of autonomy, the inhabitants of Sancti Spíritus experienced another commotion, motivated by a macabre happening: the sudden arrival at one of the most central places on the Calle Real of a Spanish guerrilla group that brought four *mambises* into the city who were already dead, horribly cut by machetes, the cruel wounds that disfigured their faces hands and arms still bleeding; their mouths covered with purulent froth; some of them with eyes out of their sockets; barefooted and half naked; their clothes turned into muddy rags."

In the middle of the day the cadavers were taken to Sancti Spíritus, their torsos and legs hanging from the backs of horses. They were unloaded and brutally piled up by their ferocious killers—in total disregard of pious sentiments—on the sidewalk opposite and almost in front of the prestigious Sociedad El Progreso.

Despite the passage of many years, the memory of that frightful spectacle even now revives in my innermost convictions the trembling indignation that such a horrible, ferocious scene produced in me. I harbor the certainty that it kindled the same harsh repudiation of such acts in all the inhabitants of the city with a Christian conscience.

In connection with the episodes synthesized in the preceding pages, but especially in regard to what happened near the Sancti Spíritus cemetery, I have paused many times to meditate on how, not only in the unrolling of those events, but throughout the course of my life (and the life of each human being) a multitude of circumstances converge, intertwine and combine—many of them apparently by chance, devoid of visible, logically inductive, determinative acts. Yet, in reality, they may obey mysterious causes, inexplicable to the clearest reason but intuitively attributable (think what they will, atheists and skeptics) to the supreme rule believed to govern the indecipherable enigmas of Creation and the designs of the evolutionary process of all and each one of the cosmological orders, as also the biological and subjective orders of the human race.

Because many circumstances of our existence, thought to happen by chance, by simple unpredictable events which have arisen without any evident or reasonable nexus with acts or things far removed, happen, nonetheless, as if they were transcendent events, interconnections or consequences related to those remote realities; just as if these new circumstances with undoubted connections to the preceding ones were brought about by express induction of the above-mentioned mysterious design.

I do not intend to formulate a capricious pseudo-scientific hypothesis with this abstract digression on such enigmas. I simply wish to express my most sincere belief that the undeniable correlation that, in the course of years, emerged with the meshing of circumstances that are so similar, I cannot attribute to mere chance or accidents. Instead, I attribute them to present-day limited human intelligence and sensory capabilities. This correlation, then, becomes evident in the intuitive light of fervent spirituality.

Limiting myself concretely to the turn of events that most intensely affected me during the first days of my residence in Sancti Spíritus (from December 12, 1895, to the end of that month), I do not hesitate to confess my conviction that accidental circumstances did not save my life from imminent material dangers, but rather that it was the influence of the apparent designs of Providence. Perhaps this was so in compensation for the pitiful misadventures that I was to suffer in my early youth, or who knows whether it might have been because a mission was reserved for me by the same inscrutable secret force: the mission, the professed manifest destiny of pursuing and successively intensifying vocational tasks with enthusiasm, always acting with honorable civic sense from the outset of my romantic adolescence. I undertook those tasks to advance and defend sacred rights and natural duties, bulwarks of authentic humanism, which are germane to the greatest mutual respect of Christian confraternity and indispensible civilized solidarity—rights and duties that I understand must be maintained worthily and strictly among all people and all social nuclei, national, political, religious of all humanity on earth.

But, as I insinuated at the beginning of this *Memoir*, I not only experienced painful impressions during my stay in Sancti Spíritus. I was also able to enjoy stimulating and comforting satisfactions such as those I've already mentioned, as well as diverse emotions awakened in my contemplative spirit by continued admiration of the houses, temples, plazas and wide streets, the monuments of historical importance in the important city, as also by the surrounding landscape and the attractive Yayabo,[49] with its moving waters, a majestic sight beneath the magnificent bridge of granite arcades.

In the midst of that urban greatness and the suggestive pantheistic enchantment that the fields and mountains on the outskirts of Sancti Spíritus inspired in me, I began to feel my liberal, republican, and democratic rebellions—traceable directly to legitimate Catalan ardor—become more robust, along with my support of the sister rebellions of legitimate and sacred Cuban Independence.

Besides the totality of immediate impressions, some of them dimmed after the passage of so many years since they affected my spirit, I very gratefully continue to evoke the mental recollections of persons, instants, places, things, and surroundings during my historic residence in Sancti Spíritus.

So, for example, among evocations of the urban monuments in the city

—its temples, regal houses, wide streets, and the attractive Plaza del Ayuntamiento, in one of its most central parts these edifices stood out: the building of the Sociedad El Progreso, Dr. Rabell's pharmacy, Dr. Weiss's optical shop, and a majestic house with spacious salons visible through the grilles behind which an adorable group of very beautiful girls used to sit in the late afternoon and early evening accompanied by a mature lady who was no less beautiful.

On the same Calle Real, beyond the church, I see the pharmacy of Dr. Cancio Madrigal, who belonged to one of the most prestigious lineages in the city. And on a nearby street, but diagonal to it, I also recall the saddlery of the robust Catalan, Chiner, and next to it the surprising reproduction of the spirited horse of natural size that was the silent guardian of the store and a possible twin of another horse, an example of the same design that I discovered years later in a saddlery on the Teniente Rey Street in Havana.

On the opposite side of Sancti Spíritus I preserve a faint image—the newspaper press run by two intellectuals with the same surname, Fernández Morera, whom I did not have occasion to meet and even now I regret it.

And on the subject of presses and newspapers, I have never forgotten, since I first heard it, a shocking and ambiguous call of a town crier who went through the streets of Sancti Spíritus in the afternoon, shouting: "The morning *El Pais!* Lettuce!"—a cry that for me was like a symbolic summary of the two main Cuban preoccupations in that anguished period: patriotism and the quest for a modest family meal.

I gathered together still-palpitating testimonials of those impressions, inspired by places, moments, or unforgettable emotional experiences in the notebook that constituted my first book of poetry, *Odes del cor*, published three years later in Barcelona with the title *Elegía de la guerra*, with a preface by Joan Maragall,[50] "the greatest and most original lyric poet that Catalonia, and perhaps Spain, had in the past and present century," in the opinion of the eminent Spanish critic Manuel de Montoliu.[51]

As a complement to this chapter, which refers to recollections of my stay in Sancti Spíritus, I shall insert here translations of some of my first poetic impressions, inspired in moments, things and places of that city:

BEAUTIFUL NATURE

Beautiful nature,
your fields form a contrast:
I find reddish earth,

as if kneaded with blood.
So many watered you
that you are now the image of horror:
so many, like thousands of mothers.
who weep here, and far away, beyond the seas.

DAWN

A thin winding sheet is spread immobile
over the "grassland."
It is the veil that covers mother earth,
It is thick fog.
But, soon the Sun comes up; and that sheet
little by little disappears,
Nature reveals its charms
and the War, its wings!

CONSCRIPT

They brought me here to a beautiful and rare world,[52]
a soldier by force, not by conviction.
Here I discover poetry,
and here in times of peace it must be Heaven.
But, ay! The acrid breath of death
spoils such brilliant prospects,
and exhales emanations from the grave,
that hampers ecstasy at the splendor of it all.

THE SMILE

I saw her behind the grille,
seated in a rocking chair.
Her fine and delicate placidity
made me exclaim: How beautiful!
Large eyes, hair unbound,
white dress, still hands,
and in her hair, flowers
that enhanced her beauty. . .
I contemplated her through the grille,
and at that moment she smiled
as if she knew me.
as if we were friends.
"Blessings on the sweet smile

that brought me to your presence!"
I said to her; and I did not know how
to continue down the street.

A good friend approached me
as I delighted in her smile: he whispered in my ear
with a pained voice "She is mad! . . ."
Then I saluted her
with tenderness and gratitude;
and slowly sent her a kiss
through the grille.
And why not? I am grateful
for the smile she gave me;
It is the only one, the first
since I have been exiled;
and even though the woman is mad,
far as I live from all love,
I kept her smile in my heart.

SENSITIVE

Near the River Yayabo
in a border of greenery,
they tell me that there is a plant
asleep in sweet drowsiness.
This morning I hastened
to the banks of the Yayabo,
and found the sleeping plant,
and gave it a light touch.
All its unfurled leaves
crumpled up at once,
and one by one, determined,
closed violently.
I moved away. A spider,
weaver in a subtle web,
moved down upon the leaves,
whistled, and the plant opened.
Then I thought I saw
ineffable confidences
between the fearful plant
and the vigilant insect.
I touched the plant again

and its mysterious defender
rose up in fury
and the plant trembled. . .
Cuba, admirable nature;
I do not wonder at your ideal;
even in the weakest plant
there are yearnings for liberty.
Jealous of your beauties,
happy in the burning sun,
you live a prisoner,
and long for your redemption.
I would give you if I could
the freedom you sigh for;
but, ay! your jailer
took mine away as well!

At the end of May 1896, the General Command of the Sancti Spíritus zone communicated an order from the Gobierno Superior to the directorship of our office for our transfer to the town of Aguacate, situated in the territory of Havana Province almost on the border with Matanzas. We were informed that the battalion column complied with a similar order.

On the morning of June 4, 1896, the same freight train that brought us to Sancti Spíritus on December 12 of the previous year took the commanders and the group of office scribes and orderlies to Tunas de Zaza. This time our troop companions were loaded with our respective arms and backpacks. They also watched over several wooden boxes containing the documents and property of the office.

From Tunas, on board the *Antinógenes Menéndez*, we sailed without delay toward Cienfuegos, where we remained for a few hours, during which time we were permitted, in two separate groups, to walk around the beautiful streets of the modern city. On the sixth we arrived at the Surgidero de Batabanó[53]; I don't recall whether it was in the same *Antinógenes Menéndez* or another ship. The next morning we continued by rail toward Matanzas[54] and Aguacate,[55] the new residence assigned to us so that the battalion column, transferred to this zone of operations, could communicate often with the office.

2

The War in Aguacate

(June to December 1896)

We arrived in Aguacate on June 6, 1896, and were very surprised to be lodged in the town's church. This was done in order to install the offices of the battalion there, as well as our barracks. It was a novel idea that for a moment seemed sacrilegious to us, although we were quickly informed that the decision was based on a legitimate accord between the supreme authority on the island and the bishopric of Havana. The accord reflected strategic considerations since the church, situated in the center of the town well apart from nearby streets, was equivalent to a fortress in the opinion of the military commanders, able to resist any aggressive action on the part of the *mambises*, and because it was possible to keep watch over and control great expanses of the surrounding area from the windows of the bell tower.

Tables indispensable to the officers and scribes were set out in the ample space of the nave. Some convenient shelves and cabinets were placed on the sidewalls for the archiving of files and documents. Brackets and racks were also distributed along the walls to hold the rifles of the guards and the office workers. In the presbytery, as well, on each side of the main altar and in the sacristy, more or less comfortable mats were laid out at night, along with some hammocks belonging to the office personnel.

The interior balcony, or choir, situated above the atrium of the church, also accommodated uncomfortable beds and served as a place to fasten hammock ropes. During the first few nights, until I found a usable space to hang my hammock in one of the corners of the presbytery, I chose to improvise a bed along the top of the main altar itself.

Upon our arrival in Aguacate we were surprised at the news that our commander, captain, and one of the lieutenants of the office in Sancti Spíritus had been assigned to other units, and that another commander, captain, and lieutenant were taking their places and were charged with assuming their respective bureaucratic functions, along with Lieutenant Resiles. The management of the office, nonetheless, was confided to the captain and the two lieutenants. The new commander was excluded from this charge. He was delegated to undertake the job of authorized paymaster only; that is to say, the representative of the battalion in its budgetary dealings with the island's military administration.

The recently incorporated commander, the captain, and the lieutenant, together with Lieutenant Resiles, chose for their mansion a nearby building situated on the side street to the right of the office, in front of the access that the office had (and I suppose still has) to that street. And the corner formed between the external projection of the church vestibule and its wall on the side street was the place chosen for the installation of the stoves where the food was prepared for the office personnel and the squad charged with maintaining the corresponding guards.

From the time that they initiated their respective functions in the management of the office, the new captain and lieutenant garnered our most respectful sympathy, sharing it with the affection we already professed for the affable Resiles. All the office workers, moreover, felt a special attraction to Lieutenant Navascués due to his leadership qualities of simplicity, openness, and democratic comportment. He was an authentic son of Zaragoza, a man of noble character, the oldest and the most competent among his comrades, for all of which he was unanimously chosen to be the leader of the office and also the friendly counselor of all the office personnel.

On the other hand, the commander in charge very quickly became the object and target of general antipathy owing to remarkable circumstances. He was about sixty years old, short, with a big belly, almost bald but with a full beard and mustache. Within a few days of moving in next to the office, to the great astonishment of his comrades, the office staff and the neighborhood in general, it was learned that the commander whose physical appearance was far from that of an Adonis, rather mysteriously went to live in the private domicile of a respectable old man and his daughter, who resided a short distance away from the church, on the Calle Real.

In stark contrast to the old man, his daughter was a beautiful young woman of twenty-four to twenty-six springs, tall, slender, with a very beautiful figure. Her features were adorable. They limned, nonetheless, a revealing fixed expression of profound sadness. Even though the old man and his enchanting only daughter were held, until then, in the highest regard and could justify the admission of the strange commander into their company as a simple boarder, as a means of relieving themselves of numerous economic reversals suffered during the war (an explanation that could prove accurate and reasonable) public suspicion, nonetheless, continued to characterize and lament the ambiguous living arrangement of the enigmatic commander in the domicile of the ruined man as a situation only explicable, in secret, as a tragic filial sacrifice of the compliant young woman.

Within fifteen days of reinstalling our office, the battalion column arrived in Aguacate. Its arrival was an emotional event for the office workers just as it was for the group of soldiers who, like us, were forced recruits.

We had scarcely had time to take leave of them six months earlier in Sancti Spíritus when they had to undertake military actions without having received any preparation whatsoever for such exhausting operations.

It is not necessary to ponder how effusive our greetings were and how inexhaustible were the confidences, news or agreeable impressions—along with painful ones—exchanged that day and the three following days between the office workers and the soldiers in the battalion column. There were exchanges describing forced marches in the *manigua* and mountain hamlets, and others describing our peaceful labors, no less anguished in a spiritual sense for being sedentary. Because both groups during our separation suffered pitiful losses of esteemed companions, and we were all also involved in risks, dangers, fears, nostalgia, and similar intimate sources of sadness.

Our conversations were more emotional and fervent when we met up again with the soldiers from Montblanc and other Catalans who started out with us from Cartagena. How brief were those few days that our battalion column remained in Aguacate!

The cordial effusions, however, of such an authentic sense of comradeship became quite disturbed and inhibited by the unexpected arrival at the railroad station of a new, unexpected, and deplorable contingent of troops from the Peninsula that had recently disembarked in Havana. They amounted to some two hundred soldiers altogether: young for the most part with the look of unhappy *quintos*, and the rest, fewer in number—about sixty—of relatively mature appearance, some already in their forties, all of them sporting brand-new striped uniforms and each one with his backpack, but without arms as yet.

The soldiers who were in their forties came without doubt from the well-known policy of volunteer enrollment according to which each man obligated himself to fight against the Cuban insurrectionists during the war and to remain under the military discipline of the Spanish Army for an additional six months. In exchange for such a singular commitment, those spontaneous combatants in favor of supposed Spanish *integridad* in Cuba, on signing up, received the sum of 50 *duros* (250 *pesetas*) in cash and a brand-new blanket.

The battalion commanders and officials of the new expeditionary force had a difficult task in distributing the recently arrived recruits among the decimated companies of the column as well as in getting arms and munitions to the new troops and instructing them in their new obligatory duties. It was also difficult for the officials of our office to negotiate the necessary funds with the battalion command and with the paymaster in order to cover the extraordinary cost of the food allowance and the salaries of the troops concentrated there.

Another difficulty arose as the consequence of such an extraordinary agglomeration of troops in Aguacate: the lack of urban spaces usable at night for lodging both units concentrated there. But this difficulty was resolved by authorizing the captains of the newly restructured companies to gather at taps in determined zones of the town so that the troops—under the guard of the respective squads—could spread their bedrolls on porches and other places that were thought to be appropriate.

Everything was solved more or less efficiently. The battalion made up for its losses with recruits and volunteers recently arrived from the Iberian peninsula, except for a few of the latter, as will be seen below. And the column then left Aguacate following an advanced guard of guerrillas acquainted with the nearby areas, in the direction of the towns and hills of Jaruco,[1] and then continued operations later throughout the province of Havana.

Within a few days the battalion received a dispatch sent from Guanabacoa[2] informing us, among other things, of the column's engagements in combat with liberation forces, the losses suffered in those fights as well as other losses caused by illness. Among the latter was a compatriot of mine, a fellow recruit and forced expeditionary soldier, the son of an honorable countrywoman (Rosa Casona, as we called her), who was an excellent wet nurse to my sister, María de los Llanos.

That companion was a healthy, charming, smiling, spirited youth, whom I wanted to retain—with the consent of Lieutenant Navascués—as an orderly in the Aguacate office. But my friend preferred to continue on active duty, tempted by a group of dissolute soldiers in his company who indulged in card games at every possible moment, when they bivouacked in uninhabited places as well as when they stopped for several hours in the country near villages.

I was deeply pained by the death of such a valued fellow inhabitant of Montblanc, and since I could not now favor him in life, as had been my intention, I took care to list his loss officially as the victim of a sudden attack of yellow fever on active duty, a designation that gave the disconsolate mother the right to a modest pension for life. Making use of the same recourse, in the book that recorded deaths in the battalion, I was careful to authorize benefits due to death in action for families of other companions who were victims of that terrible fever or any other comparable illness. Because of such initial certifications four or five modest families of Montblanc farmers as well as other Catalan comrades were able to claim and receive pensions that were miserably small but were of undoubted economic relief to the devastated parents.

In addition to the new captain and the two lieutenants designated to assume the management functions of the office, some changes were made in the scribes' auxiliary personnel and the auxiliaries of the office. Two sergeants and two corporals, who came from the contingent that was recently incorporated into the battalion, replaced former companions for unknown reasons. Three soldiers were also admitted as new scribes from among the volunteers who recently joined the battalion. And finally, the squad that took turns guarding the exterior of the office was also replaced with new recruits.

I had the satisfaction of seeing that another Montblanc recruit from my call up was included in the new group assigned to reinforce the squad that guarded the building. He well deserved protection since his uselessness was obvious even though he was classified as suitable for military service despite his evident lack of aptitude. This was due to his parents' ignorance and the lamentable inattention or indifference of the recruiters in the corresponding recruitment zone. He was simply an unfortunate, mentally retarded man, slow, incapable of taking any initiative on his own, not even able to speak with his companions, for he was limited to responding with a few words or affirmative, negative or doubtful nods of his head to all questions addressed to him. He was quick, however, to obey any order directed to him, and that led to malicious comrades making him the butt of abusive deceptions and tricks especially designed to lengthen his guard duty or to steal or reduce the little money due him.

When other Catalans in the column made me aware of these abuses, I lost no time in informing Lieutenant Navascués. I wanted to have my unfortunate countryman Marquet (that was his name) assigned to the squad on guard duty in my office for his protection. The noble Aragonese officer, sharing my compassion and without delay, before leaving for operations with the battalion, saw to it that Marquet was transferred to our guard and placed under my direct protection so that the witless and pitiful son of a sharecropper in the vineyard of my elders was freed in the future from becoming the object of the kinds of extortion I have mentioned.

With the new arrivals, the battalion office in Aguacate consisted of the following personnel: the new captain, Hernández (as I recall); First Lieutenant Navascués; and Second Lieutenant Resiles. The auxiliaries of the troop consisted of two sergeants, Fernández and Caturla, the first man from Cartagena and the second from Valencia, both from our original expedition. Two corporals, both Catalans; a soldier also brought by force to Cuba from Cartagena: Ambrosio Rull; the narrator; a soldier named Rovira; and two soldiers from the group of volunteers that was just transferred to the battalion, both older men already thirty to thirty-five years old: Torromé, from La Mancha; and Sanjuan, from Alicante. I shall sketch the outstanding traits of each one of those office colleagues.

Sergeant Fernández, a native of Cartagena, was a robust youth, tall, high-strung, and sociable. He was from the original regiment of España número 46. We were recruited in the same call up although he got out of the first sailing to Cuba; later, he had to embark with a new expeditionary group. Charming and an optimist, he was indifferent to anything unrelated to the maintenance of harmony among his companions and subordinates. Gastronomy was his main interest. He invited us frequently to contribute to the reasonably priced cost of some tasty empanadas with chorizo from La Mancha, whose preparation and cooking he entrusted to the shopkeeper who provided food for the rations of the office workers and the guards' mess. In the café near the office during periods of inactivity we ate the empanadas accompanied by several glasses of beer each that served as a digestive.

The other sergeant, Caturla, from Alicante, also came from the same original regiment in which he served until he had to come from Cartagena to Cuba in the recent sailing. Caturla, like Fernández, was easy to deal with, although he had a restless temperament. He always spoke Valencian[3] with me and the other Catalan office staff, seldom omitting the additional common locution *che*,[4] indispensable in any friendly conversation among the democratic people of the Iberian Peninsula. Caturla was also an educated man, ideal for implementing directives from the managers, but he was eager to cultivate adventures among the accessible young women in the town, preferably the light-skinned *mulatas*. To ensure the greater success of his inquiries into the availability of eligible young women, he resorted to contracting the laundering of his underwear and his striped uniforms with different desirable laundresses.

Next in the order of ranked office personnel were the corporals Ambrosio Rull Queraltó and your narrator. Rull was called up when I was, and like me, he got a job as scribe in the office of the same Regimiento de Infantería de España número 46, the original formation of the battalion that came to Cuba. More than a companion, Ambrosio Rull was for me a very noble and exemplary brother, for when we coincided under the prearranged safe quarters of the church/barracks in Aguacate, the most spontaneous, honorable, and complete friendship was established between us. It stemmed from our sharing of identical principles and convictions in all areas of ideology and sentiments, especially in those relating to our patriotic rebellions, which by their nature were very Catalan.

In regard to my unforgettable friendship and gratitude to Rull for his many kindnesses, and as a testament of praise for his heroic dignity and his notably well-integrated character, it would please me greatly—if God were to give me health and tranquility—to have more space to convey the emotional warmth of this friendship in a new series of pages evocative of my second stay and definitive spiritual and civic bond with Cuba.

Three soldiers were also assigned to the reorganized battalion office in Aguacate: one from the involuntary troops, called Rovira, from Barcelona; and two from the volunteers: Torromé, from Albacete; and Sanjuan from Valencia.

The Catalan, Rovira, was the scribe with the clearest and most elegant writing. He had perfect penmanship (he qualified as a *pendolista*[5] according to his classification in the recommendation that brought him from Cartagena to join our office). He had a phlegmatic but amiable nature, always immersed in the copying tasks he was charged with, as well as in other mysterious writings that we wanted to find out about. To my great surprise, they were lyric musings on one hand and prolix annotations on the other in the intimate journal that he had kept since he left Cartagena, supplemented with facts or things worthy of mention and recollection relative to the battalion or to his observations.

When I became aware of Rovira's labors of love, even greater sympathy arose between us as we exchanged our more or less productive poetic productions. But my surprise increased at the mysterious inclinations of friend Rovira when he reminded me, in the warmth of our mutual love of poetry, that we had met before the Cuban War began. When I asked him where that happened, he told me when we were seated next to each other by chance in the front row of the so-called henhouse[6] or stewpot of the Teatro Romea[7] in Barcelona, where we talked about the Catalan work onstage, and went on to talk about the season of mime performances (or rather pantomimes) that the then famous Onofri company was offering at that time in the Palais Real near the Calle Ancha.[8] "Of course!" I said to him. And I added: "And to be sure, I was surprised when you told me in the course of that conversation that you were preparing a script in verse for a new pantomime."

Carlos Torromé, from Albacete, was older, about thirty-five to forty years old. He was intelligent, cultivated, and possessed notable literary aptitude. He was, however, very reluctant to demonstrate his talent and to open up to the other office workers when we were not occupied. He preferred to take advantage of these periods of leisure to join a supposed fellow countryman of his—an orderly in the office. He displayed such an assiduous attraction to the orderly that it always seemed strange to the rest of us office workers.

The other volunteer soldier was incorporated into the office as a scribe, thanks to the special recommendation of some military personage in the Peninsula. This was Sanjuan, a man of thirty, robust, of medium height, with an earnest look, manners, and a demeanor that were naturally aristocratic. In the office it was rumored, based on the comments of other volunteers who came in the same expeditionary contingent, that Sanjuan belonged to a noble Valencian family. He was alienated from his family over a difference of views on a romantic matter. His elders threatened to disinherit him if he persisted in his decision to marry a young woman from the irrigated gardens and orchards outside the city who was very alluring but whose antecedents were questionable. It appears that Sanjuan, upset by the paternal threat, turned to drink, and in a depressed period of disoriented drunkenness enrolled as a volunteer. Lodged in barracks and taken to Cartagena together with other adventurers, he ended up in the Aguacate office due to the influence of his father, who meant to free him at the very least from having to risk his life in military operations.

We office workers did not know, of course, whether these rumors were true but we accepted them as well founded given that Sanjuan in every one of his inoffensive and, for him, satisfying drunken episodes would lean against the balcony railing of the church choir loft, where he improvised genuine discourses, replete with querulous allusions to traditional prejudices, authoritarian failures of understanding, and unfair prohibitions. On the advice of another sympathetic office worker, he would be removed from the symbolic tribunal and put to bed on his designated sleeping platform in the choir itself. And when he woke up, with great serenity he regained the unmistakable manners of his exquisite education.

Once our tasks were in order, the battalion column gone and jobs allotted to each one, Lieutenant Navascués (the real manager of the office) appointed me his secretary, based, he told me, on the information Lieutenant Resiles had given him regarding my duties in Sancti Spíritus as well as my university background and literary vocation. This vote of confidence with which Lieutenant Navascués singled me out did not awaken any signs of envy among the office workers.

When we were caught up on our work, we did not hesitate to spend our free moments chatting, telling stories, and engaging in interesting confidences, or we often went out to "while away the morning or the afternoon" in accord with Creole custom, in some nearby bodega. And in the evening, Rull and I, having finished our daily tasks, almost always took walks or visited some honorable families in the neighborhood while other companions pursued adventures that were more or less instinctive, feasible, and understandable.

We were often fortunate in that, during extended periods of time, no military actions disturbed the relative tranquility or forcibly imposed normality on the interior of the town. By exception, on some nights we heard shots on the outskirts of Aguacate or in the neighborhood of the Ingenio Rosario.[9] The surprising contrast of those nearby shots with the spiritual atmosphere that still emanated from inside the church—even though the bishop of Havana had deconsecrated it—led me, in moments of release from office duties, to sum up in rhyme the strong impression made on me of the church turned into a barracks, as well as some of the painful reflections inspired by the imposing image of the Divine Redeemer with arms extended, which was placed at the top of the main altar. It was an image that struck me then as a sarcastic symbol of moral anguish and philosophical doubts. The translation of that spiritual *impromptu*, which was originally included in my *Elegía de la guerra* in Catalan, follows:

Neither psalms nor prayers[10]
of believers are heard now
in the nave of the temple
now a brazen barracks.
The altars are used for kindling
the walls are cracked;
even the high pulpit
is increasingly warped;
and rifles and machetes
hang there instead of ex-votos.
Only the main altar
is preserved in its grandeur.
But the only image
that it holds between columns,
is a rare statue
of omnipotent God.
The image is erect:
it looks toward the sky and extends
its arms as a sign of preaching
with clemency, the redemptive brotherhood
of peoples and nations.
But what cold sarcasm
when without the temple
shots are heard at night
cries, denunciations
angry curses,
blasphemies and laments!

Then the figure
that gazes fixedly at the heavens
arms extended
like the symbol or spark
of redemptive brotherhood
between peoples and countries
seems rather the image
of the eternal philosopher
touching among the shadows
truths that he sees,
his heart being blind,
yet, his mind denies!

I referred earlier to the visits Rull and I made on some afternoons to honorable families in Aguacate. One of them, the Abreu family, was our favorite. It consisted of two sisters or cousins—I don't recall whether they were natives of the Canary Islands—and an adorable fifteen-year-old, the daughter of the second woman. The sister with the stronger character of the two had been a teacher of primary education and music before the war, but as the struggles for independence increased, she was losing students. At the same time, the sister's husband disappeared from the town—possibly because he joined the liberation forces. And then, thanks to the decorous recourse of laundering the clothes and uniforms of some officers, corporals and sergeants, and soldiers in the troops, that good family like others in the town alleviated their economic crisis with admirable austerity and resignation.

I confess that I, as much as Rull, and one or another office worker, admired the charming and ingenuous girl's gracefulness; our conversations with her, her mother, and her aunt, the cultivated and very discreet teacher, were most pleasant. Our relations, however, remained on the most decorous level of trivial matters or motives, which reflected our great respect for the esteemed hostesses and the understanding due their misfortune.

On one occasion, however, animated by very liberal ideals, I did not attempt to restrain my aversion to despotic regimes in general and especially the tyrannical Austro-Bourbon monarchy, determined to choke with blood what it ought to resolve by means of compromises and the recognition of natural rights. But every time Rull or I brought up the daring subject, the intelligent teacher tried to change the subject although she, her sister, and the amiable girl made it clear with their affable smiles that our frankness pleased them inwardly.

Another demonstration of the unity of sentiment which that honest

Cuban family secretly shared with the purest yearnings for liberation was revealed to me by the impressive story that the cultivated teacher told me one afternoon when she rejected my request that she let us hear some sweet Creole song on the piano. The answer she gave me was as unexpected as it was moving. She told me, in summary, that she closed the piano (still in the room) at the beginning of the insurrection and promised not to open it again until the indomitable will of Cuba should manage to end the war "in the only just way that the other countries in America ended theirs." These were exemplary concepts that I was grateful for and moved by, as much for their patriotic intensity as for the noble trust that they implied in acceptance of my mental and spiritual solidarity with Cuban patriotism.

In the course of the following months, a guerrilla unit frequently came to Aguacate and stayed there for several hours to rest or store up on food supplies. It was a guerrilla group composed of unscrupulous individuals, who under orders that anticipated those of the Decreto de la Reconcentración, were burning down the humble *bohíos*[11] inhabited by defenseless families, which were already reduced solely to women and children. In addition, they were ordered to take those unfortunate displaced creatures with their necessary belongings and yard animals to the nearest towns.

On the outskirts of Aguacate, protected by a fort located a short distance from the railroad, there was an old wooden house whose two floors—with open balconies on the second floor—were used as a mobile hospital for Spanish soldiers. Beyond that building some twenty meters to the right, there was a spacious, empty wood frame warehouse with a damaged, rotten roof. Half fallen down through neglect, it was divided into three sections and may have served originally as a pen for cows or a storehouse for merchandise since it was conveniently located next to the railroad. That warehouse, accordingly, was unsuitable for housing human beings, despite the fact that it was fitted out to take in a crushing jumble of unfortunate victims of the terrible reconcentration's first casualties.

One afternoon, accompanied by other office workers, I wanted to see the real conditions of that appalling agglomeration of people all crammed together. And the shock of pity and indignation its horrendous scenes aroused in me was so intense that even now, sixty-two years later, my Christian soul still throbs with painful vibrations triggered by the same principled protests of moral indignation. That piling up of human beings was a scene out of Dante. Beaten down, weeping, half-naked and sick for the most part; some were dying, others lacking the most essential things for survival. Nonetheless, in brotherly fashion they shared the miserable victuals, clothes, blan-

Figure 1. "Sunday morning mass in the field. Spanish officers and soldiers attend divine service between battles, and sometimes dodge bullets while they tell their beads. The priest stands near the extemporized altar." (*Greater America*. New York: F. Tennyson Neely, Publisher, 1898.)

kets, or useful items that some of them had salvaged from their modest dwellings!

Deeply affected in the presence of that horrible den of suffering—witness to the anguish of starving children and the cries of desperate mothers—from the depths of my conscience I cursed those responsible for such a detestable way of waging war. But then, feeling confused, pained, and humiliated in my human dignity by that inferno of barbaric cruelties, I left the horrendous building and walked with unsteady steps to the church/barracks. There I sought refuge in my quiet hammock in order to still the agitation I felt by focusing mentally on the purest and most righteous reflections.

Within a few days of the horror I experienced in that frightful hell of indescribable tortures, an open-air mass was celebrated on a piece of land next to the hospital and the building where people were enduring frightful suffering. Either because the battalion column had returned to Aguacate, or because the next day was Sunday, or because of I don't know what special commemoration, the civil and military authorities of the town decided to offer a mass attended by all the military units on active duty and also by our office personnel.

It was a splendid, hot morning at the end of July or beginning of August 1896. It goes without saying that because of the extraordinary circumstances of the occasion and the place where it was celebrated, the mass constituted a most interesting event. It attracted numerous faithful from the town, gathered around the armed forces that in proper formation lent greater solemnity to the occasion.

Of course, I wasn't able, nor did I try, to discern the impressions made on the souls of the troops as they witnessed the sunny mass with more or less fervor. But the emotional impact of my recent visit to the nearby Dantesque warehouse not only revived in my brain the nerve-racking anguish of the desperate people packed into that infernal space, but also revived reactions of pious condolence and impulses of instinctive protest in my heart and soul, causing a kind of delirium, intensified by the suffocating heat. And while that sensation troubled me, angry, phantasmagoric, menacing goatish figures passed before my feverish imagination, a reflection, no doubt of the emotional and spiritual reactions evoked by the sarcastic and, in a way, sacrilegious contrasts that arose from the shocking juxtaposition of two immediate realities—realities so opposed, so discordant, so repellant in their individual significance as the criminal reconcentration and the symbolic ecclesiastical rite of the Holy Mass.

The next day I felt a deep need to synthesize in rhymed stanzas the successive stages in which the unexpected mass was celebrated. Of course, I also wanted to evoke the hallucinatory effects produced in my imagination by the enormous contrast between the two spectacles that existed side by side but were so essentially opposed. I could not exclude the Castilian translation of "The Red Mass" from this memoir. The original poem in Catalan is in my book *Elegía de la guerra* and also appeared in *Juventud*, one of the most famous magazines published in Barcelona at the beginning of the twentieth century. I felt honored to be counted among its most frequent contributors.

THE RED MASS[12]

The fingers of the priest raise
the glowing, golden host.
Under the sun, the soldiers on their knees.
In unison the cornets sound
notes of a grave and regal tune.
Bayonets and rifles shine,
and murmured prayers abound.

To the right of the holy celebrant
three lines of barracks stand.
There, beyond the silent town
the *reconcentrated* woeful dwell.

With poor beasts thrown together,
women and children cluster round,
remnants of families an angry
tyrant drove from neighboring land.

To the left of the holy celebrant
stands a hospital, an old, ramshackle house;
with balcony windows opened wide,
feigning the form of a human skull.
Pale gowns of patients gleam
like roaming *ignes fatui* and then are gone.

I saw the elevation of the chalice over the altar
When the divine host had already descended.
The reflection of the sun on the golden vase
blinded me.
That shaft of sunlight made me wince,
like the thrust of a lance it pierced my brain;
and its afterglow of red left a terrible,
fevered vision in my soul.
. . . And round about the celebrant
I saw a host of phantoms suddenly appear,
and saw them fling their bodies, stripped of flesh,
against the sacred altar.
I heard their chilling cries,
I understood the meaning of their words,
and, in the midst of the din,
I heard the voices of my friends
who were dying in the War.

And I saw the specters who, in a fury were
ripping off the vestments of the priest,
tearing up the holy missal
and throwing down its ruined leaves.
And I saw more ghosts attack,
fiercely rending the host to bits,
into splinters smashing the altar
and bouncing the chalice off the ground.

Then the swarm of skeletons
in a band flew through the air,
and from on high let fade
their baleful screams of impious revenge.

The monstrous vision vanished,
leaving my mind distraught.
When freed from that delirium,
the Mass beneath the sun was at an end.

. . . As, in formation, I made my way to town,
I felt my head was spinning;
there on the altar's right
the corral was swaying in a dismal dance,
sinister as the whim of a heartless fiend
was everything I saw,
so that, from atop a fort, I spied
the red and yellow flag of Spain,
whose folds appeared to melt
drop by drop, with blood!

I took advantage of the frequent rest stops in Aguacate taken by the callous guerrillas I referred to earlier, plus different columns of soldiers, as well as the reinforcements of our battalion, to broaden my impressions regarding the most important differences that existed, in my view, between the conscripted soldiers in the Spanish Army and those who came to Cuba in the same army as the result of its well-known policy of volunteer recruitment.

I know that this topic, due to its complexity, merits an extensive psychological study rather than a simple interpretive exegesis in these pages. But I believe that the direct observations I was able to gather in those and subsequent days—right up to the collapse of Spanish sovereign power in Cuba—enable and authorize me to have an opinion on this subject, although I shall limit myself to laying out very briefly my convictions on this subject.

Moving along—I have excluded the generals, commanders, and officers of that army from this discussion because each one of them (with few exceptions on the whole) could not exist or act otherwise than in accord with the demands of the unconditional allegiance they swore to uphold. From the time of their entrance into military academies, military careers, or into the ranks of the respective branches, as well as those who rose in rank in combat, they functioned in the rigid and exclusive service of the monarchy and its representative powers. They were tools of the same regimen, serving each one of the hierarchical orders of that reactionary organization, such as governance, political rule, the judicial system, and the imposition of dogmatic religion. They were the "crutches"—as popular malice had it—that propped up the archaic and ruinous Bourbon regime. Military men were the agents and responsible parties, no less than the ultra-patriotic and venal daily press, of all the misjudgments, failures, regressions, disasters, and embarrassments brought on by exaggerated Spanish pride during that period.

On the other hand, I do not hesitate to declare my sincere opinion that the ordinary troops of that army bore no criminal responsibility in the course of the last war against the heroic *mambises*. I refer, of course, to the typical Spanish soldier; that is, to the thousands of unfortunate youths of nineteen or twenty, who lived in the enslaved provinces of the absurd Spanish State (absurd, because it was unjustly monolithic, centralizing, and antiliberal). Those men to their misfortune were conscripted, assigned to barracks, and forcibly sent to Cuba, which was, at the time, similarly enslaved by the same absolutist State. There they were obliged to oppose human beings whom they could not consider enemies, since they had no grievances against them. On the contrary, they won our sympathy as soon as Spanish soldiers got to know them.

I always doubted that I could find two or three men out of a thousand among the thousands of conscripted Spanish expeditionary troops who were capable of feeling belligerent hostility toward the Liberation Army. I was certain that if they fought them in the *manigua*, it was only due to the automatism imposed by military discipline, because of the rigid mandate of their fatal position as conscripted fighters, or out of the instinctive need for personal and mutual self-defense, which was unavoidable in many instances. For it cannot be doubted that if the troops in the Spanish Army, in that as in other epochs, had not been conscripted, it would have been very difficult and even impossible for the Spanish government to round up unfortunate recruits who lacked a military vocation and bore no ill will against separatism or the Cuban people.

Among the multitude composed of those flocks of apathetic youths, I could certainly count some ingenuous recruits who, under the influence of the deceitful propaganda heard in chauvinist speeches as the military expeditions embarked for Cuba, would let themselves be influenced briefly by the glittering childishness of histrionic discourses, by insincere flattery, by illusory promises, by the din of bands and the distribution of little flags, medals, and blessings in the midst of cheers and official enthusiasm (although also by sobs, embraces, and sincere farewells). Through direct observation, however, I can assure the reader that all the chauvinistic outbursts launched at such moments vanished into thin air when the conscripted battalions left the ports of the Peninsula. Once they arrived in Cuba, freed from the yoke of Spain's inescapable rule and the harmful influence of deceptive propaganda, the native mental and emotional equilibrium of each recruit was restored with no lingering harm to his soul.

At the same time, what we might call the idiosyncratic psychology of the volunteer soldier was, in general, very different. I have taken care not to include special cases of a romantic rather than a morbid nature, explicable at the time because such romantic types, educated in an environment that promoted an essential *Spanishness*, could not or would not free themselves from their fanatical fixations. At the urging of these fixations, they considered themselves duty bound to sign up for the quixotic military service that sought to impose those concerns. Their obsessions were similar to those of numerous functionaries in the judiciary as well as to those of participants in the triumphalism that characterized the Spanish bureaucracy during that period of confusion with respect to the exercise of authority. These were men who transformed their power into instruments of persecution and angry attacks against Cuban patriotism.

With the exception, then, of recruits with this background (sons, relatives, or friends of political hacks), the majority of the soldiers who volunteered and fought against the Liberation Army could be classified accurately as adventurers. Their main incentive was not patriotism, or even a quixotic romanticism, which was understandable up to a point. Rather, they were merely eager to throw themselves into the search and fulfillment of ambitious adventures of all kinds, without any limiting ethical, policing, or judicial scruples or qualms that might hinder them. To an extent, then, it can be said that the volunteer troops who came to Cuba during the war of 1895–1898 were just like the well-known, perverse, and audacious troops whose immoderate desire for fortune and power led them to sign on to the ships of the *conquistadores* of the Indies—the Indies that Cervantes in *El Celoso extremeño* called the "refuge and shelter of the destitute of Spain, the sanctuary of the bankrupt, safe conduct of murderers, cover and hide-out of card sharps."

During the war, as I have said, I knew many specimens of the adventurer type among volunteers through direct observation. I also knew men who were direct exceptions to this rule during the war, as well as exceptions who have already been described, who fit into the classification of romantics. Among the reinforcements for our battalion there were authentic representatives of volunteers who were rogues. Most of them had served more or less lengthy sentences for theft, fights, scandals, extortion, and all kinds of daring dodges in order to live comfortably day after day, at the expense of their fellow men and on the margin of the law.

During the crossing from Cartagena to Havana, as our friend Rovira explained to us, the hold of the ship that had been converted into bunks for the soldiers were convenient places for gangs of the most experienced adventurers to carry out all kinds of dirty tricks in order to empty the backpacks of the inexpert recruits, and to organize sessions at all hours that offered different attractive card games in which professional con artists appropriated the money that naive soldiers and some volunteers, who were ignorant of the cardsharps' tricks, trustingly handed over to those swindlers. Four of the scoundrels who worked as a gang from the time we embarked in Cartagena deserted when we disembarked in Havana with the deliberate intention of escaping as stowaways or signing up as sailors in some merchant ship headed for the United States or some other country in the Americas, just as many other rascals of the same type did during the war.

At the end of August or beginning of September, I felt ill. With a high fever and fainting spells that prevented me from standing up, I did manage to call for Rull, asking him to contact Navascués in order to excuse my absence. Then I became unconscious and was not aware of anything that happened around me. As I learned many days later, the Cuban physician Dr. Luis González O'Brien, who was summoned to examine me, concluded that my symptoms suggested yellow fever. He recommended my urgent removal to Las Ánimas[13] in Havana, as did the manager of my office.

Lying on a stretcher, put on the first train that arrived from Matanzas and placed in the care of Sergeant Fernández, once the train arrived at the stop of Regla[14] or Guanabacoa, I don't know how he was able to facilitate my transfer to the Caballería dock[15] in Havana, and my immediate admission to the historic hospital with wooden cottages called Las Ánimas. There, still unconscious, I was "discovered" providentially by a Catalan sanitation worker, Antonio Miró Beltrán, who was providing very effective services there. He was an auditor in pharmacy at the University of Havana and graduated later as a pharmacist. Antonio Miró and I, both from Montblanc, were fellow students during the two first courses of the *bachillerato* in the Colegio de Nuestra Señora de la Merced. From that time on, we remained intimate friends and later we were companions during periods of university vacations as assistants in the pharmacy in Montblanc owned by the kindhearted José María Casanovas.

With this background in mind, the reader can imagine Antonio Miró's great surprise when he found me in such deplorable condition in the hospital, and the astonishment I felt, together with hopes of better care and a prompt cure, when I learned that the gravity of my case was lessening and I was able to understand my good fortune at meeting up with my good friend and countryman. I am certain that thanks in large part to his care in supporting the appropriate treatment by the medical staff, my cure was effected more easily—three or four weeks after the onset of such an alarming illness.

During the final days of my hospitalization, however, a new misfortune, more desperate than any suffered until then, befell me. An anguished letter from my mother, forwarded to me by my fraternal companion Rull from the office in Aguacate, notified me of the death of my adored father. It is not necessary to ponder the overwhelming sorrow into which the inconsolable loss of my most exemplary progenitor plunged us all, my far-off family, as much as me.

How many steps I took and how many pleas I made to be allowed to go home, as was fitting, arguing that I was the sole male relative who was able to attend to my family! But it was all in vain. There was no remedy for my enormous bitterness other than to return to Aguacate, where with the indulgence of Lieutenant Navascués and my office colleagues, I took up my secretarial tasks again. I undertook the added effort of sending long letters of mutual consolation to my mother and sisters. I alternated these labors with the comforting relief of gathering together heartfelt poetic expressions—heartbeats, of deeply felt gratitude and perennial devotion to the sainted memory of my most honorable father, whose biography I tried to sum up years later in the pages of one of my first books in Catalan titled *El meu pare, que al Cel sía* (*My father, may he be in Glory*).

When I resumed my office duties, I caught up on the most important news and happenings that had occurred in Aguacate and in the office during my illness. Rull immediately set my mind at rest on the whereabouts of my hammock and the backpack in which I kept all of my belongings and, above all, my intimate papers. My kind colleague took good care of it all when he learned about the seriousness of my sudden illness.

I learned about the successive movements of troops that had recently crossed through Aguacate. I also learned about combat sustained by the battalion column with liberation forces in the scrubland of Vista Hermosa in the jurisdiction of Jaruco—combat in which there were sizable losses of dead and wounded on both sides. I also learned about the scarcity of food in the town due in great part to the destruction of garden produce and fruit ordered by Weyler in order to deprive the liberation forces and the miserable people displaced by the reconcentration of food.

But discreet confidantes also revealed to me that despite the terrible crisis, help arrived on a daily basis to the Dantesque warehouse. It came not only from honorable families and some stores in the vicinity of Aguacate, but also from charitable individuals in the garrison and from our office, who wanted to contribute to the support of that forced conglomeration of desperate beings with leftovers from the soldiers' mess and the office rations.

In October and November, different units of the Spanish troops continued to reconnoiter through nearby jurisdictions, in the direction of the valleys of Bainoa[16] and the hilly country of Matanzas, as also toward the plains and mountains of Jaruco. But despite the frequency of such movements, on a certain night there were alarming sounds of gunfire, which, it was thought, was coming from skirmishes between rebel forces and the garrison at the Ingenio Rosario. A few minutes later, the glow of a mounting fire that illuminated the outskirts of the town bordering on the northern part of the lands adjacent to that sugar plantation intensified.

The office guard mobilized in a state of alarm. Meanwhile Lieutenant Resiles and various office workers and I climbed to the top of the bell tower of the church/barracks in order to verify the location and seriousness of the fire. Fortunately, we calculated that the flames were quite far from the town and the plantation. They were advancing, on the other hand, toward the left, crackling loudly as they invaded the cane field spread out in that direction.

The intensity of the fire, the rays of light it cast in the atmosphere around us and in the faces of the anxious viewers in the windows of the bell tower, along with the intimate reaction that such a surprising and deafening scene produced in me—all that, I tried to describe the next day in spirited stanzas of free verse.

I confess, however, that moved by an overwhelming succession of instinctive moral protests and humanitarian reasoning, once I began to describe the event, it quickly turned into Christian imprecations against the accursed demon of war. It also became a no less severe reproach, directed at the vengeful supporters of war. I even committed the blunder—excusable in the dubious spiritual misunderstandings of my youth—of confronting with foolish boldness "the unknown entity, ruler with universal dominion," asking why it did not prevent all kinds of crimes and injuries against brotherhood and human civilization . . .

With sincere remorse for having proffered such regrettable, though well-intentioned, recriminations, here are the verses from my *Elegía de la guerra*:

THE FIRE[17]

The vigor of the cane, that joyfully
saw its sweet fruit sway in early evening
without risk or danger, now sees
its harvest twist amidst crackling flames!

The overpowering roar of the fire
as it courses on, jumbles the curses
and shots of the escaping troops.

The animals, frightened, howling
or neighing in horror, run blindly,
seeking a saving way out . . .

The graceful palm tree is lit
by the tongues of fire choking it,
its fronds raised pleading to Heaven,
as if it were crying out to Heaven in pain.

And the Heavens are dark; the Moon
dared not come out; nor does a star
appear in the impressive sweep of space.

Down below, around
the church and its tower, the poor dwellings
in the frightened town huddle together.

Round about the bells in silence,
our faces seem inflamed by
the red glow of the fire
they contemplate.

And I, with fever heightened by the blood
that quickly rises to my brain,
feel my face burn and, trembling,
I am agitated by idealistic protests.

Ah, legendary monsters! Your
acts, how slight they seem, in
the burning glow of the flames that in the field
opened a hellish trench, on the surface of the land!

Not Satan in the Bible, from his throne,
presiding amongst demons over the punishment
of the miserable damned—as the agitated mind
supposes—shows the hatred
of the destructive demon of war,
when it lets loose upon the world
floods of misery and vengeance.

Observe, blinded combatants,
how you are instruments of this monster:

whatever its sight encompasses, the terrifying fire
devours . . . now the acts of unfeeling sacrifice
of your own brothers are not enough; you
were not fulfilled by angry deeds against mankind;
your being is degraded even to depriving
most prodigal Nature of its fruit.

The hatred you feel, you cast in gushes
pitilessly upon the earth;
the pious earth created with
sublime love by the great mother!

Oh, caste of Neros, vile race
that sates your destructive urges
with acts of rancor! What is the prize
that drives you toward the miserable path
of ferocious war?

And you, mystery,
unknown Entity, origin of total dominion,
how do you permit
these disasters if your power is immense?
Say why you permit these horrendous crimes
to germinate in the human mind
if you can prevent it? A cruel sarcasm . . . !

Although the return to my office work and the exchanges of impressions with my colleagues, along with my more frequent visits to the estimable Abreu family, alleviated the deep pain that my father's death caused me, that oppressive grief continued to cause me anguish in all those moments when, by day or night, I was without those distractions. And during those moments, besides calming my spirit through frequent letters to my sorely missed mother and sisters, I looked for consolation in poetry. However ingenuous those poetic expressions may be, it seems to me that because of their subjective nature, I ought to include them here. Such outpourings of commemorative inspiration follow, translated with the greatest exactitude of which I am capable from the originals in the familiar *Elegía de la guerra*:

FATHER!

Last night I wandered
through the forests of my dreams.

I no longer found
the oak for which I longed.

I was only able to find the roots
of its memory amidst
the new shoots
growing round about.

Ah! my well-loved forests:
Always stand proud!
May storms not cower you
nor impious adversities.

We shall venerate the memory
of the oak no longer with us;
and thus one day
our children will honor ours.

WINTER MEMORIES

The sky, turned gray,
lets snowflakes slowly fall.

A frozen veil
extends along the valley and the hill
        of the town gathered tightly together.

        And fierce mastiffs
stand guard in yards and gardens.

The wind whips everything,
it spoils and ruins everything;
it punishes the trees,
it snatches away their fruits;
and when its arrogant chariot crosses by
en route to the Coast, in the forest,
it plummets to the sea in whose magic potion,
the waves' white foam, it takes communion.

My spirit, in turmoil,
frenetic with longing,
also crosses, in heedless passage
through lands of distant memories.
Like the wind it traverses the illusory
region of its lost hopes;

and when it comes to the beach of its history,
where it meant to take communion with sweet whiteness,
it finds only bitter misfortune!

DREAMING OF MY LAND

Midday sun—burns the plains,
that seem ensorcelled—in sweet ecstasy.
Nothing troubles their dream—lengthened by repose;
the far-off song—alone is heard
of the hardy farmer—who guides the plow.

"How lovely is the valley!—how straight the lines
of rows of plantings—that the plow imprints!"
Thus does the farmer murmur.—He dries the
drops of sweat—that bathe his face;
he halts the horses,—sighs and rests.

The farmer sits—beneath a tree.
In the boughs—the cicadas strident sing.
And the Sun shines brighter;—and the extensive plain
is beautiful and fertile,— ploughed and seeded,
a symbol of life—a messenger of hope.

But sudden visions—enter the mind
of the tranquil farmer—and leave him troubled:
visions of his son—who, a slave of Spain
fights against his brothers—in distant lands!
And two tears fall—from the father's eyes!

YELLOW BROOM

Now blooming in the heights,
it must enchant the morning
with its golden plumes;
it casts brightness on the plains,
on the breast of lovers
and in the hands of lovers.

It must delight the poor villages
when, copiously picked
and scattered on the streets
like illusory carpets
on solemn occasions,
the blossoms meld in light, joy and life.

Oh yellow broom:
you evoke in my memory
the vision of Corpus Christi and of flowers;
and this illusory vision
worsens and deepens
the anguish of my loves!

REMEMBRANCE

It was a joy to see
vineyards in plenitude:
turned golden by the sun,
the muscatel grapes hang;
and the sweet garnacha
its black grapes shining,
like eyes that in the grip of passion
are feverish and blind.

The cicadas were saying:
October is on the way!
And the crickets were singing
Hidden amidst clods of earth.
October is near;
and fresh, contented,
like the swallows in
chattering flocks,
the songs drew near
and the ingenuous laughter
of handsome youths
and young country women
who filled the big baskets
with fruit in season,
to the lively measure
of different songs,
of laughter and shouts,
of roguish words.

Oh unforgettable month:
your vision grieves me;
since you stir the embers
of my love for my land,
and you make my spirit wander
in its course without a lodestar,

trying to pass over
the seas that surround me,
very far from where
abundant October
bearer of harvests
of white and black grapes;
of the end of summer's heat;
of intense harvests;
of the most sublime hymn,
of the most tender song:
the song of love and life:
the song with the most beautiful notes!

VISION OF THE PYRENEES

Brief, impious dream
that deceives my spirit;
you give me a bright vision of the Pyrenees;
and evoke for me its high peaks
crowned with snow.

A deceitful vision,
for you revive the image of my land
driven by an illusion:
Is an accursed fate warring against me
and even in my dreams embittering my heart?
If it is so, bright dream,
torture me; your war does me good.
Send me often, at any hour
the vision of the Pyrenees, however brief
the vision of its snow may be!

3
The Death of Maceo and the Transfer to Havana

(December 1896 to July 1897)

On the eighth and ninth of December 1896, an unexpected event reverberated greatly in the vicinity of Aguacate, when civil authorities first, and Havana newspapers subsequently, received the sensational news that on the seventh, during a skirmish between Cuban troops and Spanish forces near Hoyo Colorado,[1] the lieutenant general of the *Ejército Libertador*, Maceo,[2] the Bronze Titan, as he was called, had died.

Official communications transmitted to the mayors on the island incited towns to raise Spanish flags on the balconies or portals of as many private houses as possible, as well as on the town halls, barracks, hospitals, and residences of societies in demonstrations of joy at the death of the great *mambí* fighter.

Numerous houses on the streets of Aguacate, especially on the Calle Real, whose inhabitants were more or less spontaneously allied with Spanish *integrismo*, apparently complied willingly with that directive. At other houses, despite the fact that their inhabitants felt no solidarity with a dubious Spanish *integrismo*, flags were also raised, but on odd parts of the houses and with red and gold colors that were so faded, their appearance, instead of being impressive, looked like a shocking mockery of patriotic Spanish symbolism.

I didn't know whether the integrationist elements in Aguacate realized that they were being taunted with such old, dull flags. Judging, however, by the real or apparent indifference with which the colonial authorities and representatives registered the ridiculousness of such symbols, I was inclined to suspect that Spanish patriotism in that neighborhood, even among its most conspicuous officials, was very questionable, and more conventional than sincere.

Comments I was able to pick up in discreet conversations with some of those supposed representatives of peninsular ultra patriotism in Aguacate confirmed my convictions along the lines I have described.

I also confirmed the real possibility that the most significant representations of Spanish *integrismo* in Aguacate were only apparent or for show because of the no less revealing fact that Maceo's death did not provoke any noisy demonstrations of rejoicing as happened in Havana and other towns on the island. Rather, despite the forcible show of flags, the sensational news of Maceo's death in the vicinity of Aguacate disclosed silent but respectful indications of a frank homage to the memory of the heroic liberationist leader, whose deeds elicited unanimous admiration.

Within two days of learning about the death of Maceo and his aide, Panchito Gómez,[3] a no less extraordinary source of concern arose in Aguacate. Captain-General Weyler suddenly arrived in the town preceded by a vanguard of cavalry, and protected—he and his general staff—by noisy transport vehicles of mountain artillery, as well as overwhelming infantry forces. Weyler and his men stayed in Aguacate for a few hours, only as long as was necessary to acknowledge the respects paid him by the local, civil, and municipal authorities.

Some of the flags raised because of Maceo's death were hurriedly raised again at the agitated instigation of the authorities. But Weyler was very impatient to get to Havana, eager to take advantage of the success occasioned by Maceo's fall, in order to intensify his ferocious procedures against the tenacious and heroic resistance of the Liberation Army.

Although Weyler's passage through Aguacate was brief, it prevented the majority of inhabitants from leaving their houses, nor did they appear at their doors, fearful that curiosity alone could provoke the well-known angry outbursts of the intolerant despot.

The confusion and terror of the sudden arrival of Weyler and his overwhelming legions in the peaceful population of Aguacate led to the deplorable demise of a victim: a poor Chinese laundryman, when he found out who the mysterious personage was who appeared in the middle of that deafening armed multitude, was so powerfully affected that he fell over dead on the spot. Such was Weyler's terrifying reputation for cruelty!

When Weyler's alarming war caravan resumed its noisy journey to the island's capital, people in Aguacate regained their tranquility. Frequent troop movements, however, continued in the streets and outskirts of the town. Among them, the column of our battalion in particular, which often needed to inform our office of significant casualties of unfortunate soldiers and an occasional officer, sustained in field campaigns in confrontations with clusters of *mambises*.

Men who died in combat at a considerable distance from the town were buried by the side of the road or at the foot of a tree that was easy to find later; or if they had fallen in action near the town, they were carried on stretchers or on the backs of mules to be buried in the cemetery in Aguacate. As for the wounded, the commander of the column ordered that the most seriously wounded were to be transported in stretchers, the less seriously wounded helped by healthy companions, and all taken as quickly as possible to the mobile hospital located at one end of Aguacate.

I shall refer later to the loss of some of the officers from our battalion that occurred in encounters with separatist forces. One of those casualties, not fatal but the victim of a bullet wound, as I shall describe below, was a second lieutenant called Onrubia, who came in the second expeditionary group composed of forced troops and numerous enlisted men among the volunteers recruited in Cartagena. I shall discuss it here because it resonated greatly in the *integrista* press of Spain.

When he arrived in Aguacate, Lieutenant Onrubia impressed us with his youthful appearance—seemingly fifteen or sixteen years old at most. According to information we received from other members of his expeditionary group, Second Lieutenant Onrubia—the son of a colonel—was a privileged student at the *Academia de Infantería* in Toledo and, at his own request, despite not having completed one or two courses that would earn him the rank of second lieutenant, he was able to join the Spanish Army in Cuba at that rank.

At the first sally of the battalion column and during light skirmishes—no one found out how it happened—Onrubia took a bullet in the fleshy part of his leg closest to his thigh. The injury was reported to the General Staff of the Captain-General and it earned him a promotion to first lieutenant. Luckily, given his impatient ambition to rise even higher, it didn't take him long to recover from that mysterious wound. However, in a subsequent battle that was fiercer (at Vista Hermosa, if I remember correctly), now First Lieutenant Onrubia was gravely wounded in the same leg, site of the previous accident. The bullet destroyed a large part of his femur a few inches from his knee so that that leg had to be amputated at the midpoint of the ruined bone.

The circumstances surrounding these accidents were much commented on among the chiefs and officers of the battalion and also among the troops, since in recompense for the wounds, the very young officer was promoted to captain and awarded the *Cruz de María Cristina*, which gave him the implicit right to display the rank of commander and receive the entire sum allotted to that rank. Operated on successfully and transported back to the Peninsula, young Onrubia was received in a special audience by María Cristina[4] herself in the Palacio de Oriente. He was praised by the patriotic press in Madrid and in the provinces, and admitted to the Regimiento de

Inválidos, as the youngest, most battle-experienced and exemplary soldier, up to that time, among Spanish cadets.

A few days later, the traditional and most fundamental Christian celebration—that of Christ's birth—took place. In the preceding year of 1895, I spent Christmas in Sancti Spíritus, having recently arrived at that time in the important city in the province of Las Villas together with the rest of the forcible recruits in my expeditionary group. The accumulation of anguished impressions and different causes for fear did not give me time to recall the ineffable enchantment of the annual Christmas solemnities.

In Aguacate, however, perhaps because I was more accustomed to misfortune, the advent of the foundational festivity of Christianity awakened a host of luminous visions and kindled flashes of emotion in my spirit that were so comforting that their very intensity moved me to consecrate a few solitary moments to the sweet memories and moral teachings that the glorious festivity impressed on my character and on all my life since childhood.

Accordingly, on Christmas Eve, with my head and arms resting on my desk, I decided to devote myself to reflections relating to the festivities. When some office companions observed my posture, they wanted to distract me, moved by similar emotions stirred by nostalgia—although less anguished, perhaps, than mine since my father's recent death weighed heavily on me. They invited me to join them with the object of celebrating Christmas Eve simply, by expressing heartfelt desires that the war would end soon and peace would make possible the longed-for return to our respective homes, where the annual succession of Christmas commemorations would gladden our souls again.

And so it happened that in a café located in a side street to the right of the church, several of us who were well disposed to comply with that sentimental proposal gathered together at small tables. Soon, between sips of *sidra* [hard cider], the conversations became more animated as each man evoked the customs and usages related to Christmas Eve and the very solemn festivity of the following day which were characteristic of their respective towns and families.

And we continued our conversation with picturesque descriptions of such customs, made more pleasant in each dwelling by ingenuous renditions of carols and roundelays accompanied by rhythmic sounds, beats, and the din of flutes fashioned from cane, tambourines, bells, and other popular instruments. All of this around a glowing fireplace or in front of the novel and increasingly original and attractive "crèche," which was the delight of all the family members, since all of them—parents and children, grandparents and grandchildren—contributed to the impressive preparation, setting up, embellishments, illumination, and appeal of the typical crèches. The diverse pantheistic conceptions embodied in the crèche are evocative as a whole of the aforementioned folkloric ways, and no doubt revelatory of the historical, religious, moral, and artistic roots characteristic, in general, of each town and each family in the geographic mosaic of the different national groups, regions, or provinces, absurdly and forcibly united and fatefully still enslaved (as Cuba was then) by the intransigent and despotic central government of Spain.

We members of this fraternal group left the reunion, comforted spiritually by the sincere expressions of such timely memories. Each one went wherever he wished until taps, which obliged us to return to the office barracks. However, I felt awake and emotionally excited by conversations that revived in my soul the urge to engage in solitude—as I had wished to do earlier—in a poetic-philosophical meditation on my Christmas memories, which were in painful contrast with the failed illusions of my youth. And I added to the opening pages of my book *Elegia de la guerra*, the following fruit of my sentimental musings, the translation of the original in my native language:

CHRISTMAS
THE TRADITION

At around midnight
you will hear a melody
that will fill
you with joy;
and when the new day is born
Dawn, desirous to excel,
will scatter brightness.

The rosebuds
and all the sweet flowers
that embellish the gardens,
will regale you in
enchanting celebrations
with delicate, delicious scents.
Jesus comes down then to earth
to redeem men from War.

THE PHILOSOPHER

When the bells of night
sound midnight,

the reign of vice will begin
in the crazed cities.

Salons in bordellos and sites of orgies
will fill up;
and dark pleasures will
surge amidst lubricious songs.

Dirty, perverted bodies,
in mockery of human glory
you will see turned into brutes
by vile drunkenness.

You will see purity, tarnished;
honor, lax;
old age, mistreated;
and amidst vices, virtue.

For then, mankind in its blindness,
does not halt its demented course
even before the Redemptive God it venerates.

THE SOLDIER
Forces of the advance guard;
rest from your exertions
for the sentinel is vigilant against an ambush
by the enemy hosts.

Sleep, poor brothers.
Dream with illusions of good fortune;
since joy does not last,
let us enjoy the moments already past.

Tomorrow, on the road,
who knows if we will find our grave.

With faces turned toward destiny;
let us not fear death nor aught!
Oh unfortunate soldier without free will,
there will be no Christmas for you!

THE POET
Twenty years of my life,
luminous Christmases of my yesterdays;

my most impatient voice
in vain calls and bids you to return.

How distant you are! Their pure image
I conserve in my memory,
for I created the painful immensity of a history
in a perjuring tear.

Return, then, to my lips
oh ingenuous glories
of my infancy;
give me back the traces
Oh Faith, of my childhood beliefs!

The poet's Christmas
I cannot sing today,
a bold and antiquated ship
stole it from me from beyond the sea.

Longed-for coasts:
will you take me in, a fortunate man?
Or will my hopes be lost
in the mysterious unfathomable depths of fate?

O, Christmas, Christmas:
I don't know how to bless you.
My song may wound you
with strophes of impiety!
Your name causes such anxiety in me!

In mid-January 1897, I was elected to the rank of sergeant. Lieutenant Navascués on behalf of his companions in the management of the office informed me of the promotion and told me that I could now exchange the faded red stripes on my uniform for the three yellow stripes corresponding to my new rank.

The promotion effected by the unanimous vote of my superiors in the office, with the approval of the lieutenant colonel of the battalion, clearly helped to alleviate my sorrows. This was so for different reasons: the two most immediate ones were the satisfaction with which my companions accepted my promotion, and the opportunity it gave me to increase the deduction from my salary every month in order to help my mother and sisters financially. I received the official notice of my new rank a few days later, authorized by General Ahumada, second in command on the island.

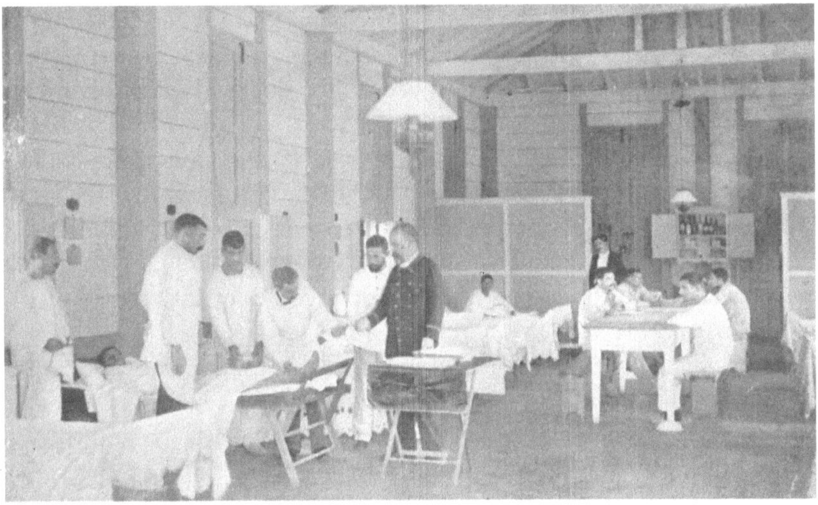

Figure 2. "Church converted into Spanish hospital." (Fitzhugh Lee and Joseph Wheeler, *Cuba's Struggle against Spain*. New York: New York Historical Press, 1899.)

The managers of the office, as well as the battalion, used my promotion to resolve certain problems that had arisen in the infirmary installed a few months earlier in an old edifice situated in the far north of the Calle Real in Aguacate, to the right of a row of palm trees near the cemetery. I will explain below the connection between my promotion and said infirmary. But first I shall provide the context for the most important circumstances that determined the improvised establishment of the infirmary.

Providing medical services was always a serious problem for our battalion and also for the personnel of the office since our arrival in Sancti Spíritus in mid-December 1895. As I noted in the first part of this *Memoir*, the young lieutenant medic who came over with our expeditionary force fell sick and died suddenly a few days after our arrival. When the battalion column left immediately for the *manigua* near Sancti Spíritus, it had to go without any medical officer. I don't know how the column of our expeditionary troops managed without the indispensable medical assistance. Surely, the lack of such necessary attention resulted in a large number of casualties.

When the battalion and its office were ordered to move to the border of the provinces of Matanzas and Havana, we were still without a doctor. For that reason, when field operations began again, it was necessary, as I already explained, to install a mobile hospital in the large, rundown old house near a fort and the railroad at the south end of Aguacate. That hospital did not have military doctors either, only the generous assistance of the two civilian doctors in the town, aided by individuals in the troops who wanted to support the effort to provide medical care.

Because of its special mission, the mobile hospital attended by preference to cases requiring surgery. Patients from the column or the office with common illnesses could not be hospitalized and only received innocuous remedies or a few spoonfuls of the handy Epsom salts kept in a big sack freely available to those who wanted it in a corner of the sacristy of the church/barracks.

Given these conditions, illnesses increased due to inevitable cases of fatigue, intestinal infections, lack of hygiene, etc., that could not be treated in the mobile hospital. Therefore, the heads of the battalion and the office, with the approval of the necessary credit granted by the quartermaster's stores, agreed to install the infirmary solely for the care of the sick and convalescent.

Nevertheless, it was still impossible to designate a military doctor to head the infirmary since there was no doctor available to serve in that capacity. The two civilian doctors in the town, in exchange for a modest recompense, took charge of the joint medical services of the mobile hospital and the infirmary. It was necessary, however, that an officer or at least a sergeant should be designated as commander of the infirmary to oversee the indispensable auxiliary personnel and the new squad of guards assigned to the building. Since there was no officer available for that post, a sergeant, who had been recruited from the last expeditionary force and had ended his service, was offered a salary to serve again, on the assumption that he possessed qualities and sufficient experience to be selected for that position.

But that sergeant's command turned out to be not only ill conceived but scandalous on account of the many atrocities he countenanced as much in his administrative capacity as in the systematic detentions and even criminal maltreatment with which he victimized the unfortunate inhabitants of the poor dwellings at the edge of town simply because he felt that he was dealing with insurrectionist informers or spies. It was even rumored that the sergeant killed one of the men who was unjustly detained.

The office became aware of the aberrant instincts of the perverse sergeant. It also learned of a civil complaint made by the owner of a food store that supplied the infirmary. The complaint revealed the demand of the insolent and corrupt sergeant that in each voucher of victuals and goods acquired by the infirmary, a margin of inflated prices should be added to benefit the bold mediator's liquid assets.

As the immediate consequence of such denunciations, the adventurer was disarmed, arrested, and imprisoned in the fort next to the mobile hospital to await being handed over to the battalion column, tried by a military court, and demoted, as might be deemed appropriate.

When the command of the infirmary was left vacant because of the scandalous events I have summarized here, the honorable but not at all easy or agreeable mission to replace the sergeant who had been dismissed fell to me. I was very sorry to leave my job in the office, where I was surrounded by excellent advantages and companionships; but I had to accept the new assignment, in part because of military discipline, which I could not evade, as well as to repay the special confidence placed in me.

I asked Lieutenant Navascués to favor me with instructions, advice, and suggestions that in his judgment were indispensable in order to implement the most satisfactory fulfillment of my new duties.

"I don't need to instruct you," he said. "Use your discretion in all that concerns your duty and the duties of the infirmary personnel, acting in accord with what is esteemed just and worthy. In short, whatever is opposite to the conduct of the insolent man who was dismissed." I took note of the words of the noble Lieutenant Navascués, but I wanted to consult him on my negotiations in the acquisition of victuals, medications, and effects indispensable for serving the patients, the auxiliary personnel, and the squad of the infirmary guard. "All of that is also entrusted to your able charge," the head of the office said to me. He added his impression that the auxiliary personnel who took care of the patients were performing in a satisfactory manner; and as for the cook, he also deserved our trust, since he wrote down his orders to the retailer every day in a little notebook, and in accord with those orders, the corresponding vouchers would be expedited.

With such guidelines and auspicious notes of support, I began to exercise my functions as commander-administrator of the infirmary, seconded by the auxiliary personnel, and also by the sick and convalescent soldiers in gratitude for the no less careful attention we accorded them.

One single problem began to worry me within a few weeks of undertaking my new duty—a problem, I was told, that also preoccupied the hospital administrator, namely, the shortage of provisions that was becoming acute in the so-called bodegas or general stores that sold different kinds of merchandise, especially foodstuffs. A variety of causes led to the shortage, all of them traceable to the war. First of all, there was the reduction in imported products from Spain. The hiked-up costs of these products, implicitly agreed upon by the importers and warehouses in Havana, also contributed to the shortage, as well as the systematic destruction of plantings and fruit trees ordered by Weyler in order to deprive the *mambises* of food.

That crisis was worsening, not only because it was detrimental to the general population of Aguacate, but also because it cut into the needs of the mess halls and food for the columns, detachments, forts, and, of course, the infirmary. Obtaining food was becoming increasingly difficult and was scarcely alleviated by the remaining provisions of crackers, sacks of flour, garbanzos and beans that had spoiled as a result of selfish speculators holding them back too long in order to make fat profits. All this led to fatal setbacks in the health of the community and the troops, since many people reduced their food intake or tried to supplement it with watered-down emergency provisions. In addition, residents of Aguacate learned of the sudden, spectacular deaths of several Chinese who lived on the street behind the church. In order to appease their hunger, they had killed a dog, cooked, and ate it, but they were unable to digest it.

Although the civil and military authorities intervened in order to alleviate as much as possible the great scarcity of basic necessities and did manage to arrange urgent shipments of vital merchandise to the retailers in Aguacate, the distribution of the shipments was inadequate to satisfy the needs of the infirmary and, more urgently, those of the sick and convalescent soldiers receiving assistance there. In the judgment of Dr. González O'Brien and of the other civilian doctor who was consulted, the recovery of these patients depended primarily on appropriate nourishment provided, in particular, by milk and meat when possible, and not by ineffectual stews.

But how was it possible to obtain those foodstuffs if the retailers didn't have them in stock? Dr. González O'Brien suggested that it would be helpful to contact the wealthy owner of the Ingenio Rosario and arrange for the temporary use of a milk cow, together with the generous donation of one of the calves that grazed on the land next to the infirmary and belonged to the Ingenio. In one of his frequent appearances in the vicinity of the infirmary, I personally solicited from the majordomo of the Ingenio the temporary use of a milk cow and the donation (for the exclusive benefit of the hospitalized soldiers) of a calf. The majordomo of the Rosario rejected the request for a milk cow right off, since, he said, he didn't have one. Regarding the donation of a calf, he promised me that he would convey my request right away to Señor Ramón Pelayo, owner of the Ingenio.

Three days later, in view of the fact that the majordomo at the Ingenio had not passed by the infirmary as usual, I met with the cook, the corporal of the unit assigned to guard the town, and two convalescent sergeants to discuss whether we could interpret the majordomo's silence regarding my request for a calf as tacit consent. Since we all agreed that we could, one of the calves was slaughtered and dressed for the exclusive benefit of our sick and convalescent soldiers.

At midday a few days later, the corporal of the guard informed me that two riders mounted on spirited horses had approached the infirmary at the rear of the building, and when he cried out, "Halt! Who goes there?" they identified themselves respectively as the owner and the majordomo of the Ingenio Rosario. When I went out to receive them, without dismounting from their richly caparisoned horses, the most important looking of the two, that is, Señor Pelayo, addressing himself to me, asked angrily, "Are you the butcher sergeant?" I responded sharply to his outburst, "Do not insult me! I am not a butcher, I am a conscript, and a man of profound humanitarian convictions."

"Why then did you order the killing of one of my calves without authorization for such an abuse?" Don Ramón demanded insolently.

I answered firmly, "I did it out of the necessity of providing food to the sick and convalescent in the infirmary, and because you ignored the courteous appeal that I sent through your majordomo, requesting that you accede to my just request."

"But I did not authorize it," the arrogant fellow complained.

"At least you ought to have answered my request," I said to him, adding, more or less verbatim, "but your response was silence, and since silence gives consent, according to the old saying, I thought that far from becoming indignant over the sacrifice of a single calf among the many that you pasture in the vicinity, you would be pleased to contribute such a small gift in view of the benefits and advantages to your personal safety and your considerable business interests provided by the proximity of Spanish detachments to your Ingenio."

And the dialogue ended in this way:

"You have no right to judge me!"

"And you have no right to quarrel with me!"

"I shall complain to your superiors!"

"And I shall be able to defend myself for my bold act of humanitarianism before them and before God!"

That gross and greedy person went to the office immediately, as he said he would, to lodge his denunciation and vent his impetuous protests against me. And to an extent, he left pleased with his visit to the headquarters of the battalion, whose head was the noble, understanding, and also very skilled diplomat, Lieutenant Navascués, who promised to relieve me of my post at the infirmary. This was a very satisfactory solution for me since I could take up my office duties once again, thus freeing myself from responsibilities and negotiations that did not accord with my character and my aptitudes.

Don Ramón Pelayo, the discourteous and very wealthy owner of the Ingenio Rosario with its innumerable head of cattle and its extensive sugar plantations, was a thin man with a yellowish complexion and very black, though lank, hair, mustache, and beard. He was sickly-looking, with a scowl on his face and an unrefined accent. He resided in a spacious mansion surrounded by gardens, close by the Ingenio, accompanied by a young niece and numerous servants, some of whom were informally lodged in nearby rural dwellings.

The magnificent residence of Ramón Pelayo and the essential outbuildings of the plantation were connected to the town of Aguacate by a broad avenue bordered by tall palms; a convenient lane that could be used for agreeable afternoon horseback rides by the officers and also by some office workers.

On special occasions Don Ramón and his aristocratic niece provided enthusiastic proof of undying support for Spanish intransigence as opposed to Cuban patriotism by seating at their table civilian or military persons who had arrived from Havana or were in transit through Aguacate—individuals representative of that colonial obsession. On such occasions the very rich sugar grower had no difficulty paying for his banquets and receptions with amounts equivalent to the value not merely of a small calf but to the cost of several bigger steers belonging to his holdings.

I had the satisfaction of knowing that my conduct in the course of that incident met with the tacit, though discreetly held, approbation of my office mates, who were rightly astonished by the ridiculous protests of that prideful and very wealthy man. One and all agreed that the indignant supporter of Spanish rule ought to have resigned himself to the loss of a single calf if only in gratitude for the incalculable advantages he enjoyed in respect to his vast holdings due to the military detachments—provided by his mother country—situated around the Ingenio Rosario and its extensive cane fields.

Given the revelation of his egoism and antihumanist nature, it was no surprise months later, when the well-deserved collapse of Spanish rule took place, that the intractable supporter of Spanish sovereignty in his disappointment—fearful, perhaps, that his ties to colonial intransigence could prove harmful to his large personal holdings—hastened to sell the Ingenio Rosario and his other properties in order to take his entire fortune to Asturias, without leaving even a miserable token of gratitude in acknowledgment of the generosity of this land and its hospitable inhabitants.

And the no less vindictive Spanish monarchy, in turn, committed the blunder of rewarding Señor Pelayo's repellent anti-Cuban and un-Christian actions by bestowing upon him the shocking title of Marquis of . . . I don't remember what, nor do I want to remember.

During my directorship of the infirmary, I took advantage of some moments of repose in order to give myself over to the deep contemplation of the green plains and elegant palm groves before me; and to raise my eyes to the intense blue of the sky, resplendent at midday and beautiful at sunset with its clouds displaying different and harmonious variations in color. And clearly, the enchanting contemplation of those tropical wonders reinforced the throbbing of my emotional anguish along with the purest longings of my spirit.

I added diverse variants of those comforting moments to the pages of lyrics contained in *Elegía de la guerra*. I have inserted some of these here:

DAWN

A thin winding sheet spreads motionless,
over the plain,
it is the veil that covers mother earth;
it is thick fog.

But then the Sun comes up, and that winding sheet
little by little withdraws,
as Nature reveals its charms,
and the War its wings!

A RAY OF SUN

It was the first that Dawn
let appear, pure and lovely;
the first that in the fields
spread its brightness.

I heard high above
a mysterious voice,
a voice of Art in the Infinite
let out a strange cry.
"Always the same," I heard its words,
"always the same!"
When will I be able to view

this thoughtless world without grief,
glorious, without battles at last,
without wars and rancor,
peoples fraternizing
and nations joined in sisterhood?

The ray grew silent. In the dew
it was reflected pure and lovely;
and in the folds of Dawn
its gleam vanished.

TROPICAL

The Sun quickens its pace,
a ribbon all alight, full of life,
    spreads in the west;
and the earth, tinged with red,
    invites us to partake of joy.

How lovely is your grandeur
Oh Sun; how beautiful your light,
    when you tinge Nature
with the color of an immense rose
    that generously opens!

But how brief is your embrace!
How quickly night falls and takes away
    this vision, this good fortune,
pleasure, dreams, beauty,
whose radiance appears to us, and does not last!

INSOMNIA

Tonight at the burst
of a loud discharge,
I awakened startled,
and through some branches,
contemplated the full Moon
in the high starry vault of the sky.

Lovely night! The encampment
trusting in your light, rests;
for the column sleeps
although shots sound,

certain that its sleep
is watched over by advanced troops by your light.

My eyes, sleepily,
look at the starry vault.
Somber presentiments
horrify my Soul,
believing pessimistically
that my sorrows will last long;
that peace is difficult,
that my anxieties will last forever!

And I even seem to observe
that the Moon, brazenly,
mocks my heart
with a pitiless laugh, cold, sarcastic!

THE FIREFLY

You remind me of the *Ronda de Lluernes*
that one night in the woods[5]
surprised a good friend amidst the mysteries
of beautiful inspiration.

But as I see you wandering through the air
under the starry sky,
you seem to me the soul of a mother
watching over her child . . .

SPIRITUAL PAIN

A soldier by force, not by conviction,
they brought me to a lovely and rare world.
Here I now discover poetry;
here, in times of peace, it must be Heaven.

But ay! the sour breath of death
darkens such brilliant qualities,
and exhales emanations of graves,
denying ecstasy at its grandeur!

One morning after I had returned to my small desk next to Lieutenant Navascués's large one, I learned about an anonymous denunciation against the estimable and generous Dr. Luis González O'Brien. The unnamed accuser—a coward like all those who make use of anonymity to satisfy a desire for vengeance, out of envy or some other unworthy, spiteful intention—urged the heads of the office to have the gentlemanly doctor detained and sent to the Havana fortress, La Cabaña.[6] He was accused of leading a gang of clever agents in his confidential service who held medical supplies for the benefit of the separatist forces located in fortifications in the Jaruco zone.

As discreetly and quickly as possible, I was able to inform that kindly, interested party about the aforementioned denunciation. My warning must have been very opportune because Dr. González O'Brien took the first train from Matanzas that passed through Aguacate to go to Havana on the pretext of assisting in a medical consultation that he could not decline.

When Lieutenant Navascués learned about the sudden departure of Dr. González O'Brien, he did not comment on it in any way. But judging by his intelligent perspicacity and the complete nobility of his character, I was inclined to suspect that since the denunciation lodged against the humanitarian doctor was anonymous, he chose to destroy the malicious accusation, without communicating it to his fellow officers in the governance of the office. My suspicion was shared by the very man who had been denounced, as he told me years later when we had the welcome occasion to renew our sympathies and affinities in Havana, at that time a free Republic. Together we recalled the hazards, unexpected turns of events, and dangers, but also the exemplary struggles of the heroic and glorious Cuban patriots.

Up to this point I have recalled the principal events that had the greatest impact on my life while I resided in Aguacate during the epic Cuban War of Liberation. I could add other recollections that were no less indelible, though they were peripheral, linked to my troubling preoccupations of that time. In order to avoid unnecessary prolixity, I will limit myself to pointing out here a brief summary of such memories.

We office workers kept up frequent exchanges, especially with my Catalan compatriots: our fraternal friend Rull, and the careful "chronicler" Rovira. We paid daily visits that were always amiable and respectful, to the Abreu family. The office workers took discreet and pious measures to avoid inspiring envy in the fighters from our column, such as not shaving and wearing uniforms that were not very clean when the soldiers returned wearing their striped uniforms, all muddy and full of lice.

The frequent arrivals of soldiers from the battalion's column or from other units provided us with an opportunity to have very interesting, fraternal chats with self-sacrificing recruits from other expeditions and other parts of the Peninsula who were also obliged to withstand the fatigue and rigors inherent in waging war. On those occasions, the men gathered together told us about their mutual anxieties, fears, and hopes as they sipped drinks in moderation, "taking the morning or afternoon nip," as was customary. The office workers acquired painful news about the dead and wounded in the battalion's troops as the result of encounters with the liberation forces, sicknesses, or accidents. Two recruits died accidentally when they suddenly expired after gorging themselves on delicious mangoes followed by strong alcohol.

Those expansive gatherings also gave rise to jovial parties which never led to lamentable excesses but, at most, to the improvisation of songs more or less typical of the singers' native regions.

The most impressive, original, and unforgettable example of those very human and enjoyable gatherings was a guitar concert improvised in the office, that is, in the church/barracks, by a recruit from Alicante whom Sergeant Caturla introduced to us. He turned out to be a highly inspired interpreter of his own musical fantasies who also performed masterful, nuanced renditions of the most varied and genuine folkloric contributions of the respective unmistakable ethnic groups on the map of Spain. Our companion Caturla, who was well acquainted with the skill of his young fellow countryman in the mastery of the popular instrument, wanted to take advantage of the excellent guitarist's brief stay among us—he was a soldier from another passing column—so that not only the office workers, but also numerous comrades of the musician, could enjoy such a pleasant event.

I didn't want to ask where the guitar came from and how it was procured in such adverse circumstances. What did it matter to the enthusiastic men who were present, captivated by the miraculous spell cast by the chords and nuances that the masterful player drew from the guitar strings? The admiration of those in attendance turned into warm applause at the end of each one of the generous offerings of the young artist. And the emotion of the audience grew most intense when, at the beginning of the chords suggestive of Andalusian arpeggios, the vocal style typical of that region emerged in the natural, untutored voice of one of the soldiers present, in perfect synchrony with the tonal filigrees of the masterful guitarist.

The collective enthusiasm at the end of the spontaneous party evolved into displays of most cordial gratitude directed at the marvelous player. How I lamented, nonetheless, in the midst of such appropriate ovations, not having the authority to prevent the fact that in a few hours that excellent artist would have to resume his abominable mission as an involuntary and forced combatant at the service of aberrant institutions and reprehensible oligarchies!

The next day, still spellbound by the charm of the delightful concert, I wanted to sketch an impromptu poetic eulogy of the guitar, a musical instrument among the most apt, no doubt—when prodigious hands play it—to reveal the intense and pure emotions of the human soul. Here is that eulogy, included in the pages of my *Elegía de la guerra*:

THE GUITAR

I do not know what mystery
lies in the guitar's strings that
transports our spirits
to regions of longing.

I do not know what mystery
lies in its strings that inebriates us
with tearful joys that please the soul.

And whether the songs entwine
with the magical instrument
heard in distant lands
by the nostalgic soldier.

I do not know what mystery
the guitar holds in its sound,
that seems to speak
with amorous accents
of consolation and hope;
and moistens our eyes
with such beneficial emotions
that our memories are dispelled
and our anxieties are calmed,
anxieties enflamed with indignation
against the evil people
who exploit our unawareness,
make us vile and deceive us.

It remains for me to note here another recollection of my stay in Aguacate. It refers to the protest I felt it was my humanitarian and civic duty to lodge against a wrathful sergeant, whose name was Ibañez, in connection with the ill treatment in word and deed that he permitted himself in order to punish the unfortunate soldiers in the squad of guards.

Sergeant Ibáñez was a disagreeable type with an angry look about him and a brusque manner—a man incapable of calm conversations with his colleagues for he always took them in the direction of unpleasant remarks or outbursts. He was a mature man of some thirty-five to thirty-six years of age. A native of Murcia, discharged from the army fifteen years earlier with the rank of sergeant, he reenlisted for active duty when volunteer recruitment was enacted, with the purpose of coming to Cuba to fight against the "spurious sons of Spain" (that's what he called the Cuban liberators), and also to free himself, it was said, from some difficult family problems that embittered his life in his native country and because of which he tried but failed to commit suicide.

Once he joined the second expedition that arrived from Cartagena to reinforce the battalion's column, Sergeant Ibáñez expected that it would be easy for him to be promoted to lieutenant as recompense for his long service in his previous rank or because of meritorious service in the war. When time passed without producing the illusory promotion, the angry, sick behavior of Sergeant Ibáñez became more pronounced, leading him to relieve his anger with frequent oppressive and outrageous actions against the self-sacrificing recruits in his company. For those reasons his captain, assuming that the irascible conduct of the veteran sergeant was due to serious nervous fatigue, requested the head of the battalion to place Ibáñez under the direct orders of the office for several weeks to see whether he might calm down.

But Lieutenant Navascués, aware of his background, did not want to admit the sergeant—whom he considered an intruder—as an office worker, although he appointed him as an alternate to serve in the command of the squad of guards, a charge that Ibáñez thought somehow humiliating, although he couldn't refuse it because of army discipline. Being forced to perform that job exacerbated his ill nature, and caused him to mistreat the recruits of the guard as punishment for simple or supposed trivial misdeeds.

One day, by chance, I witnessed how Ibáñez allowed himself to insult and hit a poor soldier in the guard, and indignant at that act of angry aggression, I criticized the brutal abuser. Surprised by my angry reproach, the irascible soldier tried to justify his iniquitous behavior, alleging that I lacked authority to place limits on what he called his powers, nor could I judge them, since, although we were both sergeants, his stripes were older than mine and I had to respect them.

"You do not have any such powers," I responded, "nor is it a question of anything other than the rights and respect that are reciprocal and fitting between human beings who consider themselves civilized."

Inflamed by my protest and conscious that he looked ridiculous before the squad of soldiers who witnessed the episode, Ibáñez tried to intimidate me by threatening to accuse me in writing to the battalion commander of the supposed insults I allowed myself to direct at him.

"I am not afraid of your threat," I answered, "since you can't be unaware that the testimony of the soldier you attacked and those of everyone present here will make the denunciation revert back to you, confirming your inhuman behavior against the long-suffering soldiers."

The incident led to many comments in support of my quixotic attitude, but there was also a thoughtful attitude of compassion for the impulsive aggressor. An exchange of impressions among the office workers showed that we agreed that from a psychological point of view we should judge Ibáñez not as an authentic case of a man who was excessively cruel, but rather as a man with an acute neurosis produced by the painful adversities of his desperate life (as he himself confessed when the column returned from operations), and also because of his not being promoted to lieutenant as he expected when he reenlisted.

In accord with that charitable interpretation, a few hours later, confidently guided by a Christian impulse, I invited Ibáñez to discuss amicably the widely known incident and exchange our interpretations of it. And the interview was satisfying for both of us. I was able to expound moral considerations of profound commiseration for the respect-worthy human dignity of the unhappy soldiers. In addition, I laid out opportune concepts of friendly exhortation with a view toward having Ibáñez seek consolation for his personal bitterness in the cultivation of a Christian, healing brotherhood with all the members of the squad of guards and the office.

Ibáñez, for his part, moved by my reasons and advice, did not hesitate to declare himself guilty and grateful for my understanding interpretation of the sorrows afflicting his soul.

I sketched an emotional reflection of that lamentable incident and its psychological consequence in another original page of my *Elegía de la guerra*. Here is my version of that sketch:

Hold back, comrade!
Respect the poor soldier!
Think of your own honor
before you strike out at him.

Exercise your judgment
without abuse or rancor,
and don't arrogantly resort to
wrongful power.

Examine the spirit
of the soldier you assault,
and you will find a shrine of sorrows
instead of faults.

Each man bears a mystery
worthy of respect within himself
and that mysterious essence
determines every action.

At times, the most inept action
is inspired by righteous motives.
Don't then, be abusive:
treat the soldier without anger!

With the evocation of the preceding episode, the series of my principal recollections linked to my stay in Aguacate from June 1896 to the middle of June 1897 comes to an end. In subsequent chapters, I shall relate my transfer to Puentes Grandes,[7] followed three months later, by my stay in Havana until the felicitous end of the Separatist War.

4
In the Cuban Capital

(July 1897 to January 1898)

My transfer to Puentes Grandes and Havana from Aguacate came about because of the spontaneous gesture of an affectionate companion of my youth, Buenaventura Vallespinosa, a tax collector at the time in the province of Tarragona. When that good friend heard about my obligatory embarkation to Cuba and the promotion to sergeant that I had received in the military offices of Aguacate, he wrote to a brother of his, a colonel in the General Staff of the Captain-General in Havana, Don Benito Vallespinosa, asking him to favor me in whatever I might need and lay in his power to grant.

To my delighted surprise, the result of that generous recommendation came into my hands in the form of a letter from Colonel Vallespinosa, telling me that he would take great pleasure in acceding to the request of his dear brother Ventureta. He wrote that I could inform him of my wishes by mail or by meeting with him in his office at the Captaincy General if it was possible for me to travel by train to Havana for that purpose.

I thought that a personal interview was preferable; consequently, I solicited and obtained the appropriate authorization and pass, and one morning in the middle of June 1897, I boarded the train from Matanzas that took me to the station in Regla. From there I went by launch to the Muelle de Luz in Havana, the end point of my journey.

Carlos Martí[1] awaited me on the dock. He was a friend of mine from Barcelona, where he had been the director of a newspaper in the maritime neighborhood of the Barceloneta. Carlos Martí had come to Cuba at the beginning of the war, and his former job at a newspaper got him the job of collator at the *Diario del ejército*. (The press office was on one of the parallel streets, either Obispo[2] or O'Reilly.[3])

When I met Carlos Martí on the Muelle de Luz, he was wearing civilian clothes, but I had on the striped uniform that was obligatory for all the armed forces of Spain in Cuba. We walked along distractedly, exchanging our respective impressions without at all noticing the passersby. But as we crossed the plaza where some of the streets of colonial Cuba converged, an authoritarian voice suddenly cried out, "Sergeant! Stand to attention!"

Alarmed as I was, I obeyed immediately when I saw that the cry burst from the mouth of a totally authentic Excellency and Illustrious Señor General of the Spanish Army, clothed in a uniform displaying the undoubted attributes of his picturesque rank in the hierarchy: gilded twigs on the cuffs and on the collar of the jacket; a red sash with fringes, also golden; a sword with a chiseled hilt, a baton with little decorative acorns hanging down from it; a display of decorations on his chest, etc., etc.

> "Why did you fail to salute me," asked the harsh high-ranking authoritarian.
>
> "Pardon me, Your Excellency, my General. We were distracted as we walked along. I did not see your Excellency," I responded.
>
> "Well, salute me now, it's required!" he rudely insisted.

And so I had to comply, conforming to the showy procedure of the archaic Spanish military regulations applicable in the case of generals—that is, a salute in three phases of successive movements. First phase: When a general approaches, one must stop with feet together, head raised in profile, the left arm at the side and the right hand at the level of the cap with a visor (or the straw hat in Cuba). Second phase: A turn facing the general, in the same posture. Third phase: Another turn at the same rate of speed, but lowering the right hand quickly in a salute.

I don't need to say how annoying that outburst of the unknown but fearsome general was. After such a disagreeable incident, my companion and I were very careful to exercise vigilance so that our passage across the Plaza de Armas wouldn't cause some cantankerous general to subject me again to an identical bit of unpleasantness.

When we arrived at the Captaincy General, Carlos Martí waited for me in a nearby café. Soon after, I was received by Colonel Vallespinosa in one of the offices of the Gobierno Superior of the colony.

In contrast to the repulsive harshness of the general I had just encountered—whose image still made me nervous—Colonel Vallespinosa received me with the most natural and welcoming manner. In summary, the amiable colonel said to me: "It was preferable for you to come personally so that we could understand each other better for I want to comply with the recommendation of my dear brother Ventureta. I suppose," he went on, "that since you are a sergeant, you must aspire to become a lieutenant. If this is your purpose, you have only to spend fifteen days in a column of your battalion while it is in operations, and there will then be an opportunity to include you in the first proposal of recommendations for promotion in order to arrange your promotion to lieutenant."

I was surprised by the suggestion of the benevolent colonel. I told him that that was not my desire. I made it clear to him, immediately, with all sincerity, that I was grateful for the generous offer he made me, but I honorably confessed to him that the prospect of a military career did not tempt me at all because I had no vocation for it. And besides (I added), in fifteen days of operations, I could be the target of fifteen bullets or worse.

"Then what is your wish?" the colonel asked me.

"To remain close to Your Excellency," I responded, "in some office position that would free me from going out on operations and, if possible, would allow me to resume here in Havana my literary and journalistic vocation, which along with my university studies I had to suspend in Barcelona because of the *quinta* and my forced embarkation for Cuba."

The colonel was silent for a moment, and then he smiled at me and said:

"Good! I shall try to comply with your request. Go back to Aguacate and I shall arrange your transfer to Havana as soon as possible."

I took leave of Colonel Vallespinosa, expressing my heartfelt gratitude in advance. And moments later, having rejoined Carlos Martí, my friend took me to the office of the *Diario del ejército*, where, with the help of a large pair of scissors (the equivalent, he said, to the editor-in-chief of the editorial department), he collected some informative pieces destined for the next issue of the newspaper.

Carlos Martí and I then walked to the Parque Central to have lunch in one of the most famous establishments in Havana at that time—the Café Alemán situated at the corner of Neptuno and the Paseo del Prado (today the Paseo Martí) facing the Parque Central. This café was then the property of a Señor Pujol, a Catalan, and later of a son of his who became a good friend of mine in the months that followed. After we ate, Carlos Martí and I chatted about our recent impressions, reliving, in particular, the fright caused by the famous general's offensive act in the Muelle de Luz. In the late afternoon, after boarding a launch across the bay, I got on a train that took me back to the church of Aguacate, which had been converted into a barracks and battalion office.

Some two weeks later, when I was beginning to fear that Colonel Vallespinosa might have forgotten his promise, the order for my transfer to the Regimiento Provisional de España número 2 of the garrison in Puentes Grandes was received in the headquarters of the Batallón de España número 46. The commander, head of the Aguacate office, communicated the order to me. I was surprised at first by that order because I didn't know whether Puentes Grandes was a Havana neighborhood, or how far it was from the capital. Trusting nonetheless in the good intentions of Colonel Vallespinosa, I took leave of the commanders, of the officers, and all those who had been my office companions, as well as some Cuban families whose residences were nearby. And one morning at the beginning of July 1897, provided with a small suitcase carrying my few belongings, I settled down in the Matanzas train that was to take me to my new but still unknown destination.

When I arrived at the Muelle de Luz, I wanted to find out where I was to present myself. I engaged the first agent of the militarized body of public order who was passing by, to accompany me to an inn or safe place where I could leave the suitcase while I went to present myself at the General Staff of the Captaincy General.

The public order policeman took me to a nearby inn. Its owner took charge of my suitcase, and in a few minutes I was in the Headquarters of the Palace Guard, showing the document attesting to my new position, with the intention of presenting myself to Colonel Vallespinosa, who had authorized it. But Colonel Vallespinosa was no longer in the offices of the General Staff, where he had received me two weeks earlier, as the head of the guard told me; rather he was in Puentes Grandes, where he had been placed at the head of the military co-command, an annex to the Regimento Provisional de la Habana número 2.

After a most welcome light meal at the inn near the Muelle de Luz and after I was informed of the itinerary that I should follow to Puentes Grandes, I picked up my suitcase and in a coach for hire arrived at the Concha Station (situated in the current location of the new market in the Avenue of Carlos III), from which the train left for Marianao[4] with an intermediary stop to go to Puentes Grandes, or to take the return train to Havana. The stairway of that stop led very near to and almost in front of the headquarters of Puentes Grandes in the street of the same name.

Once again in the presence of the amiable Colonel Vallespinosa, he informed me that when he was designated provisionally for that post, he wanted to place me close to him until the period elapsed—which he hoped would be very brief—of being replaced, since he had to rejoin the General Staff of the Captaincy General. And since the command at Puentes Grandes already had enough office personnel, he placed me under his direct orders so that I could make frequent trips to Havana, in accord with my plans and his own for complying with the recommendation of his dear brother.

The satisfaction I felt when I received the kind welcome of the understanding Catalan colonel may be easily imagined. I want to declare that, in return, during the three months in which I found myself favored by such an excellent situation, I always comported myself as appropriately and discreetly as possible. I acted as I did to avoid abusing the confidence of my protector, and also to justify myself before the officers and companions in the command. As a result, no one in the office found it strange that except for my rotations as part of the nucleus of the guard in the building, I left alone for Havana many afternoons, provided with the appropriate official pass, on the condition that I return to the command in Puentes Grandes before midnight.

In one of my first trips from Puentes Grandes to Havana, I took care to visit Dr. Francisco J. Rabell, the illustrious personage from Sancti Spíritus who had lavished such kind attentions on me during my stay in that town. Dr. Rabell had his family residence and the laboratory of the famous creosote emulsion that bears his name on San Miguel Street, a few blocks from Galiano.[5]

I was gratified by the demonstrations of affection with which I was received by the illustrious autonomist of Sancti Spíritus and by the verbal exchange of our adventures since the painful afternoon when he was to be taken to Havana along with other autonomists from that town, under threat of deportation to one of the Spanish extraterritorial prisons—Ceuta, Chafarinas, or Fernando Poo—by order of General Pin, Weyler's designated assassin.

Fortunately, it was possible for Dr. Rabell to avoid deportation. Although he was removed from his native city, he was able to renew his patriotic efforts in Havana in coordination with the top leaders of the *Partido Liberal Autonomista*.[6] Some months later, when the autonomist regime was established, he was one of the most effective members elected to the Chamber of Representatives.

Dr. Rabell was happy, for his part, with my transfer to Puentes Grandes and with the special concession authorized by Colonel Vallespinosa that allowed me to go freely to Havana. When he learned about that authorization, he indicated that he wanted me to visit him often, as I did, although I did not abuse his laudable kindness.

I usually spent mornings in the office working on some assignment from the colonel, busying myself with letters and literary tasks or in the company of some other vagabond sergeant, walking around the surrounding neighborhoods, up and down the streets of Marianao, sometimes toward the Puente de la Lisa, and at other times in the opposite direction, where the paper factory was located on the banks alongside the stone bridge beneath which flowed the waters of the Almendares River.

I recall that by association with impressions I gathered and never forgot, on one of those walks toward the paper factory, our attention was drawn to piano music coming from a large house situated at the bend of the river. We were told that "some sisters who were poets and painters, the daughters of a very learned gentleman" lived there. How far I was from thinking that after the war, when I returned to Cuba in 1905 to live here and identify myself definitively with the Cuban people, I would have very amiable conversations with "that very learned gentleman," at the house beside the river of Puentes Grandes! He was the eminent patriot, doctor, writer, and educator Dr. Esteban Borrero Echevarría, father of six Borrero sisters, equally deserving of admiring remembrance, especially Juana[7] and Dulce María, both excellent poets, and the oldest sister, Dolores, who inherited all the great pedagogical gifts of her worthy progenitor.

Later, in another series of my memoirs—if God allows me the consolation of continuing them—I will enjoy referring to very interesting revelations Dr. Borrero Echevarría made to me at the end of 1905 in one of the delightful chats with which he favored me in the editorial office of *El Nuevo País* located on Teniente Rey Street in Havana, next to the Sarrá drugstore.

I have never forgotten some episodes among those that made the most intimate impressions on me, dating from my stay in the large house on the Calzada de Puentes Grandes, where the military command of the Marianao neighborhood was located.

As for the amiable contact I always enjoyed with Colonel Vallespinosa, and with the officers and my office companions in that bureaucratic team, there was never any kind of conflict, intrigue, envy, or upset despite the dissimilar temperaments of the men involved. Days passed there without complications, each one attending to his tasks, without going beyond the limits set for us or engaging in actions that were not tolerated. This tacit companionship owed a great deal to the affectionate respect that Colonel Vallespinosa's benevolence inspired in us, and also to the fact that the nucleus of the group, officers as well as troops, was composed of men assembled by the very personal appointments of the colonel himself or through recommendations from other high places, with the objective of avoiding our exposure to dangerous situations in combat operations in the *manigua* since Puentes Grandes and its urban perimeter, due to its proximity to Havana, were considered exempt from incursions from the *mambises*.

On a certain night, however, when everyone had already retired to their respective dormitories, from the colonel and the officers to the contingent of troops (the officers resided in a building situated facing the big house of the command), something surprising happened which did not have disagreeable consequences but did give rise to an incident that would have cast ridicule on Colonel Vallespinosa's respectable reputation if that risk had not, fortunately, been quickly avoided.

That night at around eleven thirty or twelve when I, as sergeant, was serving in the squad of guards in the command post, the sentinel situated at the entrance of the house sounded the voice of alarm when he heard the loud, ever-closer hoofbeats of a suspicious group of riders coming from the neighborhood of the Ceiba.[8] The guard squad mobilized quickly. Then we learned from a pair of mounted soldiers whom we called out with the order to "Halt!" that the alarming sounds did not come from an insurrectionist squadron but from the mounted escort of the general in chief of the day, who was reconnoitering that district.

When Colonel Vallespinosa heard the cries of the sentinel, the hoofbeats of the horses in the advance party of soldiers, and the confused shouts of the guards, he dressed quickly and left the side room, where he had his sleeping quarters, to find out what the commotion was about. Since the disturbance took him by surprise while he was half asleep, he did not realize that he was still wearing his customary nightcap. I immediately went up to him in order to discreetly point out what he had neglected to remove in his distraction, and to explain the reasons for all the confusion. As a result of what I had told him, he was able to go out to the main entrance and receive and exchange greetings and opportune information with the general in chief of the day who was the cause of all the uproar.

I discovered one day soon after, that among various soldiers and a colonel, who were new to the troops assigned to the command of Puentes Grandes, were two poets. It is unnecessary to say that when I learned of the romantic proclivities of both colleagues, I was not long in informing them of my affinity for poetry. I shall recall here how I was able to meet and converse with them.

The first man was León Ichaso.[9] He already possessed the mature character of a genuine Basque, energetic, not very communicative, but natural, unpretentious, attractive, and highly cultivated. I do not know what circumstances of chance or destiny caused León Ichaso, despite his age at the time—twenty-five to thirty years—to enroll as a volunteer in the Spanish Army. I don't know whether he enrolled in Spain or in Cuba. On the other hand, I do remember with gratification a very original infraction of military regulations I caught him in one day. It was an infraction that could have cost the audacious sentinel a severe correction if an officer or some other sergeant with scruples regarding regulations had found him out. It happened this way:

One afternoon when it was my turn as sergeant to head the squad of the guard on duty in the command, I noticed with great surprise that the soldier Ichaso, as he was serving as the sentinel on guard, was leaning against a column of the outer door of the building, and while he was standing up, he wasn't holding his rifle in the prescribed manner. He had the mouth of the Mauser on the ground and, in a most original manner, was using the butt as a desk in order to write on a sheet of paper with a pencil.

I approached the abstracted sentinel to inquire about the strange reason for that very novel maneuver. And smiling serenely, he confessed straightforwardly that he had taken advantage of the calmness of the hour in order to write down some strophes of a sonnet that he was working out mentally.

"Stupendous!" I said to him, also smiling. And I added, "But take care that some officer or perhaps the colonel doesn't catch you in this infraction, because it could cost you a serious reprimand."

That episode sealed the beginning of the sincere friendship that I renewed on my return to Cuba at the beginnings of independence with the illustrious and very cultivated journalist. Later, he achieved well-earned renown as a masterful litterateur, exquisite poet, and thoughtful columnist who wrote for the press in Cienfuegos, and later in the best Havana publications, especially the *Diario de la Marina*.[10]

Adding to the agreeable memories I retain of León Ichazo, whose son Francisco[11] inherited his great intellectual gifts, it is a pleasure for me to recall another anecdote, related, to be sure, with another sonnet, also written by the unforgettable sentinel of the historic military command in Puentes Grandes.

Some twenty-five or thirty years ago, here in Havana, a certain unabashed imposter committed the blunder of submitting a sonnet by León Ichazo to a questionable journal and then substituting the name of the illustrious author with his own—that of the contemptible plagiarist. I will abstain from revealing the name and the surname of the rash, hack writer out of consideration for family members who are still alive and deserving of respect. But as an example of León Ichazo's integrity, I do want to note here that when he discovered the literary theft of which he was the victim, he limited himself to making fun of the scandalously brazen fellow by saying: "What stupidity! As if everyone who knows him doesn't realize that he is incapable of composing a couplet, much less a sonnet!"

The other poet and journalist from Spain, who was incorporated into the military command of Puentes Grandes in the third trimester of 1897, was José Muñiz de Quevedo, a Spaniard of some twenty-five to twenty-seven years of age at the time. He was self-assured, a talker, intense, attracted by the excellence of Cuban rum from the moment he disembarked in Havana, and an admirer of Creole female beauty. But at the same time, he was an impulsive adversary of the patriotic ideal of independence and often denounced it. This was a prejudice clearly inherited from his father, Don José

Muñiz de Terrones, a colonel in the Spanish Army and author of a book on *Las Ordenanzas de Su Majestad*, a text used in Hispanic military academies.

Since he was born, raised, and educated in a militarist environment that exemplified passionate repulsion to the ideals of the Cuban people, and since he also worked for the jingoistic Madrid press of those days, it did not strike me as strange that he should have come to combat the defenders of Cuban independence, branded by him and by Spanish chauvinistic opinion as traitors or spurious sons of Spain.

According to what he told me, when he arrived in Cuba, Muñiz de Quevedo was posted to the Batallón Cazadores de Llerena, where he was assigned the job of quartermaster, that is, the coordinator of everything pertaining to the acquisition of foodstuffs and the means used to prepare and serve on a daily basis not only the so-called mess for the troops, but also (with the appropriate differences of quality and variety) the menus for commanders and officers. Those culinary duties were often very difficult for the romantic quartermaster when his battalion suffered attacks by rebel forces or when that same battalion had to join other armed units, without his being able to think how and when he could make use of the circumstances and recourses at hand to improvise something—even if it was only a comforting watery soup for the troops.

Muñiz de Quevedo often told me that he had written a series of reports on the tumultuous times when those experiences unfolded, with the intention of collecting them into a volume. Nevertheless, he never showed me any of those articles for as long as he remained in the command of Puentes Grandes. He only told me that they contained facts, anecdotes, and episodes that he hoped would attract curious readers when he published the book. On the other hand, I had some friendly conversations with him on literary topics to begin with, but which soon diverged into his systematic prejudices against the *mambises*.

In view, however, of the explosive concepts he used to denounce the patriotic rebellion, a conflict between essentially opposing political criteria soon surfaced between us since, acting on very liberal ideological and sentimental impulses—as sincere as his own, but certainly more understanding—I pointed out to him reasons, antecedents, and undeniable evidence that justified the Cuban insurrection against the stubborn intransigency of the Spanish governors. And since I voiced those arguments in the most temperate and friendly tone, our discussions never ended in quarrels but rather in a discreet return to literary subjects and, preferably, to poetry.

Later, I don't remember how or why, Muñiz de Quevedo disappeared from the nucleus of the command in Puentes Grandes. And I heard nothing more of him or of his projected book until my return to Cuba in 1905.

At the end of that year, I discovered a copy of *AJIACO*,[12] Muñiz de Quevedo's book, when I stopped, as I often did, to look around the store and warehouse of secondhand books on Obispo Street owned by a Señor Ricoy, who was a buyer of private libraries and remainders.

I bought the book immediately. It was not in good condition and I asked Ricoy to exchange it for a better copy if he had one, but that was impossible because the bookseller informed me that that copy was the only one that had come to him in a pile of various books bought from a widow.

As I leafed through the book, I could not wait to read it. I was interested, but fearful at the same time, to learn whether the author had presented his obsessions against Cuban patriotism in his former crude manner or whether the experiences he had had during the campaign and, at its end, with the disaster that befell Cervera[13] in Santiago de Cuba, had provided more than enough lessons for reflection so as to rectify his prejudices against the defenders of the ideal of independence.

The honest impression which I drew and still retain from reading *AJIACO* in a spirit of understanding is that despite gathering together in some chapters, and especially in the one titled "Por la Patria," deplorable examples in verse of stupidities against Cuba (under the pretext that they constituted folklore) signed by the most popular representatives of Spanish poetry of the period, along with shameless insults directed against the most outstanding leaders and apostles of the Liberation Army—I do not doubt, nevertheless, regarding the direct responsibility Muñiz de Quevedo bore for the denigration of Cubans, that when he was on the point of launching his book, he tried to attenuate his views by including a piece titled "Descubierta" by way of a prologue. This was an article written, it appears, after his trials in the war in which he dedicated enthusiastic, unmatched praise to the divine poet Julián del Casal,[14] to the great poet and artist Juana Borrero, and to her sensitive biographer, Carlos Pío Ulirbach,[15] declaring—astonishingly—in regard to Casal—"that many supposed geniuses (an allusion to Spanish poets) would be satisfied with the crumbs fallen from the hands of the unfortunate Cuban poet."

In the same article, "Descubierta," Muñiz de Quevedo affirmed, rather paradoxically for those days, that in his opinion, "No noble Spanish breast harbors systematic rancor against our compatriots, the Cubans." And if that was not indicative of a rectification of his criteria and sentiments toward the defenders of a free Cuba, he added the two following lines: "When peace comes, I shall be able to speak of the causes of our equivocations." One must suppose that such equivocations would not be attributed to the conquerors but to the conquered alone.

I also sincerely believe that I contributed to the discreet, corrective evolution of Muñiz de Quevedo's thought in favor of Cuban patriotism with the solid accumulation of arguments with which I refuted his stubborn prejudices against the heroic *mambises* during our friendly conversations in the command of Puentes Grandes.

All of this leads me to suppose that quite possibly the impression or recollection of my friendly and frank contentions in defense of the separatist ideal dictated the following paragraph, whose discovery on page 164 of *AJIACO* pleasantly surprised me when I bought the book in 1905.

> This campaign for whatever reason, since the same was not true of the previous struggle, has brought forward many writers. There has been a raft of emulators of Pedro Antonio de Alarcón.[16] Of all of them the only one who is worthwhile is José Conangla, a Catalan poet, with whom I got along well because, beside the fact that we both served in the troops, he has a lot of common sense.

Since the war of 1895, I have had no news of Muñiz de Quevedo. I don't even know whether he is still alive. But when I found and was gratified by his spontaneous praise, I assumed that he would not have attributed a lot of common sense to me only in regard to literary and poetic matters, but also, and especially, to topics connected to my defense of the Cuban rebellion in the face of the mistakes and obstinate intransigence of the Spanish governors and Spanish chauvinism in general.

During my frequent trips to Havana, I always carried an official pass from the command in case I might be subjected to an incident similar to the one brought about by the repulsive general who caused me such unpleasant embarrassment in the plaza of the Muelle de Luz, as I related previously. The military uniform, however, did not prevent me from acquiring successive relationships with journalists, as well as affable literary friendships with some of the writers for the most popular dailies and magazines in Havana.

One of the first professionals in Havana whom I met at that time was José Manuel Fuentevilla. The Catalan commission agent, Don Salvador Torra Pous, who was also an accredited correspondent for Spanish and French newspapers, introduced me to him. Señor Terra Pous's office and residence was in the street of San Rafael, at the top of the very house where at the beginning of the Republic, Nonell, Llerandi y Cía, dedicated to administering the collection of revenue from the lottery, was legally registered.

By a happy coincidence, one morning when I visited Torra Pous in his office to exchange impressions on the increasingly grave course the war was taking, I was fortunate enough to have my visit to the Catalan correspondent coincide with a visit from Fuentevilla, who was there for the same reason. That was the origin of the reciprocal and fraternal friendship between Fuentevilla and me. And very soon, through Fuentevilla, I widened my friendly relations with other Havana journalists, among them Don Antonio San Miguel, the famous native Catalan, director of *La Lucha*[17]; with José Triay,[18] the editor of the *Diario de la Marina*; with Manuel Serafín Pichardo, director of the magazine *El Fígaro*[19]; with Antonio G. Zamora, director of *El Hogar*[20]; and in addition, with Ubago, Alfredo Martín Morales, Aniceto Valdivia, Rafael Santa Coloma, Enrique Fontanills, Carlos Guardiola, and others.

As a result of those friendships with journalists in Havana, I also began making frequent contributions solely of a literary nature in magazines and supplements of the *Diario de la Marina*, as well as articles on diverse matters and reports in *La Lucha* and other dailies. I signed my work or used a pseudonym in the literary articles, but I did not sign the other articles, whether unprompted or solicited.

The *Diario de la Marina* was located in the building now occupied by the Hotel Plaza (before it was expanded) on Zulueta[21] and Parque Central.[22] Its editorial and administrative offices were located on the first upper floor and the press on the lower floors, where the obese but untiring worker Don José Triay, united the functions appropriate to his role as editor with those of director in order to prepare the layout of the newspaper in its two editions. There, Don José Triay, who was always courteous, accepted my collaborations (free, of course) for the columns of brief notes, curiosities, and literary digressions for the afternoon edition.

Along with friendly relations with professional journalists, I made friends with a trio of bohemian intellectuals whom I met around the table of a café next to what was the Albisu Theater (on the block of the present Centro Asturiano of Havana).[23] Riera, Peche, and Niebla were the names of the members of that group of would-be writers like me, enthusiasts—each in his own fashion—of the free exercise of creativity in prose or in verse.

Of the three romantic musketeers, Riera and Peche were older than I, Niebla the youngest. All three, in unanimity, were very fond of comforting alcoholic beverages and zarzuela performances. Out of discretion I always refrained from asking them—since they never told me—what their *modus vivendi* or respective jobs were that allowed them to meet at their leisure, stroll around the Parque Central, and enjoy nocturnal walks through the libertine neighborhoods of Havana, where I took leave of them to catch the train from Concha to my hammock in Puentes Grandes.

I have always recalled with sympathy the most outstanding traits of those three bohemians. Riera, the Catalan, strong, corpulent, euphoric, dressed in a kind of dark frock coat, a tie with long ends, and a black bowler hat (*bonbín* in Creole parlance). Angel Peche was of medium height, stout with a serene air and measured speech, an enemy only of bad prose and padded verses. Policarpio Niebla, a native of the Canary Islands, was energetic, decisive, with firm ideas and pithy concepts. His firmness of character led me to predict that he would exercise great influence on the political evolution of his island homeland, and in fact, as I learned twenty years later, Niebla held a very outstanding position representing his native land.

Before I learned the abovementioned fact about Policarpio Niebla, a report appeared in Havana's daily press describing the tunnel that connected the Castillo del Príncipe[24] with the side of the hill of the same name. The exit from the tunnel was visible when a large part of said hill was leveled to connect the present Avenida or Paseo de los Presidentes, in the Vedado, with the road leading to the Colón Cemetery. The author of the article included, among other curious facts pertaining to the tunnel, that different explorers of that mysterious passage discovered signatures on one of its walls. Among others, the reporter copied the names of the unforgettable colleagues I often consorted with in the latter part of the 1895 war: Riera, Peche and Niebla. I kept the clipping of the report in which this detail appeared and proved very suggestive for me, but I haven't been able to locate it since then. Vagaries and links between life and history!

I still remember another pleasing impression of my conversations in cafés with the charming trio of those bohemian intellectuals: the indirect criticism I received, voiced by the purist Peche when he noticed that an article published in the supplement of the *Diario de la Marina* on the monologue *Tirando la llave* by the Mexican poet Juan de Dios Peza, was signed with the pseudonym Jocofó.

"How could it occur to the author of this article to sign it with a *ñañigo*[25] pseudonym?" Peche exclaimed, unaware that it was my article.

I responded sincerely to the critic's timely query that that pseudonym consisted of the three first syllables of my name and my two surnames. And so the incident ended with mutual explanations, but also with the promise that I would never again use a pseudonym that Cuban culture found so repugnant.

I don't recall what reasons there may have been for a commemoration of some kind, or for the display of Spanish *integrista* propaganda, that led to the gathering of a contingent of ardent members of the historic body of volunteers of commerce of Havana[26] under the broad overhang of the first beer and ice factory, La Tropical,[27] in Havana, near Puentes Grandes. The fiesta was held on a splendid Sunday at the end of July 1897, and was attended by numerous militia sporting their familiar uniforms with the typical fitted jackets with blue borders at the neck and sleeves, their light-colored straw hats decorated with showy rosettes of red and gold, and their shiny black boots.

In addition to the majority, consisting of that fatal militia with their well-starched uniforms, different units of the regular army came to the function, along with a group of relatives and friends of the volunteers—all of them impatient to applaud the fervent agitator, Eva Canel,[28] whose speech was billed as the main attraction of the event. But the boisterous crowd in attendance was no less avid to savor for free the cold brew with its head of foam provided by the first, and already at that time, most popular Cuban beer.

I was repelled by the noise, the shouting, and the guffaws of that multitude gathered together for anti-Cuban reasons. I would gladly have left a situation so opposed to my convictions if I had not been drawn there with the aim of using that annoying opportunity to form a correct idea of the spiteful craziness of the irascible, chauvinistic agitator whose pamphleteering venting in the daily columns of *La Unión Constitucional*[29] earned her the fanatical admiration of the anti-Cuban mob.

When she arrived at the spacious overhang of La Tropical, the peninsular crowd enthusiastically greeted the anticipated protagonist of the event with fervent *vivas* to her, to Weyler, to Spanish *integrismo*, to the body of volunteers, to the Spanish Army, to the Marqués de Azpeteguía, etc. Some commanders of the volunteers bearing the insignia of their honorary rank, and other men, who must have been representatives of the organizing commission, sat down in the place reserved for them, after helping Señora Canel climb up to a sturdy platform, at the rear of the overhang, facing the expectant assembly.

I have preserved through the years the repulsive mental picture, the carnivalesque appearance of Señora Canel. She was in her fifties, with masculine features, of medium height, clothed in a uniform similar to that of the volunteers of commerce, but with a skirt down to the middle of her ankles to discreetly conceal her most pronounced physiological protuberances.

A cornet's sharp note signaling silence, ordered by the president of the fiesta, quieted the chattering of the crowd jammed together along the length of the overhang. Eva Canel began her speech immediately with explosive praise for Weyler, attributing to him genial gifts of command, strategy, and energy, which led—the orator stated to great applause—to the death of the most ferocious among the separatist bandits, namely, Antonio Maceo. Following his disappearance, she added—more or less verbatim—we will see the extermination of all the mobs of blacks and whites without God and country in the insurrectionist bands since—thanks to the reconcentration—those savages will have to surrender or die of hunger, for very soon they will lack the help and the traitorous intelligence of the deceitful countrymen residing in places more or less distant from the towns.

The emboldened agitator went on to apply the grossest, most slanderous adjectives to the heroic commanders of the Liberation Army. She attributed all kinds of crimes to those leaders and to the separatist fighters. She even denied that the defenders of the ideal of freedom were Cubans, an absurd ideal for natives of the country, she explained, for it was unrealizable and unnecessary: What abounds in Cuba, she stated, is nothing other than freedom, too much freedom. The excess of freedom and tolerance granted to the evil, spurious sons of Spain, traitors to their country, made the war possible.

In summary: The injurious and slanderous charges that the speaker, convulsed with spite, leveled against the idea of liberation were so insistent and shameless; and in addition, the scandalous words of adulation which the cynical agitator heaped on the governors, the military, the volunteers, the *guerrilleros*, and everything that signaled the tyrannical domination of Spanish intransigence in Cuba, were so repugnant to my ears and to my liberal support of the rebellion, that in resolution, not wishing to listen further to more absurdities from the superpatriot, I left, putting distance between me and that atmosphere saturated with morbid obsessions. I was indignant and ashamed at the same time for having had the patience to put up for so long with the overwhelming pandemonium taking place there with impunity. Nonetheless, on my way back to the command in Puentes Grandes, my indignation subsided because the insolent superpatriot from the Peninsula dressed, carnivalesque style, in the uniform of the volunteers of commerce seemed ridiculous to me. Her audacity seemed laughable more than anything else, deserving of the satirical scorn with which the popular commentator of that period, who later served as a magistrate, Wenceslao Gálvez, treated her when he discovered that Eva Canel was the theatrical pseudonym for the anti-*mambises* agitator. Her real name was Agar Infanzón Canel, and in accord with this fact, the ironic Wenceslao Gálvez, in referring to the scandalous and rude remarks of the histrionic anti-Cuban, addressed her from the weekly *Gil Blas*, with the following witty pun, which was much admired: VEN ACA . . . AGAR; VEN ACA . . . [By eliding the two A's in the first phrase, this can be pronounced, "VEN A CAGAR; VEN ACA . . . " (Come here to shit; Come here . . .)].

By the end of July in the same year (1897), the campaigning carried out on behalf of an exalted Spanish patriotism was increasingly inflamed. And as if the criminal reconcentration was not enough to plunge thousands of families condemned in this way to a slow and certain annihilation in conditions of misery, helplessness, and the most horrendous tribulations, Weyler's pre-Hitlerian ferocity ordered other punishments which were no less harsh. He ordered the operational military columns and especially the cruel volunteer guerrillas to destroy *bohíos*, small plots of land, and fruit trees of all kinds, so that lodgings and food could not be used by the liberation bands. Additionally, as much in Havana as in other important towns in the island, investigative procedures were honed to discover and punish *infidencias* (a word equivalent to disaffection or simple antipathy) attributed to any Cuban suspected of separatist inclinations.

The worsening, serious crisis, which was not only political but also economic in many aspects, became graver when the unexpected and sensational news arrived of the assassination of Cánovas del Castillo,[30] president of the Spanish government, by the anarchist Angiolillo[31] in the seaside resort of Santa Águeda. The shock of that assassination in the lands governed by the Spanish monarchy, in Cuba and the Philippines, in the United States, and in the entire international political world, is well known.

The immediate replacement of Cánovas, head of the Conservative Party, by Sagasta,[32] head of the Party called Liberal, mobilized feverish meetings among the elements representative of colonial intransigence. And making itself the echo of those elements, the *integrista* press labored to point out the grave dangers that in its opinion would threaten the essential shared interests of the colony and the mother country if the new government in Madrid were to recommend a change of procedures to General Weyler in the face of separatism, since the *mambisa* forces, in the judgment of those individuals, were on the brink of complete disaster because of Weyler's implacable tactics.

The truth, however, was very different from the way it was presented by the spokesmen for obtuse Spanish *integrismo*, because the liberation forces, despite the ferocity with which Weyler tried to annihilate them, maintained their heroic rebellion, courageous as always, and resolved to prevail.

Sagasta's government, meanwhile, was already at odds with the systematic intransigence of the Marqués de Azpeteguía's troops, backed by the despicable battalions of volunteers. With impudent protests from their presses, and with frequent demonstrations in the streets and plazas of Havana, the stubborn agitators wanted to prevent any change whatsoever in the governing procedures that Weyler imposed against the rebellion for liberation. But when a direct diplomatic incitation from McKinley,[33] the president of the United States, was received in Madrid in the middle of September, threatening the government of Spain if it did not abolish the inhuman measures of the reconcentration and prevent armed demonstrations by the volunteers and the aggressive mobs in Havana, Sagasta was quick to obtain authorization from the Queen Regent of Spain to relieve General Weyler of his superior command in Cuba, replacing him with General Ramón Blanco.[34] He also obtained authorization allowing Don Segismundo Moret[35] to initiate a project destined to establish a supposedly autonomous government in Cuba.

In connection with the second of these authorizations, I recall that the version of the following dialogue between Queen María Cristina and Sagasta appeared in the North American press and in newspapers in Havana:

"You are not afraid, Mr. President, that (as the opposition insists on affirming) the concession of autonomy will bring about the loss of Cuba for Spain?"

"Madam," Sagasta replied, "how is it possible to lose what has been lost for a long time!"

The Royal Decree according to which General Blanco was to take Weyler's place was made public in Madrid and was communicated to Cuba and the international press on October 9. But General Blanco didn't arrive in Havana until the thirtieth of October, 1897. Official delegations and others of a semi-official character received him in a prudent way, that is, without extreme displays of adulation, and accompanied him to the seat of the Captain-General's government, where he immediately relieved his spiteful predecessor of his post.

On the other hand, groups of agitators saw Weyler off with loud ovations during the short trajectory from the Palace to the Muelle de Caballería, They were not prevented from mounting those scandalous displays by the Military Governor of Havana, General Arolas, who was present as head of the cordon of regular troops deployed to preserve order during the farewell to the deposed despot. (It is true that General Arolas, an ill-mannered military man, was thought to sympathize with the republican ideal in Spain, but in Cuba he always showed himself to be as firmly attached to the anti-Cuban absolutist intransigencies as the rest of his colleagues in the decorated military hierarchies.)

As soon as the new Captain-General took command, he ordered the suspension of all the measures Weyler had implemented in the Dantesque reconcentration and in the systematic persecutions of supposed disloyal subjects. He fired different military men, police chiefs, and vigilantes who had stood out for their extreme animosity in the application of Weyler's cruel orders.

In addition, General Blanco expended great effort into attracting the confidence, sympathy, and help of autonomists and reformers. At the same time, he laid down rigorous instructions aimed at preventing the volunteer militias sympathetic to *integrismo* from producing new disturbances. He also initiated tireless soundings of important liberation chiefs in the hope of attracting them to an accord, but with the exception of Masó Parra,[36] all of them refused to accept the tempting offers made by the government. Some of the leaders of the Cuban Army even formed a Military Tribunal and approved the execution by firing squad of the mediator. Since all of this is well known because it is confirmed by history, there is no need to recall it in these *Memoirs*.

Ultimately, General Blanco's provisions, which were inspired by a desire for peace, along with official announcements on the organization of the promised autonomous regimen, far from reining in the stubborn intransigence of Spanish colonial patriotism, inflamed it even more. In the face of both irreconcilable tendencies, the separatist army pursued its irreducible objectives with maximum determination. As the corollary of such struggles, the inopportune solution of the supposed autonomous regime provided little hope.

Moreover, as if all that were not enough to understand the inefficacy of the inadequate new regime, and to foresee intuitively the proximity of the catastrophic collapse of stubborn Spanish imperialism in Cuba, on a daily basis the intrigues that North American advocates of annexation were instigating became more visible and threatening, aided by the more or less evident complicity of Washington's diplomacy in some European chancelleries. Despite such adverse circumstances, on January 1, 1898, in the Salón de Actos of the Captaincy General the solemn installation of the scheduled autonomous government, decreed on November 25 of the previous year, took place.

Since I wanted to see how that event would unfold—its consequences for the immediate political future of Cuba were unclear—I hastened to the Plaza de Armas in Havana, in front of the Palace, as a simple spectator, in the company of another sergeant from the command at Puentes Grandes.

The public that flocked to the Plaza de Armas, attracted by the event, was not, in fact, overflowing, since it only covered half of the plaza and the immediate neighborhood of the Palace on Obispo Street.

Precautions had been taken in advance to avoid or suppress any attempts to incite the crowd, but they were unnecessary. From ten to ten thirty in the morning, luxurious open coaches escorted by military forces on horseback began arriving, carrying the personages who would compose the cabinet soon to be constituted: Don José María Gálvez, president, and the five secretaries or ministers—Rafael Montoro, Antonio Govín, Francisco Zayas,

Laureano Rodríguez, and Eduardo Dolz[37]—followed by the invited diplomatic, official, and special representations.

A cordon of infantry soldiers was situated around the palace. Meanwhile, the public (dominated, I supposed, by supporters of autonomy) limited itself to saluting with applause the arrival of the aforementioned personages at the mansion of the executive colonial power, and it redoubled its applause before the joint appearance of General Blanco and the nascent cabinet on the central balcony of the royal edifice once the ceremony was over.

The animosity of the battling political elements was inflamed with clear signs of increased seriousness in the capital of the island, especially within the Hispanic nuclei opposed to what they termed the "shameful surrender on the part of Spanish sovereignty." And the animosity of those nuclei of *integristas* exploded a few days later (on the twelfth of that same month of January) when an angry squad of uniformed officers of its army took to the streets and regrouped in the Parque Central of Havana, shouting *vivas* to Weyler and *mueras* [death] to autonomy, and interjecting bold exclamations such as, "General Blanco must resign."

But the furious demonstrators were not satisfied with their shouts. They broke into the offices and the printing press of the newspaper *El Reconcentrado*,[38] situated at the end of the Acera del Louvre, destroying the job cases and the machines, in reprisal, as they said, for the commentaries made by the very popular and valiant director of that newspaper, Ricardo Arnautó—the Rochefort of patriotic Cuban pamphleteering—who had written about the supposed cowardice of some lieutenants of the Spanish Army.

Although General Arolas, the military commander of Havana, hastened to disband the furious mutineers, those acts of violence provided the consul-general of the United States in Cuba, General Lee,[39] with a motive for asking the government in Washington to send a warship immediately in order to protect Yankee interests and citizens in Cuba. And it wasn't long before the battleship *Maine* sank in Havana Harbor.

5
The *Maine* and the Disaster

(January to July 1898)

The request for the battleship and the arrival of the *Maine*[1] in the port of Havana on the twenty-fifth of January, 1898, led to great indignation on the part of the most vehement partisans of Spanish *integrismo*, but it clearly obliged them to repress their street demonstrations. Nonetheless, in their newspapers and in their private meetings, they did not curtail their intrigues against General Blanco, and they indicated that they were ready to have Spain declare war on the United States. I well remember that in blundering support of that obsessive spite, a doctored fact sheet was widely circulated in Havana and in all the towns on the island that presented a comparative study of the respective war flotillas of the United States and Spain. The deceptive graphics used in the comparison presented Spanish naval power as very superior in number and destructive power to that of the great northern republic.

At that time, a scandalous diplomatic episode increased the serious tension that existed between the governments in Washington and Madrid. A letter from Dupuy de Lôme,[2] the Spanish ambassador to the United States, contained astonishingly offensive remarks about McKinley, the North American president. Dupuy de Lôme had sent the letter to Don José Canalejas,[3] a prominent Spanish politician who had come to Havana on an information-gathering mission. However, Dupuy's epistolary blunder was mysteriously taken from among other papers contained in Canaleja's suitcase by an agent of the Cuban Directorio Revolucionario, who was resident in Havana. It was then sent to Mr. Rubens in the United States and handed over by him to the State Department, which lost no time in publicizing it.

That unheard-of scandal prompted the immediate resignation and precipitous return to Madrid of Dupuy and Canalejas. But the international commentaries on an instance of such diplomatic imprudence aggravated the growing reciprocal nervousness between the governments of Washington and Madrid. It also increased the expectations and animosity of the two groups in Cuba that were more irreconcilable by the day: that of the followers of the harsh colonial *integrismo* and that of the advocates of the irreducible objectives of Cuban patriotism.

The presence of the battleship *Maine* in Havana harbor seemed to silence the anti-autonomist agitation. Meanwhile (as I pointed out in another historical evocation of those days), the nascent autonomous cabinet reorganized and adjusted their administrative procedures for the better as much as possible. It yanked innumerable venal functionaries from their warrens, replacing them with genuine Cubans. It made elections for representatives of the island in positions of authority possible and decorous. Above all, it sought untiringly and generously to remedy the overwhelming needs of thousands of victims of the war, especially the victims of the reconcentration—the elderly, women, and children who were crowded into towns, sick, beaten down, starving, half-naked, dying.

The widely known and highly sensational explosion[4] of the battleship *Maine* occurred one month[5] after its arrival in Cuba. On that day, as was the case on almost all preceding days, I was in Havana from early afternoon, dressed in civilian clothes (with special authorization from Colonel Vallespinosa). I went on my accustomed rounds during which I would visit newspaper offices, join some companion for a frugal meal, and in the evening with friends and other colleagues meet in cafés near the Albisu theater, or seek distraction in another of the theaters then putting on performances: Tacón,[6] Pairet,[7] Alhambra, or Irijoa.[8]

On that evening (February 15, 1898), when José Manuel Fuentevilla, Carlos Guardiola and I met as we usually did at the entrance to the Albisu theater, instead of waiting for the performance of one of the Spanish zarzuelas we had already seen, we opted to go to the Alhambra theater to enjoy the festive humor of the actors and the very typical Creole scenes that made the historic salon in Consulado Street[9] so famous.

We three companions were in the second box on the side reserved for the press. A few moments later, Don Justiano García Delgado arrived to take a break from his rounds in Havana. He sat in the first box, next to the proscenium arch. General Blanco had confided the leadership of the Policía de Orden Público to him, by agreement with the autonomous cabinet, bearing in mind the special gifts of intelligence, equanimity, discretion, and exquisite tact that characterized him, very opportune gifts in those days for the prudent exercise of the difficult leadership of the Havana police.

At about ten or ten thirty,[10] while we three companions were chatting with the refined lieutenant colonel, we heard a huge explosion. Everyone—the public, the actors—was instantly stunned, irresolute. We asked ourselves where that tremendous explosion could have happened.

The magazine at the Santa Clara Battery must have blown up, a voice shouted. But the truth wasn't long in coming.

"The *Maine* has exploded!!"[11]

Needless to say, the theater quickly emptied. People hurried home under a misty rain caused by the explosion. The chief of police with his adjutant and two agents of public order got into a coach and headed rapidly for the Muelle de Luz. Fuentevilla and Guardiola ran toward the portals of the Parque Central, eager for news on all the commotion. And I climbed into the first coach for hire I could find, to get to the Estación de Concha, in order to catch the train, as soon as possible, for the command in Puentes Grandes.

When the captain paymaster and other officers, seated in the portal of the residence in front of the command, saw me, they wanted to know where the explosion took place. When I told them that the *Maine* had blown up, they stood up, quite awestruck, and besieged me with questions on the formidable explosion without my being able to satisfy their quite natural impatience.

"Now the war will end!" the captain paymaster exclaimed.

"Unless another worse one breaks out!" one of the other officers objected, speaking in a low voice.

Before I retired to the interior room of the command, where I had my hammock, I asked the guard squad at the portal and in the offices inside whether Colonel Vallespinosa had been informed about the explosion, but they couldn't even tell me whether the colonel had retired to his dormitory. Thinking, nonetheless, that the officers or the squad would take care to transmit the news about the explosion obsessing us all to the colonel when it became available, I tried to go to sleep. But I failed because of the intense nervous excitement and worries that such a serious and mysterious accident produced in me.

In the morning, I tried again to contact Colonel Vallespinosa, but when he came out of his room, it turned out that he already knew what was known about the sensational explosion thanks to information that the officers of the command had garnered since my return the night before. Moreover, Colonel Vallespinosa, in full-dress uniform, was getting ready to go to the capital immediately to confer with General Blanco, not only in reference to the immediate consequences that might arise from the deadly explosion, but also—as we were not long in finding out—to seek permission from the Captain-General to be relieved from the military command of Puentes Grandes and reintegrated, as was promised earlier, into his ideal job in the General Staff under the direct orders of the supreme colonial leader.

And, in fact, four days after the troubling explosion of the *Maine*, Colonel Vallespinosa, an old friend of General Blanco, on the latter's orders ceased to be the provisional leader of the military command in Puentes

Figure 3. "*Escribientes y ordenanzas del 2° Batallón del Regimiento de Cuba.*" (Scribes and orderlies of the 2nd Batallion of the Regiment of Cuba.) (Courtesy of the Biblioteca Nacional de España.)

Grandes and was reincorporated into the post appropriate for him as a member of the General Staff under the immediate orders of the governor general of the island.

The officers, noncommissioned officers, and soldiers lamented the departure of the generous colonel from the command at Puentes Grandes. The author of this *Memoir*, however, and two other companions from the office were fortunate in that the return of the understanding leader to the General Staff coincided with our transfer to the Batallón de Escribientes y Ordenanzas [Battalion of Scribes and Orderlies], as our considerate protector had promised to arrange on our behalf.

Immediately after the alarming explosion of the *Maine* became known in the United States, North Americans attributed it to a mysterious torpedo launched by Spanish hands. The government in Washington, however, did not share that conjecture. It limited itself to the appointment of a technical commission to investigate the mysterious origin of the catastrophe. In its report, the commission stated that the explosion was caused by an underwater mine.[12] That thesis did not satisfy popular opinion in the North and even less Spanish *integrismo*, because although the text of the

North American judgment did not identify the direct origin of the presumed mine, the vagueness of the thesis maliciously implied confirmation of the assumption that the horrible explosion could only be attributed to Spanish hands. Another commission of Spanish naval engineers, in turn, asserted concretely that the explosion was definitely caused by a deadly fire in the powder magazine of the *Maine* itself.

The invariable commentaries in all sectors, public and private of Havana, revolved around the two versions, both exaggerated, with reservations of an impassioned kind that increasingly embittered the respective prejudices of each side—especially the spitefulness of Spanish *integrismo* in the face of the enigmatic intentions of the government in Washington.

In reaction to the alarming explosion of the *Maine*, the angriest Spanish superpatriots did not balk at charging the Yankee government with the Machiavellian aim of taking advantage of that mysterious explosion in order to justify the imminent declaration of war against Spain. And in support of that suspicion, a malicious ultra-Spanish contingent also tried to spread a rumor damaging to the democratic spirit of the American people with the inhumane and absurd charge that a few hours before the horrible explosion, the commanders and officers of the ship were removed from the *Maine* and taken to a festive social gathering, so that the only victims of the catastrophe were the hundreds of unfortunate Marines who comprised the trusting crew. (!)

In the midst of that whirlwind of patriotic and ultra-patriotic obsessions, as I noted earlier, I was transferred to the Battalion of Scribes and Orderlies, lodged at that time in the Castillo de la Fuerza,[13] the great wall next to the residence of the second highest authority in the colony, that is, the general *2*° corporal,[14] at the end of O'Reilly Street, in front of the Plaza de Armas in Havana.

The Battalion of Scribes and Orderlies was a conventional entity that had no military obligations since its duties were strictly barracks related. They were reduced to carrying out the innocuous duty of renewing the guard squads in the fortress on a daily basis as well as in the nearby residence of the military governor of Havana, in front of the embarcadero of the Captaincy of the Port, in the Muelle de Caballeria.

In reality, the Battalion of Scribes and Orderlies answered to the sole purpose—although it was discreetly concealed—of providing a kind of refuge for avoiding the possibility that numerous individuals of the troops, family members or men recommended directly by influential personages, as well as a few commanders and officers deserving of being singled out in Havana for some explainable motive, should be sent out to fight.

No one told me about the truly privileged conditions that we members of the Battalion of Scribes and Orderlies enjoyed. From the time I entered into that mysterious fortress, I was able to ascertain for myself what it really was. I was convinced that whatever immediate directions the war might take, based on the two most important conflicts during those days in Havana, the atmosphere of relative personal freedom—analogous and in many ways even better than what I enjoyed in Puentes Grandes—could not be more favorable. In the Castillo de La Fuerza, the utmost circumspection reigned among the components of each one of the companies that formed the battalion. Every man comported himself with the most judicious discretion and the most delicate mutual respect, in order not to commit stupid abuses (if they were individuals in the troops) or abusive acts of intolerance (if they were officers). Neither group forgot that our post in such a favorable situation was owed to recommendations from high places. We put great effort into not defrauding the laudable trust of those recommendations.

I do not allude expressly to the commanders of the battalion because I never had the opportunity to meet them. Those unknown commanders, who had greater motivation to be discreet than the officers, must have thought, prudently, that since the unit they governed existed because of special privilege—an exception, in a way, depressing and contrary to strict barracks regulations—it would be useless and dangerous for the commanders themselves to dare to disturb the situation with unnecessary restrictions—and even to cause disturbances by their very presence in the castle. It was a matter of privileges and well-known attitudes of tolerance, thanks to which, a community composed of favored individuals whose good sense was apparent, was governing itself.

My youthful sensibility continued to suffer pain and sorrow caused by the anguish of remaining in a forced exile from my country and my family, far from the most satisfying stimuli and with impatient dreams of redeeming my life and reorienting it along the best path for an honorable and acceptable freedom. Nonetheless, I must confess in this *Memoir* that the relative independence I enjoyed in my post in the Castillo de la Fuerza, thanks to Colonel Vallespinosa's understanding benevolence, brought me intense spiritual comfort and compensated, in a way, for those abiding anxieties. I was able to forge the hope and even the intuitive confidence that whatever the consequences might be of the warlike conflicts between Spain and the United States that were becoming more serious and pressing by the day, for the moment I could consider myself safe from having to join an occasional combat unit against the very legitimate Cuban ideal of independence. This ideal was clearly and decidedly deserving of a glorious triumph, as all democratic, civilized nations on earth have a natural, imprescriptible right to win and enjoy independence.

"Until now"—I said to myself mentally and sincerely—"in the midst of the hazards of my obligatory stay in Cuba, I have had the great luck of being freed from armed dangers in the *manigua*, and I was also able to survive the cunning ambush with which yellow fever tried to bring me down! Grant me the grace, Oh Lord"—I continued my musings—"so that when this war ends with a well-deserved Cuban victory, I may be able to repatriate myself to Catalonia in good health and with the deep satisfaction of never having had to use my Mauser, not even to fire it into the air!"

When my spirit became calmer due to that encouraging situation and also by my sense that an end to the obsessive conflicts around the unthinking arrogance of the prideful superpatriotism of the Spanish government was not far off, I took prudent advantage of the privileges explained above in order to continue the frequent cultivation of my friendships with literati and journalists. I also had contacts with some elements of the Catalan colony in Havana, among them, by preference, with the young José Pujol y Roca, the educated and estimable son of the owner of the Café Alemán at the Parque Central, corner of the Paseo del Prado, and with Salvador Torra Pous, the very cultivated and active correspondent for Spanish and French newspapers among others.

Through Carlos Martí and Pujol Roca, I also made the personal acquaintance of Julio Talavera, founder and director of the weekly *La Opinión Catalana*, the regional, literary, and informational publication for all the news about Catalonia and Catalans living in Cuba. Talavera, originally from Lérida, came to Havana before the *Grito de Baire*, the recipient of one of those positions, definite or illusory, arranged in Madrid for the occupancy of a particular sinecure in the Havana branch of the Ministry of Finance. But after a few months in his post, Talavera was let go, for reasons I do not know. With the help of *La Opinión Catalana*, he was able to create a new modus vivendi, aided by Carlos Martí in the production of the magazine. During the last days of the Cuban-Hispano-American War, Carlos Martí was obliged to join a battalion in Holguín, and at that time, I replaced him at Talavera's side in order to help with the literary responsibilities of the Catalan weekly.

Protected, as I have said, by the privileges granted me in the Battalion of Scribes and Orderlies, I took care to make the most of such advantages by submitting myself spontaneously to a kind of careful regulation of those privileges. In accord, then, with this norm (discounting the only days, every three or four weeks, when I had to "stay in barracks" in order to confirm the roll call and the distribution of bread and the mess for the troops, and cover the changing of the guard in the castle or in the nearby residence of the governor general of the Plaza), on all the remaining days of that unforgettable period, I was able to distribute and employ my time freely. After the morning bugle call, showering if possible, shaving, and after a frugal breakfast in the Café Escanriza, situated in front of the Castillo de la Fuerza in the Plaza de Armas, I sometimes preferred to return to the castle to take care of some literary project. On other occasions, I set out alone, or with another unoccupied sergeant, to wander through the streets of Havana, eager to observe people, gather curious impressions, and find popular shops where merchandise could be bought at modest prices (as the grave economic crisis of the time demanded). Or sometimes I discovered modest restaurants, such as one run by Chinese situated in the first stretch of Revillagigedo Street, entrance at the Calzada del Monte, where for a few centavos we were given a good portion of rice with milk, or a kind of tasty Cuban stew.

Later, after having coffee and chatting for a while with my friend Pujol Roca, I visited the offices of newspapers and magazines to hear more about the most relevant and disquieting facts, rumors, and preoccupations. Especially in *La Lucha*, because of the amicable consent of Don Antonio Sanmiguel, its very popular director, and because of my friendship with some of its writers and reporters, I was able to learn a great deal about the real actions of the Cuban liberation forces—victorious in combat with the Spaniards—that contradicted the latters' official dispatches. I also learned about Mr. Woodford's[15] intrigues on behalf of annexation seconded by those of other American diplomats.

News reports concerning intrigues stemming from the insistent North American push for annexation of Cuba arrived directly and persistently to *La Lucha*, but the government's department of censorship on the island did not allow their publication. They were only available in other dailies when editions or clippings of the major North American newspapers came in, provided that the above-mentioned official censorship did not intercept them. That was how the Cuban press, for example, was prevented from echoing the sensational measures that Yankee diplomats—backed by North American political personages and financiers, in more or less disguised complicity with some European chancelleries—proposed to individuals around the Spanish Minister of State and Queen María Cristina. These measures were designed to persuade the governors of the Spanish monarchy to favor the annexation and even the sale of Cuba to the United States.

Nevertheless, whether or not that information was published in Havana newspapers, it was inevitable that it should become widely divulged, amplified, and the source of disquieting rumors, giving rise to more intense enmity among their supporters or adversaries. I well remember that one of the most impressive rumors spread in Havana at that time was connected to the alleged plan that the well-known superpatriot Eva Canel attributed to General Weyler—that he would return to Cuba with a formidable expeditionary force of revanchist legionnaires to overthrow General Blanco, abolish autonomy, confront anew all the enemies of Spanish sovereignty in Cuba, and finally, assault and invade the United States in order to impose an obligatory peace on the Yankee government in the capital in Washington. (!)

In support of such a laughable, but disturbing, piece of nonsense, I was told in the pressroom of *La Lucha* that they had seen a copy of a letter from Weyler to Eva Canel, announcing the madcap project.

After the mysterious explosion of the *Maine*, the rumor that the North American government would actively intervene very soon in the Hispano-Cuban War was spread about in Havana and in all the towns in Cuba. Added to this rumor was the arrogance with which the pens and tongues in support of Spanish military aggression confronted the imminence of the North American intervention—in a tone of burlesque defiance against the pork butchers of Uncle Sam.

However, according to confidential reports that arrived at *La Lucha*, thoughtful warnings issued by illustrious republican thinkers, and especially, by the most celebrated and venerable of them all, Don Francesc Pi i Margall, did appear in Spain. Pi i Margall advised the governors of the old metropolis to aim for a judicious compromise with separatist Cuban patriotism by granting Cuba unconditional and immediate independence since that commendable solution would satisfy the legitimate desires of the ultimate Cuban ideal, and would cut off at the root any pretext or motive for a dangerous North American military intervention in the island.

But in Spain (in the Royal Palace, to be exact), the thoughtful admonitions of the honorable federalist-republican apostle were rejected and even scorned by the monarchical oligarchs in office at the time, who were perhaps fearful that Weyler's haughty threats might ignite a bloody military uprising on the Peninsula if the government was so cowardly as to form a pact with the *mambises* in order to avoid a war with the Yankees.[16]

The entire month of March 1898 transpired in the midst of such anxious expectations. At the end of that month, the president of the United States proposed to the Spanish government that it should arrange an armistice with the Cuban separatist forces in order to negotiate peace. An analogous proposal had been made simultaneously by the Pope and several European powers. But Sagasta and his ministers, instead of supporting these promising suggestions, responded only that they had transmitted them to the autonomous government of Cuba in case it might consider them worthy of consideration. General Blanco and the autonomous cabinet, for their part, without counting on the consent of the Army of Liberation, thought a provisional suspension of hostilities against the rebel forces was the only feasible action in the immediate future.

As the result of such opposed and worrying circumstances, combined with the vigorous pressure of genuine public opinion among the American people, who opposed the permanence of Spanish dominion in Cuba—responsible in their view for the sacrifice of the *Maine*—and who were in favor of Cuban independence, the president of the United States sent the expected message to Congress, soliciting authorization to end hostilities in Cuba and organize a stable government on the island, capable of maintaining order and observing international obligations.

Six days later, on April 19, the House of Representatives and the Senate of the United States not only accepted McKinley's initiative, but also broadened and clarified it in a literal sense, asserting the following:

> That the people of the island of Cuba are, and by rights must be, free and independent. That the government of Spain must renounce its authority and sovereignty over the island, by immediately retiring all its land and sea forces. That the president will be enabled to use North American land and sea forces to put this resolution into effect. That the United States has given the lie to any intention or desire to exercise sovereignty over Cuba; and has affirmed its determination to leave the governance of the island to its own people.

One day after the preceding resolution passed, President McKinley sanctioned it. With that act, war between the United States and Cuba was declared before the world.[17]

The reactions produced in the government of Madrid and in supporters of Spanish ultra patriotism by the vigorous manifestation of Yankee power are well known: the mobilization of its battleships, cruisers, and every kind of artillery to reinforce the defense of the Peninsula's coastline, and the urgent dispatch of a naval squadron to the tropics, to impede and fight against, as far as possible, the blockade of the island's ports.

As for Havana, the first reaction that the tremendous decision of the North American Congress elicited from the Captain-General and the autonomous government was the natural fear that angry public demonstrations of whatever kind could aggravate the different current crises, especially the economic crisis, which was more intense every day among the popular classes. To forestall such possibilities, General Blanco, in accord with the autonomous government, ordered that substantial armed military squads in every important locality of the island should dramatically declare martial law, threatening rigorous sanctions against people responsible for crimes against the observance of public order, due respect to constituted authority, or aid to the opposing forces.

In laughable contrast, the mission of declaring martial law, applicable as an extraordinary recourse to the besieged populations, was to be promulgated by the innocuous and very pacific Battalion of Scribes and Orderlies, among whose favored members (thanks to God and to the benevolent Colonel Vallespinosa) I was fortunate to count myself. On the morning of April 21, appropriately equipped squads of the paradoxical battalion roamed the city, stopping at the cry of "Halt!" in designated places, where in the position called for by "Stand at attention!" and in anticipation of the accompanying cornet's sounding "Attention!" the Governor-General's edict was read aloud for the benefit of Havana's neighborhoods.

On our return to the barracks, tired and sweaty from our fatiguing rounds, I was convinced that most people were indifferent as they listened to the dramatic reading of martial law. In the expressions of a good number of attentive attendees, far from reflecting disgust or repulsion at the North American decision, one saw that they, like me, trusted that the war resolution of the United States against Spain would turn out to be favorable in the end to the triumph of the ultimate Cuban ideal of independence.

During the days that followed—when the blockade was already visible with American warships at the Havana coastline and before the other principal ports on the island—I had the opportunity to compare my impressions with friends and companions at the principal newspapers (some of them still opposed to liberation ideology). I confirmed that all of us, deep inside, believed that no matter what consequences might come of North American military power in the formidable fight, it was possible to predict, with no risk of being mistaken, the crushing defeat of Spanish resistance, the subsequent liberation of Cuba, and the final expulsion of Spanish dominion in all the rest of what constituted the vast Spanish colonial empire.

In one of those conversations with colleagues at *La Lucha*, I learned about a sensational episode that was publicly silenced by the censors, but was divulged by clandestine spokesmen for some of the separatist units. Briefly, the version of the sensational episode, later confirmed by direct reports from the liberation military command, revealed that General Blanco, either on his own initiative or following desperate suggestions from the government in Madrid, had committed an act of supine imprudence by authorizing a Señor Menéndez, a confidential agent of General Pando (the Colonial Intendant) to be the bearer of a letter from Pando to Máximo Gómez.[18] The letter guaranteed the supreme leader of the liberation forces the rank and immediate posting of Lieutenant General of the Spanish Army if he would expedite a peace with Spain through his recognition and support of the continuation of the autonomous regimen on the island.

It is not necessary to add that the commission entrusted to the reckless agent was carried out in vain, for General Máximo Gómez rejected it with indignation and had the mediator appear before a very severe war tribunal that ordered him shot, a sentence that was duly executed.

The literal clarity with which the Joint Resolution of the North American Congress against Spain was written, voted on, sanctioned, and proclaimed was very precise and could not at all be interpreted as a cunning deception designed to conceal intentions to annex Cuba. Nevertheless, it did not fail to inspire understandable suspicions among some Cubans aware of the insistence with which astute and ambitious Yankee personages in diplomacy and big business, both within and outside the United States, were developing plans to absorb Cuba.

But the revolutionary leadership tacitly rejected such suspicions with timely public declarations by Don Tomás Estrada Palma[19] and General Máximo Gómez, expressing the gratitude, trust, and mutual support of the Liberation Army for the North American naval and land forces already blockading Cuban ports.

Nevertheless, however fantastic and inadmissible such suspicions of the more or less remote danger of annexation were in those moments, the angry ultra-patriotic Spanish press continued to make use of them to agitate in the Peninsula as well as in Cuba. General Blanco alluded to those very spontaneous suspicions in a desperate and ineffective letter directed to General Máximo Gómez, supreme leader of the *mambí* army. It was a surprising document, revelatory of the astonishing lack of judgment on the part of Spanish patriotism that in those days, as on many preceding occasions, had been incapable of understanding and respecting the honor and essential rights of genuine patriotic adversaries or enemies, for whatever reason, of the injurious and absurd ultra-patriotic Spanish mandarin class.

In order to contribute to the greatest possible diffusion of the psychological lessons—conveyed in a genuine and exemplary mode of political and civic enlightenment—that can be gleaned by contrasting the inept and boorish letter of General Blanco with the commendable response with which

Máximo Gómez rejected it "in terms of rigorous and noble simplicity, worthy of figuring in any anthology of democratic ideas" (as Herminio Portell Vilá,[20] one of the most conscientious and civic-minded historians in Cuba, deservedly praised said response), I have transcribed both documents below, certain that most prospective readers of this *Memoir* will thank me for it.

The Spanish Governor-General's letter, dated at the beginning of May 1898, read thusly:

> General Máximo Gómez
> Supreme Commander
> of the Revolutionary Forces
>
> Sir: With the sincerity that has always characterized all my actions, I address you here, not doubting for a moment that the clear intelligence and noble sentiments, which I recognize in you as an honorable enemy, will lead to your favorable reception of this letter.
>
> It cannot have escaped your attention that the Cuban problem has changed radically. Spaniards and Cubans are now confronting a foreigner who belongs to a different race, is possessed of a tendency that is acquisitive by nature, and whose intentions are not only to deprive Spain of its flag on Cuban soil, but also to exterminate the Cuban people because of their Spanish blood.
>
> The blockade of the island's ports has no other object. Not only is it harmful to the Spaniards, but it also affects the Cubans, by completing the work of extermination consummated in our civil war. The supreme moment, therefore, has arrived in which we must forget our past differences and Cubans and Spaniards together must repel the invader for the sake of our common defense.
>
> Spain will not forget the noble aid of its Cuban sons and daughters and once the foreign enemy is driven from the island will, like an affectionate mother, open her arms to another new daughter of the nations of the New World who speaks her language, professes her religion and feels noble Spanish blood coursing through her veins.
>
> For these reasons, General, I propose that we form an alliance of both armies in Santa Clara. The Cubans will receive the arms of the Spanish army and to the cry of "Viva España!" and "Viva Cuba!" we shall repel the invader and free the descendants of a new people from the foreign yoke.
>
> Your devoted servant,
> (Signed) Ramón Blanco

The response of Generalísimo Máximo Gómez:

General Don Ramón Blanco
Captain-General of the Spanish Army in Cuba

Sir: I am astonished at your boldness in once again proposing peace terms when you know that Spaniards and Cubans can never live together in peace on Cuban soil. On this continent you represent an old and discredited monarchy, and we fight on behalf of an American principle: the very one shared by Bolívar and Washington.

You say that you belong to the same race and you invite me to fight against a foreign invader; but you are again mistaken, because there are no differences of blood or of race.

I only believe in one race: humanity; and for me there are only good and bad nations. Spain has been bad up to now; and the United States is fulfilling a duty of humanity and civilization toward Cuba. From the bronzed Indian savage to the refined and wise Englishman, a man, to my mind, is worthy of respect according to his honor and sentiments, whatever his country or the race to which he belongs, or the religion he professes.

That is what nations mean to me; and up to now I have had nothing but motives for admiration toward the United States. I have written to President McKinley and to General Miles[21] thanking them for the American intervention in Cuba. I do not see the danger of our extermination by the United States to which you refer in your letter. If that were to happen, History will judge them.

For now, I can only say to you again that it is very late.

Your attentive servant,
(Signed) Máximo Gómez

Here, narrated in summary fashion, are my impressions in connection with the historic blockade of Havana and the definitive end of Spanish sovereignty in Cuba.

On the morning of April 22, the blockade of the Havana coastline began with battleships and destroyers from the United States. The lookouts at the Castillo del Morro[22] informed us that the blockading squadron was composed of two great battleships: the *Iowa* and the *Indiana*,[23] various destroyers, and some auxiliary ships situated far enough from the shore to evade the reach of coastal batteries.

People in the capital were hopeful, but also cautious, about the mysterious plans behind the blockade. The spiteful Spanish ultra patriots feared that Sampson,[24] the admiral of the Yankee fleet, would begin a vigorous bombardment against Havana's defenses in preparation for an attack on the city before Cervera's squadron, which was nearing tropical waters as they supposed, could prevent it. In turn, people in Havana, including those sympathetic to the autonomous government, trusted that the bombardment feared by the Spaniards would not happen, since they interpreted the blockade as an indispensable means of impeding the commercial traffic of merchant vessels in the major Cuban ports.

But the greatest fear provoked by the blockade, especially among the poorest classes, centered on its consequences for the distribution of provisions. The calculation was that the supplies available in the city would run out in fewer than twenty days. Day by day, that worry heightened the economic crisis latent in all sectors of the city. This crisis was due as much to revolutionary contingencies as to the increasing discredit of the last issues of nominal pesetas in bills from the Banco Español in Cuba. It was claimed that they were made and put into circulation surreptitiously during Weyler's absolute command without the consent of the Spanish government. Consequently, when the supposedly fraudulent origin of those bills became widely known, it was difficult to use them in many stores, thanks to clever excuses passed on to the consumers.

In spite of those worries, for as long as the blockade lasted, groups of curious people went every day to the end of the Paseo del Prado,[25] next to the Castillo de la Punta[26] on what was then a reef beaten by waves and is now the beginning of the Malecón sea wall. Someone had the good idea of installing several telescopes on improvised tripods that allowed viewers to observe far off in the distance the imposing bulk of the battleships and cruisers blockading the port. Whoever installed the spyglasses collected a few centavos from those who wanted to use them for that purpose.

Some Spanish steamships, one French, another Norwegian, and several schooners succeeded in evading the blockade and unloading their merchandise in Matanzas, Batabanó, Cienfuegos, Caibarién,[27] and Nuevitas.[28] The *Montserrat*, a transatlantic ship sailing under the Spanish flag, entered the port of Matanzas and then the port of Havana. This feat carried off by the captain was considered very difficult. It earned him an enthusiastic homage in the press for such a deed, and he was the object, in person, of a warm salvo of applause one night in the Albisu theater on the part of the public who regularly attended its zarzuela performances. On the other hand, a very different fate was reserved for another ship belonging to the Compañía Transatlántica Española, the *Alfonso XII*. When the blockading squadron sighted it near the Havana coastline, it had to veer toward the Pinar del Río coast,[29] but it was pursued close to the Bay of Mariel,[30] where the Yankee destroyers shelled it, set it on fire, and abandoned it when it was half-sunk.

At the end of April and during the first part of the following month, as the blockade of Havana was eased, contradictory reports circulated about the supposed victory in the Bay of Matanzas by Sampson's squadron and by its attack on the battery at El Morrillo. But the victory in the bay in the Yumurí[31] region was not confirmed, and as for the bombardment of El Morrillo, if it took place, its only casualty, according to official press reports, was an inoffensive mule that was grazing on pastureland near the battery.

Other news circulated in Havana of artillery encounters between North American and Spanish ships that were exchanging cannon fire near Cárdenas[32] and Tunas de Zaza. But during that period, the greatest anxiety and impatience in Havana affecting each one of the three sectors of the population linked to the three armies at war centered on the imminent outcome of the land and naval battles that would be fought in the hills and on the coast of Santiago de Cuba.[33] Those battles would decide—as each faction hoped—the definitive end of the exhausting war.

In connection with the whereabouts of the Spanish squadron (the ghost squadron, as the *mambises* called it), the Spaniards forged grand illusions when the blockade was announced, in the belief that a decisive battle would soon take place between the squadrons of Sampson and Cervera. But the disillusion of those who held such illusory opinions was enormous when sensational news broke successively of Cervera's squadron wedged in a bottleneck by Sampson's fleet in Santiago Bay, of the battle, defeat, and capture of that squadron by the North American squadron when Cervera's squadron moved out from its confinement, and finally, when all the Spanish forces in Santiago de Cuba surrendered, followed by the bombardment of the capital of Oriente Province.[34]

The commotion that this news caused in Havana was extremely distressing to the masses that adhered to an obtuse ultra Spanishness. It supposed a profound impatience in the autonomist cabinet, functionaries, and sympathizers. It gave very legitimate patriotic satisfaction to the Cuban elements dedicated to the separatist ideal, even though this satisfaction was embittered, in part, by word of the inconceivable rudeness and oversights with which General Shafter[35]—the prideful and unsociable head of the North American forces who landed in Santiago de Cuba—disdainfully treated the *mambí* General, Calixto García,[36] and the heroic Liberation Army. When advance notice appeared in Havana newspapers of those huge disasters that had befallen the Spanish squadron and land army in the sea and in the hills of the Oriente region, numerous groups of agitated neighbors instinctively headed for the Plaza de Armas, to demand loudly from the Captain-General that he confirm or give the lie to those crushing accounts. And, in fact, General Blanco, in deference to the crowd's request, appeared on the central balcony of the Governor's Palace. He extended his hands in a gesture meant to calm down the demonstrators' impatience, and once he had quieted them, he pronounced in a strong but unsteady voice that historic sentence: "Fortune does not always accompany valor!" He continued with a few words that were an unnecessary addition to the veracity of the disasters that had been announced.

At the polite requests of the numerous police, the demonstrators began to disperse, each one's face reflecting the disillusion or the satisfaction that moved them profoundly.

With my mind deeply affected by that noisy confusion of people and circumstances and with General Blanco's words of regret still vibrating in my ears, I returned to my room in the barracks of the nearby castle, anxious to devote myself to the most honorable and thoughtful meditation possible on such extraordinary circumstances. I wanted to draw from those circumstances appropriate moral, political, and ecological lessons applicable to the mutual respect that ought to govern all the peoples and countries for the Christian achievement of civilized pacific coexistence.

The immediate fruit of my plan that was conceived so impulsively was a pile of sheets containing vehement accusations against the continuous errors committed in their American domains by the monarchical governments of Spain. However, the central theme of my ambitious study referred, in particular, to the responsibilities of all the governments of the Austro-Bourbon oligarchs in past years in refusing insistently and systematically to recognize the very just demands of Cuban, Puerto Rican, and Filipino patriots. With the title "Gabinete negro" ["Black Cabinet"], I meant to symbolize the lack of compassion, goodwill, and thoughtfulness that characterized the intransigent and disastrous oligarchs who in the last three decades of the nineteenth century alternated in holding power in the government of the Spanish state and in its transatlantic colonial exploitations, without having known how or without having wanted to deduce any judicious lessons from the successive revolutionary emancipations of the heroic peoples of Central and South America.

That impromptu of mine expressing ardent condemnation of the recalcitrant stubbornness of the Spanish politicians of the second half of the nineteenth century and my no less open satisfaction at the glorious dawn (which at that time, seemed imminent) of Cuban national redemption—that spontaneous impulse, I say, of entrusting to my pen the thoroughly

Catalan sincerity of my sentiments—brought about a consoling spiritual and soulful expansion. In no way did I entertain prejudices, animosities, or antipathies of any kind toward the Spanish people of the Iberian Peninsula, for neither then nor later in my life have I felt the slightest ill will toward them, but rather only for the successive governments (monarchical and also republican *unitaristas* [a term used at the time to characterize those who called themselves federalists but were, in reality, supporters of a disguised centralization], as well as the inflexible top men in the military), all of them directly responsible for the major misfortunes and public tragedies of the absurd Spanish state.

I discussed the unedited sheets of the "Gabinete negro" with Dr. Rabell and my fraternal companion Fuentevilla. Two months later in a noble article, accompanied by my photograph, which he published in *El Hogar* of October 9, Dr. Rabell referred to the "Gabinete negro": "Conangla, the author of several pamphlets, lets his fecund pen lash out vigorously at injustice, error, evil, and tyranny in his work "El Gabinete negro." His highly generous and redemptive ideas glow with the light of lively enthusiasm and faith."

José Manuel Fuentevilla, in turn, proposed coordinating a large part of my pamphlet with a work of his, which expressed analogous tendencies. Thus, in a timely and harmonious collaboration a new work emerged that we called "Unión y olvido" ["Union and forgetfulness"]. On Fuentevilla's initiative, we offered it to the civil governor of Havana, Dr. Rafael Fernández de Castro,[37] with the request that he pay for the printing of the pamphlet if he thought it appropriate. Days passed, but "Unión y olvido" was still unpublished and possibly lost, notwithstanding the amiable reception we received from the illustrious republican in his study in the large colonial mansion at the Plaza de San Juan de Dios, where the civil government of Havana functioned for several years during the colonial period and the first years of the Republic.

The many tasks that took up the time of the very popular governor assuredly drew his attention away from our pamphlet. Even now people well remember the untiring activities Fernández de Castro carried out during the blockade in order to remedy the tragic misery of thousands of homeless, hungry children and old people for whom he procured lodging, food, and care in hospitals and asylums. It is understandable, then, that in the course of those difficult circumstances, followed by the armistice and the preparation for the disappointing period of the intervention of the North American flag in Cuba, the only original manuscript of "Unión y olvido" should have remained not only unpublished, but lost.

In confirmation of that frustrated effort, I have reproduced below some paragraphs from a long article that the unforgettable Fuentevilla published

Figure 4. "Relief station in Havana. On certain days and at designated hours, portions of codfish and cornmeal are doled out to the starving. These sights were and are common tragedies." (*Greater America*. New York: F. Tennyson Neely, Publisher, 1898.)

some years later (October 1909) in *El Comercio*[38] of Havana, on the occasion of an homage that enthusiastic Catalans offered me at the Hotel Trotxa[39] del Vedado on the day of the patriotic Cuban celebration of the *Grito de Yara*.[40]

> Conangla wrote for Cuban newspapers as a result of the 1895 war, the period when our friendship began. He returned to Spain where he continued to write, never deviating at all from his liberal ideas, a pure, honorable liberalism à la Pi, for the immortal apostle of Spanish democracy was his teacher and always considered him an outstanding student.
>
> Conangla, who always defended the aspirations of the Cuban people, seconded Pi and other illustrious Spanish republicans, resolutely advocating in the Catalan press for Cuba to achieve its goal, since the laws of history would lead it to independence.
>
> We have spoken briefly of Conangla as a political journalist, recalling the time when we were fortunate to meet and fraternize with him and when, like-minded to the point where his brilliant pen and the very modest one of the man who is writing these lines, collaborated on a work when the war was barely over, that came down to em-

> phasizing what a great man and patriot Martí[41] was, even as it asked that the Republic be well-disposed toward everyone and act on behalf of everyone. The work was written but it was not published. It attested to the beating of two young hearts before the resurgence of Cuban nationalism, which they wanted to be grand, based on love and work, prosperous, rich, and happy as complete proof of the capacity of Cubans to govern themselves.

On July 21, 1898 (five days after the extremely grave Spanish disasters in Santiago de Cuba), the Spanish government sued North America for peace through the mediation of the French ambassador in Washington.[42] At the same time, the suspension of hostilities between the opposing forces was agreed upon for the entire island in anticipation of the provisional protocol for pacification that was being worked out in Washington. On August 12, the accord was signed with these principal conditions: the total renunciation of Spain to Spanish sovereignty in Cuba and its immediate withdrawal from Cuba and Puerto Rico; the occupation of Manila by North American troops until the fate of the Philippine Islands should be determined in the definitive peace treaty. The protocol also stipulated that the complete withdrawal of Spanish troops and functionaries be completed by January 1, 1899.

Nevertheless, the structure of the autonomous government, with General Blanco at its head, continued its provisional rule. The provincial governments and the town councils were authorized to apply their disposable funds to help families in need, as well as to see to the health of the people; and also to aid, as far as possible, the liberation units that were returning to each locality as the detachments of the Spanish Army retreated.

There was no reported instance, however, of any act of vengeance committed by Cuban or Spanish forces. Not a single Spaniard, whether military or civilian, was the object of reprisal or maltreatment by Cuban patriots. Nor was any violent incident reported in Havana perpetrated by the defeated against the victors. Despite the murky unknown provisions concerning the liberty of Cuba that would result from the definitive peace treaty between Spain and the United States and Cuba, the victors, for the moment, were joyful at their emancipation from colonial domination and hopeful that the North American government would not fraudulently fail—before Cuba or the international world—to fulfill the solemn declarations and promises signed off on in the well-known *Joint Resolution*.

And as for the Spaniards, in general, the commanders and officers of the defeated army as much as the civilian elements, even though they were deeply disappointed, were able to reciprocate the exemplary and incomparable kindnesses of the victorious patriotic insurrection. They accepted the defeat with silent conformity although it profoundly grieved them, resigning themselves to the well-deserved misfortunes that the defeat had in store for them and their far-off mother country, and they refrained, therefore, from provoking imprudent reactions that could prove fatal to them.

As the result of those realities, recent animosities quieted down in Havana, and little by little a political climate of tacit civility arose between elements, which until then had been adversaries, but were for the most part desirous to assume their respective situations peacefully and in an orderly fashion. The mercantile establishments, generally owned by Spaniards, were the first to show themselves respectful, docile, and contrite in view of the new realities. They had to restrain themselves in view of those realities if they wanted to maintain and secure their businesses in Cuba. The immediate consequence was that the annoying parades of the baleful battalions of volunteers of commerce disappeared from Havana streets and plazas, and the uniforms worn by their nominal colonels, officers, and mercenaries were not seen from that time forward.

6
Peace and the Return

(July to November 1898)

In accord with one of the clauses in the peace protocol, as many steamships as could be mustered by the Spanish transatlantic companies to carry out the evacuation of the colonial army began to arrive in the port of Havana. Successive contingents of men to be repatriated were assembled in the Castles of the Morro, La Cabaña, and Príncipe. Many commanders and officers of those troops took advantage of the occasion to stroll discreetly through Havana to buy tobacco and liquor, and why not? To distract themselves by going to the theater, and by preference, to the Albisu, where a lyric company of notable artists was performing the most popular Spanish zarzuelas of the time, among them, *Agua, azucarillos y aguardiente*; *La verbena de la paloma*; *El rey que rabió*; *El Padrino de El Nene*; *El tambor de granaderos*; *Al agua, patos*; and *El pobre Balbuena*.

The main attraction at the Albisu, at that time, was Rosa Fuertes, an excellent prima donna with an elegant and attractive stage presence. Another, younger singer, whose surname was Ibáñez, and who possessed a charming and appealing gracefulness, came after her in the esteem of the public. And as for the men, the ones who stood out were the baritone Piquer, the bass Villareal, and the comic actor Alen, who possessed genial histrionic talents. Years later, the baritone Piquer married a daughter of Doña Pilar Somollano de Toro, who was the director of the Hotel Telégrafo, located on the famous Acera del Louvre. Doña Pilar became very popular when General José Miguel Gómez was elected president of the Republic because she had made a gift to him of a splendid chair that symbolized the presidency.

In connection with the performances at the Albisu, which were the favorites of Spanish commercial and other societal groups toward the end of the colonial period, I recall that the famous matador Mazantini[1] was in Havana, contracted to fight in the bullring in the terrain of Ayestarán,[2] near the Calzada del Príncipe. During the stay of the aristocratic matador in this city, the Albisu presented the zarzuela about bullfighting, *El Padrino de El*

Nene. Mazantini, who, according to widespread rumors was in love with Rosa Fuentes, directed the rehearsals and performances of the zarzuela.

Since the most faithful members of the audience at the Albisu during the 1895 war consisted largely of partisans of Spanish ultra patriotism, it was natural that the works performed there belonged to the so-called Spanish *género chico* [short plays with music]. As an exquisite act of deference, however, to their Cuban constituents and as a gesture toward an opportune and discreet adhesion to the autonomous regime, the impresarios of the Albisu surprised the public with the announcement of the upcoming opening of *Yumurí*, a Cuban opera in three acts, written and composed by two Cubans eminent in their respective fields of inspiration: Dr. Rafael Fernández de Castro and Maestro Don Eduardo Sánchez de Fuentes.[3] Because of the unexpected plot, which was wholly Cuban, the announcement of the opera caused general anticipation, but also undeniable displeasure among the spiteful Spaniards who assiduously attended their favorite theater.

Rumors spread in Havana that the performance of *Yumurí* would lead to protests. The fact that the author of the music was also the author of the habanera *Tú*, which was well known, admired, and sung by everyone in the cultivated Latin world was ignored, as well as the fact that the lyrics of the work were by the eminent figure and tribune of autonomy, the civil governor of the province at the time. He was an untiring benefactor of thousands of starving, sick, and homeless old people, women, and children, the survivors of poor families submitted to the inhuman reconcentration—survivors who received lodging, food, medicine, clothing, and other indispensable help donated by the civic-minded governor.

All the seats in the theater were taken on the night of the opening of *Yumurí* (October 26, 1898). Thanks, however, to precautions taken by the police to prevent serious disturbances, it seems that at the last moment, word spread not to stamp one's feet during the presentation of *Yumurí*, but rather to substitute silence for that action in order to achieve an equivalent effect: In short, it was a deliberate decision not to applaud any of the most inspired musical scenes in the work. A good number of spectators, however, attracted by very understandable sympathy and admiration—personal and patriotic—for the eminent Cuban authors of the opera applauded frequently, even though most of the audience in the orchestra section maintained a reserved silence, accompanied in cowardly fashion with hypocritical hisses.

Yumurí had only two performances—one on the night of its opening and one more the following night with few people in attendance. The authors themselves, despite the Albisu's offer to present more performances of the work, considered it prudent to withdraw it from the playbill in order to avoid possible disagreeable incidents caused by some spiteful troublemaker.

On the days that followed, instead of passing by different newspaper offices in the mornings as I often used to do—the offices of *La Lucha* and *El Hogar* in particular—I preferred to stay in my room in the Castillo de la Fuerza in order to set to work eagerly on the task set aside during the previous months of poeticizing the accumulation of emotions, illusions and motives for impatience that agitated my heart and spirit, since—once the war ended with the defeat of Spain and the liberation of the Cuban people—I glimpsed my return to Catalonia quickly approaching.

Some rhymed reflections in Catalan flowed from my pen that would figure among others in my *Elegía de la guerra*, published six years later in Barcelona with a preface by the great poet Maragall. It seems appropriate to me to insert the translations of some of those frank poetic expressions, which are revelatory—from that time forward and taken altogether—not only of my pure and very liberal ideological convictions, but also of the intense sentimental identification that before, during and after the war I have always maintained for the independence, the progress and the happiness of Cuba.

WAR AND PEACE

I have seen them both in dreams,
each one with her retinue.
One dressed in mourning;
the other in Court dress.

One, spirits failing,
was leading her cohort
to an inferno of misery,
and disaster for her children.

The other, lovely, smiling,
was spreading knowledge abundantly,
establishing new industries,
ensuring the development of the arts,
strengthening labor,
increasing commerce,
and baptizing her children
in the temple of Progress.

The two queens exchanged looks
heedful of their retinues:

one was dressed in mourning:
the other in Court dress.

The party of War
went over to the other party
and War was left alone
now, without her kingdom, and without children.

And Peace, beautiful and smiling,
gathered friends and converts
and in the temple of Life
celebrated such a grand Event.

EXAGERATED PATROTISM

A traitorous current
that invades nations
and disguises the glory of Life
with a false mask
of gilded visions.

A gloomy, heartless sentiment,
that imposes where it likes,
the value of the color of a flag
at the bloodiest price.

Fanaticism that in seas of harmony
and human affection
buries the tenderness of poetry
and lets the most disgusting slime float free.

Deceitful sentiment of wrongdoers
who defend vile deeds
and assassinate soldiers.

If, suddenly one day,
seized with noble ire,
an ardent genius should transform this world,
how swiftly mothers would build a pyre
of relentless punishment
against that abominable sentiment!

CRY OF PEACE

Oh Europe, longed-for in my exile!
Oh Iberia, which my memories traverse!

Oh my sweet and beloved Catalonia,
land of my longings and my sorrows!

Oh beautiful places where the Villa
of my childhood and my dreams lives on!
Oh smiling faces that await me!
Oh hearth, oh mother of mine whom I venerate!

At last, if the rough Atlantic permits
its jaws not to swallow up my body,
I shall return to see smiling beaches,
I shall live again amidst embraces and kisses,
my being will be inundated in pure joy!
I shall hear words of consolation!

But oh, the venerable visage
of my beloved father will not see it:
and the absence of that very austere face
will embitter such a sweet welcome!

As I explained previously, the interior vestibule of the Albisu during the last months of the war was converted into a meeting place at night for the most active theater commentators as well as for a group of spirited practitioners and sympathizers representative of the literary and journalistic professions, which were very free at that time in Havana. The impresarios of the Albisu always warmly welcomed visits by the enthusiastic masters and disciples of theater commentators, who were, as a whole, called *El corrillo de la Peña* [The Circle of the Reunion]. Before the shows began, as they were in progress if we were already familiar with the works, or in the intermission, we conversed on all kinds of topics, except those that might disturb the tranquility of the friendly fellowship that united us. When differences of opinion became dangerous some Creole witticism or some good-humored irrelevant remark never failed to attenuate or resolve them, which was an invitation to end the discussion with general approval.

We faithful members in that group wishing, however, to continue our conversations in a more favorable place and ambiance, resolved to organize ourselves into a cultural entity with the same name of *La Peña.* We chose to establish its new venue for our Atheneum-style activities, in a welcoming corner of the Café El Casino (next to the Albisu theater), where we continued our chats for two or three months.

Although the sessions of *La Peña* began again in the Café El Casino at the end of September, the inaugural session was postponed until the last part of October to give time to Benítez Veguillas, who was the president by acclamation, to finish the report on rules, which, on completion, was enthusiastically applauded by the founders of the original society.

The minutes of the definitive inaugural session were published in the dailies *La Lucha*, *El Noticiero*, and *La Unión* with some reminiscences at the bottom of the page (the twenty-second of October) serving as anticipated testimonies of friendly farewell motivated by my repatriation, which was by then imminent.

The text of the minutes follows:

> Section of *La Peña.* Inaugural session of October 23, 1898. In attendance the founding members Don Mariano Benítez Veguillas (President), Don José A. Losada (Secretary) and Members: Don José Conangla, Don Carlos Guardiola, Don Emilio Fernández, Don José M. Fuentevilla, Don Juan Subirana, Don José Alonso, Don Nicolás Suárez Inclán and Don Leopoldo Sánchez. Following a reading of the regulations for the society, the president delivered his opening discourse as follows:
>
> It was an undeserved honor for me
> to be chosen president
> but I definitely accept it
> because it has struck me,
> quite frankly, as delicious.
> Since there is not often an occasion
> for winning an election
> that is spontaneous and friendly
> nor is the association, on the other hand,
> just any old thing.
> Obliged to preside
> I am also obliged to toast:
> and though I am sparing with words,
> you are to be advised
> of what I can wish for:
> lots of fellowship and good humor;
> money, when it's available;
> the cult of Art and Love;
> and in matters of honor
> doing what is best.
> I think that nothing is lacking
> unless the above-named membership

> should insist on other goals;
> the opening of *La Peña*, then,
> is hereby solemnized.
>
> In accord with Sr. Fuentevilla's proposal, it was agreed that the full membership should gather at the studio of Otero y Corominas for a group photograph, a copy of which, comrade Conangla, who is leaving on the fourth for the Peninsula, can take with him as a souvenir.

Amidst general approbation, Sr. Guardiola proposed that we take leave of Sr. Conangla on board the ship that will undertake the voyage.

The session ended at one in the morning.

At the same time as the publication of the preceding minutes, a pleasing article appeared in the magazine *El Hogar*, which alluded to the cultural significance of each one of the board members of *La Peña* and to their stated preferences in a humoristic manner, revelatory of the exemplary union and healthy optimism that existed between us.

Those sessions of *La Peña* and other equally unforgettable friendships forged in the offices of dailies and magazines in Havana constituted one of the most pleasant and compensatory emotional connections of my forced stay in Cuba during the war. When I returned to that wonderful country on May 26, 1905, to emancipate myself from all servitude to the absurd unitary and monarchical Spanish State, and to avail myself and my family of voluntary and honorable citizenship in the Cuban Republic, it was very pleasing to renew some of those friendships. I refer especially to the fraternal Fuentevilla, editorial director of the daily *El Comercio*; to Antonio G. Zamora, director of *El Hogar*; Rafael Santa Coloma, theater critic during the war, converted later into an indispensable photo journalist at the time of the fully established Republic; to Alfredo Martín Morales, the rigorous litterateur and creator of the Associated Press. I also include the famous social chronicler of the *Diario de la Marina*, Enrique Fontanills, whose colleague I was honored to call myself during the first period of the daily *Cuba*, and to Carlos Guardiola Rendón, theater reporter and humorous writer.

Regarding the new and definitive stage of my voluntary return to Cuba, a move that confirmed my identification with the highest ideals and sentiments of the Cuban people—a spiritual and patriotic extension, to my mind, of Catalonia on Cuban land—regarding all that, it would be very agreeable for me, God willing, to evoke my intense recollections in the last part[4] (already sketched out) of my *Memoir*.

Before what may be called the official reopening of *La Peña* in El Casino, the first weeks of October were a time of constant disquiet for me, thinking that the yearned-for return to "the fatherland of my longings and my sorrows," as I defined it in a stanza of my poem "Grito de paz," transcribed on a previous page, was drawing near. Deep inside, two emotions, opposed in a way, stirred me even as they fused together and troubled me with redoubled, intense agitation: the consolation of my immediate return to Catalonia and, at the same time, the distress I felt at leaving Cuba because of so many spiritual connections that bound me inseparably to the splendors of its prodigious nature and to the noble friendships I had formed here.

One of those friendships, the one formed with Dr. Francisco J. Rabell, the outstanding figure in Sancti Spíritus and representative in the autonomous chamber in the last days of that ephemeral government, had just favored me with new proof of his kindness through a spontaneous and very gracious article which, accompanied by my photograph, he published in *El Hogar*, an extremely popular weekly at that time (issue of October 6).

I had the consolation of receiving other amiable testimonials of friendship and sympathy as the date of my return to the Peninsula drew near. The article by Dr. Rabell, however, and his two original autographed sheets (given to me as a gift by Antonio G. Zamora, the director of *El Hogar*) have always constituted the most treasured credential attesting to my convictions and characteristic activities in the service of the highest ideals in all categories of honor, dignity, and human fellowship.

The sincere confessional nature of this *Memoir* cannot exclude Dr. Rabell's article. I have included here a copy of the article:

> JOSÉ CONANGLA FONTANILLES
>
> Conangla Fontanilles is a young man of upright principles, a friend of study, and a man characterized by a fertile intelligence. The most commendable modesty envelops his merits with a mantle of sympathy. Those who meet him even once easily hold him in high esteem.
>
> We met him in Sancti Spíritus and there, unable to limit his vocation to journalism, he brought to the columns of *La Fraternidad* diverse writings, historical, or essentially literary, in which he revealed his greatness of soul, the passion he felt for the beautiful ideals of justice and progress. His writings in prose revealed his poet's sentiments, his joys and his dreams.
>
> He believed that Spain could only progress if it accepted federalism. He admires Pi y Margall, whom he calls his mentor. He has undertaken strenuous campaigns in that political party's press.
>
> He came to Cuba because of the demands of military service, and

he has maintained his ideals with an iron-clad will; but if he has not manifested them openly, he has, on the other hand, with his poet's lyre, left his impressions of the destructive war in a voluminous volume titled *Odes del cor*, poems from his noble heart that will surely find an echo in his native Catalonia.

He collaborated in the *Diario de la Marina*, *El Fígaro*, and *El Hogar*, while he was also an enthusiastic and prolific writer for *La Opinión Catalana.*

He is the author of several pamphlets, and has dealt out vigorous lashes with his pen to injustice, error, evil, and tyranny in his piece "*El Gabinete negro.*" There his most generous, progressive, and redemptive ideas shine with the light of lively enthusiasm and faith.

Conangla is a noble component of those Spanish youths who do not commune at the altars of fanaticism and political error.

The nation that has a majority of such like-minded young people is worthy of liberty and progress.

Conangla combines with his other merits one that is quite singular; he is a sincere friend.

Who does not freely applaud someone with such attributes?

El Hogar, as on so many other occasions, has done well in providing the portrait of the sympathetic and valiant, as well as enlightened and gifted writer, Conangla y Fontanilles: honor to the man who is meritorious.

Francisco J. Rabell

The visit I paid to Dr. Rabell in his residence and laboratory to express my lively gratitude for his article, was prompt and cordial. Some days later I returned to his house to take leave of him with a strong embrace, to reiterate my undying devotion to him for his kindnesses and, at the same time, to express my affection and best wishes for the liberty and happiness of Cuba.

On two occasions I also went to the offices of the General Staff of the Captain-General in order to comply with similar debts of gratitude owed to Colonel Don Benito Vallespinosa, the providential protector and redeemer of my hopes for returning to my native land. I was very sorry, however, that my genuine desire to greet and bid farewell to the generous colonel was thwarted since he was absent from his office on both occasions, and I was unable to find the address of his family home.

I spent the second week of October in continuous comings and goings to take leave of the other friends I was fortunate to have in Havana. There were companions belonging to the literary and journalist bohemia, as well as some Catalan compatriots established in the city, among them Salvador Torra Pous, the correspondent for foreign newspapers; Pujol Roca, the son of the owner of the Café Alemán; and especially the family of Ramón Queralt, who was from Montblanc and the accredited owner of a barber shop located in Obispo Street. And once I had complied with those friendly acts, but with three or four days still left before I was to join the body of the nominal Battalion of Scribes and Orderlies that was to proceed to the Castle of La Cabaña, to await our departure, I had a few moments favorable for stimulating an ardent spiritual state that led to the expression of the highly emotive Catalan verses "Adioses a Cuba," and a stirring farewell "A Cuba libre," incorporated years later into my first book of poetry *Elegía de la guerra*.

Here are the translations of both poems:

GOODBYE TO CUBA

Despite my profound impatience
to return to my yearned-for land,
I leave you with sadness, daughter of the Tropics,
Island of blazing sun. Gracious Cuba.

I leave you in sorrow; for your
noble influences speak to me with affection;
and I also take with me emotions
impressed on my soul of your
nature, your concerns.

I leave you in sorrow; for my conscience,
rebellious like yours, for the same reason,
was consumed by oppression,
like yours it demanded Independence.

And, how could I not love you, if a great number
of my friends now rest in your bosom!

If I was brought by force to your shores
because of a tenacious and shameful fight;
and the Spanish fiat, in its blindness,
impelled me to treat you with hatred,
responsive to my sentiments, day after day
I secretly protested in your favor;
and I suffered outrage and fury
at our calumnies, just as my soul was also affected by
the punitive actions of the rebel forces.

Oh, cursed, dismal war
that makes brutes of soldiers in acts of reprisal!
Cursed be those who incite armies
as if they were starving and enraged packs of dogs!
And accursed be the justice of people
who balance reasons with killings!

Why does humanity let itself
be led by evil guides like docile sheep,
and become the instrument of blind passions,
and not wish to avoid base acts
and not listen to the voice of rebellion
against unjust, fratricidal laws
contrived by ambitious pride?

Now the fighting has stopped and now the serene
dawn is breaking, heralding a new day
for you and my brothers
that will bring us all light and calm.

Beautiful is Peace, liberator of people!
Beautiful is the day on which War comes to an end!

TO FREE CUBA

Don your finest raiments again,
oh Cuba of the blazing sun:
bring to life again
the delights of your gardens:
sing again your songs as sweet as honey;
awaken the harmonies of your mockingbirds;
braid your celestial fantasies
with the moon's rays;
fashion the most appealing hymn
from your lovely qualities,
enjoy the long-awaited
and solemn day
on which, you see yourself
free at last from your jailor!

But guard your good fortune well,
oh Cuba of the blazing sun;
for you might encounter
iron bars that are even stronger!

Watch your wings, Cuba!
Ascend! Be prudent!

As a commemorative complement to my recollections of my last days in Cuba during the war of liberation, I shall note that on the morning of November 5, 1898, after receiving our pay, as well as another month's pay to help us on our journey, all of us with our duffle bags were transported in several small boats and transferred from the Muelle de Caballería to the maritime landing of Casablanca,[5] from there to climb on foot toward the fortress of La Cabaña.[6] We crossed over the horrific *Foso de los Laureles* [executions by firing squad were carried out on this esplanade] and entered the fortress through its main portal.

We were lodged in one of the cells with grilles that open onto the esplanade referred to above. There we left our backpacks, watched over by some kind recruits. A group of us walked along the castle's passageways, went up to the old wall where the historic cannons of the fortress were placed, and looked around in other parts of the castle.

At nightfall in the canteen we ate some frugal sandwiches washed down with beer or whatever drink we men wanted. Then we entered the cell where we were to spend an interminable night of discomfort and insomnia, sharing the floor's cold flagstones with the rest of the men crowded together there awaiting repatriation.

The next day after reveille and the ablutions we were able to perform in a nearby washing place, we went to the canteen again in search of food and the customary cup of coffee. Following the necessary formalities of roll call and other preparations and needs for each man in the different units, with duffle bags on our backs, we went down from La Cabaña, and from the dock at Casablanca we were taken on board the *Patricio de Satrústegui*.[7]

Several Catalan friends and the members of the board of *La Peña* approached the steamship in launches to bid me farewell, although they were not allowed to come aboard as they wished. We had to take leave of each other with effusive good-byes expressed in words and mime in the midst of the hoarse booms of the transatlantic ship belching smoke and the cordial shouts exchanged between the troops lining the ship's rails and the people surrounding the ship cheering the voyagers.

I could offer a long series of impressions of the voyage home on the *Satrústegui*, many of which I shall omit in order not to prolong this *Memoir* overmuch. I cannot, however, exclude some of the things that happened during the crossing from Havana to Cádiz.

After three days of sailing, we were painfully shocked by the first death among the returning troops. The man was a soldier from one of the infantry units that constituted the group of forces gathered together in the hold of the ship. His body was cast into the sea wrapped in a coarse piece of burlap with an iron ingot tied to his chest, after a simple prayer for the dead was offered by the *Satrústegui*'s chaplain in the presence of the head of the dead man's unit and an officer of the crew.

On the days that followed there were similar scenes, although an accord between the commander of the forces on board and the ship's captain saw to it that the conveyance of the dead from the infirmary to the railing, where they were piously cast into the sea, was effected at night so that the voyagers could not witness the sad ceremonies.

Scenes just like this happened inevitably on board each ship used for the evacuation of the Spanish Army, according to international newspaper agencies. The urgency with which the Spanish government was obliged to complete the evacuation did not rule out the pressing removal of numerous ex-combatants who were at that time in hospitals, convalescent, or with little hope in some cases of arriving at their respective hometowns alive.

As a consequence, the thousands of soldiers whom the Spanish government impiously sacrificed in Cuba's martyred land during the three years of stupid intransigence against the heroic patriotism of the *mambí* were augmented by the no less tragic streams of ex-combatants (the vast majority having been forcibly recruited), whose skeletons paved the sea bed of the colonial routes between Spain and Cuba.

In contrast to such pitiful scenes, very different situations did exist. Helped by the good weather—the steamship navigated in favorable atmospheric conditions and calm seas—at every hour of the day in the lower decks assigned to the troops, there were many groups of happy soldiers confiding their reciprocal illusions and plans for a new life, or relating each one of the difficult moments, as well as the most reassuring moments they had experienced while campaigning.

Other groups of ingenuous soldiers amused themselves by describing customs of their native regions or the memorable types and things found in the ethnic and folkloric mosaic of the Peninsula. Those groups of soldiers also sang popular songs in the different vernacular languages of the Iberian Peninsula. And the anticipated pleasure of the ever-closer return to their native towns led to a euphoria that transformed some singers into ardent interpreters of their respective local dances.

On the other hand, clandestine betting was organized in the cargo compartments that were converted into spaces that accommodated pallets or makeshift beds for the troops. Skillful card deck cutters also offered analo-

Figure 5. "Final. Lo que hi hem deixat / Y lo que n' hem tret." (The End. What We Left Behind / What We Got Back.) (*La Campana de Gracia*, September 24, 1898. Drawing by J. Lluis Pellicer.)

gous attractions in some of the roomy intermediate class cabins destined for the sergeants of the expedition. In each one of the betting games the slippery pesetas of incautious or vice-ridden gamblers passed easily into the possession of opportunistic cardsharps.

Meanwhile, the commanders and officers of the units on board shared their leisure time and preoccupations during their agitated pacing back and forth on the first-class deck conversing about the dangers that could be ignited in the Peninsula because of the humiliating and total collapse of Spanish colonial despotism. In the days preceding our disembarking, international cable agencies already reported in the Havana press on the grave fears felt by the government in Madrid as much as by important generals and Spanish Army juntas of defense in connection with the revolutionary or merely "regenerationist" unrest that was increasing in regard to the monarchist regime and its historical "mainstays," and in particular, against the military's abusive privileges and demands.

As I walked in front of the small stairway that led from the intermediate deck to the top deck, where commanders and officers paced, by chance I was able to overhear their words and phrases, which clearly revealed the fact that their main topic had to do with the above-mentioned revolutionary ferment and the ineludible necessity—as they understood it—for the Spanish government with the help of the army to prevent conspiracies in order to safeguard the interests of the monarchy and also, in the interest of solidarity, the hypertrophic integrity of the costly military ranks.

What the indispensable recourses might be—draconian or Machiavellian—that the Spanish government could resort to in order to destroy or at least divert revolutionary aims in the Peninsula at the time, I was not able to overhear from the nervous pacers on the first-class deck. But without any fear of being mistaken, I assumed that among the most effective means of destroying dangerous conspiracies, the Spanish government would not hesitate to avail itself (as it has done in successive periods) of one or another or both of the following recourses, which were always easily effective in finding favor with the varied sectors representative of the systematic and baleful exaggerations of Spanish patriotism: invention of whatever pretext to increase military hostility against the Berber tribes in the Rif[8] region; and the renewal of similarly insidious malign campaigns against the legitimate aspirations of renascent Catalan nationalism . . . !

Early in the morning of November 25, 1898, the *Satrústegui* entered the broad bay of Cádiz. Hours later, those of us in the repatriated units on board that ship were disembarked onto the wharf. Later we were taken in military ambulances to the fortress above the city where we were lodged for three days in order to organize the transportation of the travelers by rail to our respective locations.

That brief stay in the castle on the hill above Cádiz provided me with the opportunity (accompanied by two fellow travelers) to walk around the principal streets, plazas, markets, and avenues of lively and carefree Cádiz, overflowing with picturesque sights and extremely interesting customs, as in each one of Andalusia's favored cities.

On the third day, provided with the official ticket to travel to my part of the country, I boarded the exceedingly uncomfortable third-class cars in connecting trains on my route, not without spending some peaceful hours in Sevilla. I crossed through the dry plains of La Mancha, the scenario of Cervantes's immortal idea. I enjoyed the sight of the evocative fields of Elche and Alicante, dotted with date palms. I admired the well-designed Moorish irrigation canals and the prized orange groves of the famous Valencian gardens. I crossed the Ebro River where it slowly flows by the very singular Tortosa. I stopped several hours in august Tarraco [modern Tarragona], the classic preceptor of my first poetic ventures and later of my idealistic convictions opposing every kind of tyranny, despotism, injustice, and attacks on the imperishable rights and natural respect owed to persons, families, peoples, and nations.

And once I exchanged my striped uniform for my civilian garb, I finally ended the tiring journey of my early youth with my yearned-for arrival in Montblanc, where I threw myself into the arms of my mother and sisters, for me, the purest and most consoling affection!

When that difficult period of my youth had been left behind, I asked myself what would be the surprises, the vicissitudes, the joys or the disappointments, the new unknowns, in short, compensatory or adverse, that destiny might hold in reserve for me in my immediate future?

Immersed in such preoccupations, I did not take long to confront them resolutely and worthily, with the help of plans aimed enthusiastically at liberation. As I have stated before, I would be very pleased to narrate all this in new chapters of this *Memoir*, if divine grace were to grant me health, serenity of spirit, and sufficient time to do so.

J. Conangla Fontanilles
Havana, December 27, 1958

Appendix

In this appendix commemorative of my stay in Cuba in the last days before I embarked on the *Satrústegui*, I have transcribed several farewells dedicated to me in Havana dailies and magazines. I was not able to read the texts of these tributes until the beginning of December of that year when my amiable friend Fuentevilla sent me the following clippings by mail:

Farewell in *La Lucha*:

> *Conangla Fontanilles.* Yesterday, Monday (November 6, 1898), our good and particular friend, Señor Conangla y Fontanilles, left for the Peninsula, after fully complying with the fatherland, having earned the rank of sergeant in military service. He is returning to the Peninsula leaving here much goodwill and the reputation of an excellent litterateur, based on numerous and deeply felt literary works which were well-received by the principal newspapers and magazines on the island. Possessed of the soul of an artist, always captivated by every ideal and completely indifferent to conventionality—and therefore distanced and opposed to harmful skepticism—his works have been read with pleasure by lovers of literature. His works demonstrate that he does not and has not held the distinguished literati Apelles Mestres and Santiago Rusiñol[1] as his masters in vain, writers for whom his admiration is great, bordering on a cult. He has thus benefited the public on this island, acquainting them whenever possible with the best and most notable productions of those masters in the art of letters.
>
> We wish our friend Conangla a felicitous return to his beloved country. We also hope that just as we will not easily forget him, he will not forget us in his delight at being in his home once again, and that he will allow us to savor from time to time something of his visions and sentiments by sending us publications in which some of the solid productions of his artistic and literary temperament have appeared.

Despedida de *El Noticiero Universal*:

Parenthesis. "Farewell!" A very dear companion and a noble and generous friend, Conangla Fontanilles, leaves us tomorrow on the steamship *P. de Satrústegui.*

Conangla is not a novice in letters. The Republican press in Spain, from *La Autonomía* in Reus to *El Pueblo* in Valencia, always accepted his spirited works in defense of democracy, which the Catalan journalist who is leaving us fought for as an experienced soldier. Filled, if not with illusions, with enthusiasm, with his pen of steel, tempered progressively in the furnace of our misfortunes, replete with truths that will fill the abyss of blank paper that the journalist necessarily has to cover with ideas—there in that virile Catalonia whose maximum grandeur is his ideal, Conangla will fight tirelessly as he has done here, enlightening people on the complex problem of the war in Cuba. Friend of my soul, I regret his absence. Together in those days of trial we speculated on our future fortune, and fortune has protected him. I celebrate it: the good fortune of my friends far from inspiring envy in me, I make my own.

Bon voyage, my dear Conangla. *"La Peña,"* which was born in the warmth of the most sincere friendship and the purest ideals by a group of enthusiastic companions and friends like you, regrets your departure and wishes you good fortune in your country; and as we say "farewell," nostalgia for love of country penetrates the hearts of that group of honorable men.

Juan Claridades (Juan Subirana)
November 5, 1898

Farewell in *El Eco Montañés*:[2]

Bon voyage. Last Monday our fellow writer for the press and particular friend D. José Conangla Fontanilles sailed for the Peninsula in the magnificent steamship *P. de Satrústegui.* Friend Conangla, who wrote for *La Opinión Catalana*, came to this island a little more than three years ago for the same reasons as I: because of the accursed war; as soldiers (forced).

From the first moment we met, we got along so well that the most unreserved friendship arose between us, undoubtedly due to friend Conangla's happy nature and the affinity of ideas we both held regarding our national literature. Regionalists and great admirers of Pereda,[3] Narcís Oller,[4] Guimerá[5] and many other masters of regionalism rightly understood, it is not unusual that we should often have enjoyed talking about things from those parts—from his beloved Catalonia and the no less beloved *Montaña* region—so identical in some of their customs that it seems that one region is the prolongation of the other. How can one forget those pleasant hours in which strolling through the beautiful garden of the Trijoa theater during the intermissions or through the extensive salons of the Tacón and Albisu in the company of friends, who were fond, as we were, of filling up pages, we delighted in commenting, after having applauded them, on the dramas of Feliu y Codina,[6] or the witty little comic pieces of Narciso Serra[7] and other Catalan and *montañés* writers. Happy you, friend Conangla, who, in a few days (when the newspaper in which these lines are published), will already have seen and held in your arms your beloved mother and unforgettable sisters in Montblanch, content to see yourself far from where there is still something to suffer through for those of us who can't leave when we should like to. Receive, then, these lines as a memento and proof of the friendship your friend has unconditionally professed for you from the instant in which we both presented ourselves at the print shop where *La Opinión Catalana* and *El Eco Montañés* were published.

J. Gutiérrez de Gandarilla
November 9, 1898

Farewell from *La Opinión Catalana*[8]

J. Conangla Fontanilles. Today (November 6, 1898), our esteemed reporter Don José Conangla Fontanilles is embarking for Spain. After almost four years of absence, he is returning to his beloved home. He leaves a vacuum in this editorial office that will be difficult to fill, for during his stay in Havana he has worked with a fervor and enthusiasm worthy of our utmost gratitude on behalf of whatever might heighten Catalan renown in Cuba, a country for which our friend and companion feels sincere affection. He won many friends on this island due to his modesty and fine character traits; and as a conscientious writer his signature is well known to our readers. Our esteemed friend will not stop bringing his writings to *La Opinión Catalana*, for, as a correspondent in Barcelona, he will inform us from the capital of Catalonia of everything notable that happens in those four provinces of our region. He will also send us articles and poetry, his, as well as those of other Catalan writers, so that our paper may always move forward in regard to improvements and attractive features. May our dear José Conangla's journey be swift and happy so that he can embrace his idolized mother and family in Montblanch (Tarragona) as soon as possible, a goal that constantly invigorated him during his stay in Cuba—for him, very long, and for *La Opinión*, very short.

Julio Talavera

In addition to the clippings of the preceding farewells, I had the satisfaction, which was no less moving, of receiving at the same time, a copy of the magnificent group photo of the directorship of *La Peña*, reproduced in *El Hogar*. I much appreciated each one of those honorable and very generous testimonies to our genuine fraternal bonds and, most especially, the useful dedication that appeared on the back of the group photo, which was added and matched with the autographs of the unforgettable companions pictured there, as may be seen by its graphic reproduction, which was attached and reads as follows:

To our friend and comrade,
with a fraternal embrace:
because in this original
nothing was erased by absence.
And "*La Peña*" today as yesterday,
harbors a sincere affection
for the worthy comrade
who assisted here in its birth.

Havana, November 24, 1898

(Signed) Mariano Benítez Veguillas, Emilio Fernández, Juan Pérez del Río, Juan Subirana, José Alonso, J. M. Fuentevilla, Carlos Guardiola Rendón, Nicolás Suárez Inclán, José Antonio Losada.

Notes

Introduction

1. *Cuba/España, España/Cuba* (Barcelona: Grijalbo, 1995), pp. 278–92.

2. According to the strict standards of official documents, only 782 Spanish soldiers died in combat and 8,627 from wounds. More than 40,000 were afflicted with one or another disease, among them yellow fever, which killed 14,000. These numbers have been interpreted from a patriotic Cuban point of view as depreciatory in regard to the harm inflicted by the troops fighting for independence, since the causes of the Spanish defeat are thereby reduced to illness caused by the Cuban climate and the final intervention of the North Americans.

3. "Those who are not buried in the *manigua,* either die in the jungle, victims of fever, anemia, tuberculosis, or as a result of the ambushes carried out by *filibusteros.*" (*La Unión Republicana,* Asturias, February 7, 1892). Transcribed by Francisco Erice, "Patriotismo burgués y patriotism popular: asturianos ante la guerra en Cuba (1895–1898)," in Jorge Uría (ed.), *Asturias y Cuba en torno al 98: Sociedad, economía, política y cultura en la crisis de entresiglos* (Barcelona: Labor, 1996, p. 160), an admirable and pioneering compilation in the period preceding the commemoration of 1898, an example that ought to be imitated in other communities and autonomous regions.

4. According to official figures, the amount of expenditures for Cuba was 1,554,447,449.64 *pesetas.* In his early work, Luis Morote cited figures from the Ministry of the Treasury, and added up 1,796,269,462.91 for the conflict in Cuba and 165,988,257.63 for the Philippines for a total of 1,962,257,720.63 [sic]. The result was a floating debt of 1,445,000,000 *pesetas.*

5. This is the complete title of the original that is conserved in the Conangla family archives. All of this material was temporarily ceded to the Florida Catalan Society (*Casal Català* de Miami), for its conservation and scholarly access on April 23, 1986, the Day of Sant Jordi.

6. "*El meu pare que al cel sia . . .*" (Montblanc: Imprenta Monmany, 1920), pp. 46–47.

7. This thesis has been rejected by a broad consensus of Cuban historiography, among other reasons because Maceo was only promoted to lieutenant colonel in 1869, a rank he held until 1872, so that he did not have sufficient military prominence to be accepted as the leader of a Haitian-style revolution.

8. Barcelona: Tipografía Catalana, 1904.

9. Barcelona: Artis, 1921.

10. *Memorias*, pp. 6–7. The original in Catalan is included in *Elegía de la guerra*, pp. 18–19.

11. Carta-prólogo. *Elegía de la guerra*, pp. 6–7. Unless otherwise indicated, all quotations from Conangla's work originally written in Catalan and not translated by him to Castilian have been literally translated by the author of this study. [Translated passages from Joaquín Roy's Castilian to English have also aimed at a literal rendering of the texts.]

12. The lucid work by Joaquim Marco titled "Modernisme literari a Catalunya," the introductory chapter of the volume titled *El Modernisme literari i d'altres assaigs* (Barcelona: El Punt/Edhasa, 1983), pp. 11–81, is recommended.

13. [*Noucentisme* was a movement propelled by Catalan intellectuals and politicians and conceived in opposition to modernism and naturalism. Designed to introduce new ideas and projects to improve the country, it was inaugurated in 1906 with the publication of the *Glosari* by Eugenio d'Ors. See P. Anguera, *Literatura, patria i societat: Els intellectuals i la nació* (Vic, 1999); Jaume Aurell, "El noucentisme: La regeneración del compromiso nacional y el esfuerzo institucionalizador (1900–1930)," in "La Formación del imaginario histórico del Nacionalismo Catalán: De la Renaixença al Noucentisme (1830–1930)," in *Historia Contemporánea*, vol. 22 (2001), pp. 277–84; N. Bilbeny, *Eugeni d'Ors i la ideología del Noucentisme* (Barcelona, 1988), pp. 175–200; J. L. Marfany, *Aspectes del modernisme* (Barcelona, 1975).]

14. This is not the appropriate place to include an exhaustive bibliography on the concept of the "generation of 1898," but it is fitting, at a minimum, to note some texts, above all those that deal with the connections between the social environment and those that connect the "group" of 98 with contemporary literary movements or their successors: José Luis Abellán, *Sociología del 98* (Barcelona, 1973); Azorín, "Aquella generación," *La Esfera* (Madrid, April 25, 1914); "La Generación del 98," *Obras completas*, Vol. II (Madrid, 1947), pp. 896–914; Pío Baroja, "Tres generaciones," *Obras completas*, Vol. V, (Madrid, 1948), pp. 574–80; Guillermo Díaz-Plaja, *Modernismo frente al 98* (Madrid, 1951); *Estructura y sentido del Novecentismo español* (Madrid: Alianza Editorial, 1975); John Englekirk, "El hispanoamericanismo y la generación del 98" *Revista iberoamericana*, Vol. II (1940), pp. 321–51; Pedro Laín Entralgo, *La generación del 98* (Bs.As.: Losada, 1947); Luis S. Granjel, *La Generación literaria del 98* (Salamanca: Anaya, 1966); Juan López-Morillas, *Hacia el 98: literatura, sociedad, ideología* (Barcelona, 1972).

15. Joan-Lluís Marfany, *La cultura del catalanisme* (Barcelona: Empúries, 1996).

16. Founded in Barcelona by Jaume Massó i Torrents. It appeared bimonthly or monthly in two different periods between 1881 and 1884 (a period in which it defined itself as an advocate of positivism), and from 1889 to 1893 (a stage in which it concentrated on artistic phenomena). It was directed initially by Ramon D. Perès with the collaboration of Apeles Mestres, Narcís Oller, and Josep Ysart, and later under the influence of Santiago Rusiñol, when its nationalistic, anarchistic content made it polemical.

17. A Catalan weekly published in Barcelona between 1900 and 1906 under the direction of Lluís Via y Alexandre de Riquer, similar to the *Unió Catalanista*, which fomented cultural activism and became the most representative voice for modernism.

18. In addition to those cited directly in the text, the Conangla archive has copies of other magnificent reviews of this book (except for the last, all from 1904):

A. Palau i Dulcet, *La Conca de Barberà* (Montblanc, May 21); *La Veu de Catalunya* (May 28); *El Diluvio* (May 25); Antoni Rovira i Virgili, *La Avanzada* (Tarragona, May 28); Arnau Martínez y Seriña, *Joventut* (Barcelona, June 2); Alfredo Opisso, *La Vanguardia* (Barcelona, June 3); P. Redón, *La Justicia* (Tarragona, June 4); E. Moliné y Brasés, *La Renaixensa* (Barcelona, June 5); J. Mallafré, *El Programa* (Barcelona, June 4); *Resumen Bibliográfico* (May); Rata Sabia, *La Esquella de la Torratxa* (Barcelona, June 10); *Diario de Albacete*, *La Democracia de Olot* (June 19); Román Jori, *La Lucha* (Girona, June 18); Francesc Martí, *El Igualadino* (June 19); *Germinal* (Sabadell, July 2); J. M. Mallafré, *La Defensa* (Barcelona, July 1); Francesc Pi i Arsuaga, *El Nuevo Regimen* (Madrid, July 9); E. González, *Llevor* (Sant Feliu de Guixols, July 24; Joan Ruiz i Porta, *El Camp de Tarragona* (November 5); Manuel Morplu, *El Comercio* (La Habana, June 4, 1905).

19. Specifically, Rovira points out the affinity with *Volianas* (*La Avanzada*, Tarragona, May 28).

20. Sant Andreu del Palomar 1871–Barcelona 1928. Iglesias was a prominent writer for the theater, influenced by Ibsen and Maeterlinck and well known for his dramas critical of social conditions, also a collaborator in *L'Avenç*. He received the *Flor Natural* in the *Jocs Florals de La Habana* in 1923, organized by Conangla.

21. *El Autonomista* (Gerona, June 19 1904).

22. *La Avanzada* (Tarragona, May 28, 1904).

23. Barcelona, May 21, 1904.

24. Gerona, June 12–19, 1904.

25. La Habana, June 1905.

26. First published in *El Nuevo Ideal*, Mataró, June 4, 1904. Original in Castilian.

27. His correspondence with Maragall continued after his second departure for Cuba in 1905. *Eternel*—the volume of poetry and prose—contains a letter from Maragall responding to Conangla's farewell from Havana: "[. . .] I wish you prosperity and glory in that land of liberty" (Barcelona, February 18, 1906).

28. The wretched conditions marking the transport of the troops to Cuba are better documented by anonymous descriptions, minority exceptions to the bogus patriotism found in the doggerel of the time:

> From the forecastle to the hold
> scrambled, stacked and mixed together,
> the nation "packages" its soldiers
> and delivers them to implacable death.
> (*El Domingo*, January 23, 1897)

See the complete poem in the edition of Carlos García Barrón, *Cancionero del 98* (Madrid: Cuadernos para el Diálogo, 1974), p 114.

29. Here is a fragment of the text of the October 21, 1896, edict: "1) All the inhabitants in the countryside or outside the line of fortification of towns will gather together within eight days in the towns occupied by the troops. Anyone who is found in the countryside when this time limit expires will be considered a rebel and judged as such. 2) It is absolutely prohibited to take goods from the towns and transport them from one town to another by land or by sea without the permission of the military authority at the point of departure. Those who break this law will be

judged and penalized for aiding the rebels." Let the following illustrate the effects of this measure: " [. . .] next to the large barracks built by official charity there is a starving mob that inspires compassion and horror at one and the same time; little girls wasted by misery and prostitution; thin, squalid men, near automatons, with hunger painted all over their yellowish faces; mothers who are no longer mothers because they have lost even the instinct of motherhood; all of them piled up in a heap like an unformed mass of discarded human flesh; they are the victims of the war." ("Los que lloran y los que ríen," *El Carbayón*, October 24, 1897, transcribed by Erice, in Uría González, p. 160).

30. Among the "gems" recovered in the opportune compilation directed by Jorge Uría, these verses, "A Yanquia" published by Ramiro Blanco in *El Comercio* (Asturias), stand out:

> Hybrid public, upstart people;
> Vile mix of the vile dregs
> Spat out by the old continent.
> Spurious race without honor or history!
> Stinking rodent warren
> where everything ignoble and ill born
> finds its center and natural sphere.
> Filthy brothel, fetid nest.
> Refuge of repulsive reptiles . . . !
> How, unworthy nation,
> scum of the earth, how did you dare
> to awaken the Spanish lion
> from its sovereign slumber and insult it?
> (Francisco Erice, in Uría, p. 164.)

31. "Adiós mi península hermosa," a traditional habanera.

32. In addition to the pioneering and very well-documented book by García Barrón, *Cancionero del 98*, replete with examples of popular poetry published in a dozen newspapers of the period, and the prologue by Roberto Mesa ("Mitología del 98," pp. vii–xvi), it is also advisable to consult Miquel del Sants Oliver, *La literatura del desastre* (Barcelona, 1973); and the text by Fernando Díaz-Plaja, *1898* (Madrid: Editora Nacional, 1976), intended to make the movement accessible to a larger public.

33. "Soñando con mi tierra," "Recuerdos invernales," "La retama," "Remembranza," and "Padre," whose context is referred to below.

34. *La Avanzada*, May 28, 1904.

35. See the testimony of J. Gutiérrez de Gandarrilla, in his note of farewell to Conangla published in *El Eco Montañes* in Havana: "You came to this island a little more than three years ago and for the same reasons I came for: because of the accursed war; *we are* soldiers" (November 9, 1898).

36. [*Las Ánimas* Hospital in Havana was a site of important experimentation on the cause and treatment of yellow fever before, during, and after 1898. See Mariola Espinosa. *Epidemic Invasions: Yellow Fever and the Limits of Cuban Independence, 1878–1930*. Chicago: University of Chicago Press, 2009.]

37. *La Avanzada*, May 28, 1904.

38. This historical episode, reflected in the *Memoir*, has frequently served as

an epigraph or introduction to historical works that have as their theme the colonial disaster or the later contemplation of the present and future history of Spain brought about by the Generation of 98. In the Catalan context, it could serve as a graphic (and cinematic) literary illustration to the first passages of *La ciutat cremada* (1976) by Antoni Ribas, the film that marks the rebirth of Catalan cinema.

39. On another voyage begun on August 23 and ending in Santander, the *Satrústegui* registered 74 deaths at sea: Moreno Fraginals counted 18 expeditions with repatriated soldiers of whom 4,000 died (*Cuba/España*, p. 289). Numerous descriptions of those scenes have become classics and are anthologized repeatedly. The most numerous and dramatic come from Asturias and Galicia. Let these samples serve as illustrations: "The troops formed with the clothes they were to wear on the voyage, ragged, dirty, producing a disastrous effect. The soldiers were cleaned up by bathing them in tepid water. Then they were given a complete outfit" (*El Heraldo*, La Coruña, September 11, 1898); periodically, "piles of Spanish flesh . . . fearful skeletons, with thin faces and sunken eyes, with trembling legs and heads bent over their chests arrived in ships to Spain" (*El Corbayón*, September 9, 1898, transcribed by Erice, in Uría, p. 165). Several months later, after the momentary trauma, when everything returned to normal, Baroja penned these classic lines: "The government, which like most governments, had no idea of what the people were thinking, believed that when they heard about the defeat, they would start a revolution . . . and nothing happened. When the news broke in Madrid, people went to bullfights and the theater as calm as could be; not only didn't they mount protests, they didn't even comment on what had happened. It was then that Silvela said that Spain didn't have a pulse" ("Desde la última vuelta del camino," *Obras*, VII, Madrid, 1949).

40. Letter of March 22, 1905. Conangla Archive.

41. The most recent transcription of this document is included in my edition titled *La Constitució de L'Havana i altres escrits* (Barcelona: Edicions de la Magrana/Diputació de Barcelona, 1986), which includes a selection of Conangla's texts that deal primarily with nationalism.

Chapter 1

1. In popular parlance, the *quinta* refers to the annual call-up of men for the army—all those born in the same year (once they turn twenty) and are recruited at the same time, at which time they are also termed *quintos*.

2. Catalan anarchists liked to change the famous phrase used by Cánovas into: "Down to the last man who doesn't have the 1500 pesetas to redeem himself." See the context of the sociological profile of the recruits in the last chapter of the book by Moreno Fraginals y Moreno Masó, *Guerra, migración y muerte*.

3. This is the name of the declaration of independence issued on this day in Baire, a town in the municipality of Jiguaní in Oriente Province.

4. Printed in a limited edition by the Imprinta Monmany de Montblanc in 1920.

5. Situated at an altitude of 223 meters, it is a municipality in the province of Barcelona, founded in the twelfth century. It is the seat of the judicial district and the capital of the region of Penedès, known for its wines.

6. Lluís de Castellví i Vilallonga (1840–1918). He was an officer of the General Staff of the Spanish Army in Cuba during the Ten Years War.

7. A municipality in the province of Tarragona, capital of the district of the

Conca de Barberà. At an altitude of 352 meters, it is situated beside the Francolí River. Cereals, vineyards, and vegetables are cultivated in this zone. Among the commercial activities and the most important industries, viticulture, alcohol, soap and feed, textiles, plastics, wood, paper, and plaster works stand out. The urban center preserves its medieval walls raised by Pedro the Ceremonious between 1366 and 1372 with their sixteen towers and two portals.

8. A military and naval administrative center. The original city was founded by the Carthaginians under the rule of Hasdrubal, and conquered later by Publius Cornelius Scipio, who gave it the name of New Carthage. During the Muslim colonization, it bore the name of Karthadjena. Situated in one of the finest sheltered natural bays in Spain, it occupies an ancient spit of land bordered by a series of hills that assures its great military importance as one of the best-defended ports. Among its important industries, the oil refinery of Escombreras stands out.

9. As may be noted, this figure is often used by a multitude of authors. See my commentary in the introduction.

10. Conangla does not mention the intimate relationship that this maritime company had with the wars in Cuba, given that its great expansion depended on the transport of Spanish soldiers in order to suppress the successive attempts at independence. This Spanish shipping company had its origin in another company called Antonio López and Brothers, founded in 1849 by Antonio López y López (Comillas, Santander 1817–Barcelona 1883), first Marquis of Comillas and senator for life, who made an enormous fortune in Cuba. When he was very young, he went to Santiago de Cuba and dedicated himself to amassing a notable fortune in the commerce (legal, for the most part, and illegal according to critical biographies) of slave trafficking. See the succinct references in the recent book by Francesc Cabana, *La burguesía catalana: una aproximación histórica* (Barcelona: Proa, 1996, pp. 65–71). When he returned to Barcelona, among other companies, he founded the Compañía de Tabacos de Filipinas and the Banco Hispano-Colonial. In 1856, he obtained exclusive rights to the maritime transport between Spain and Cuba, and in 1863, he was already covering this route with eight steamships. In 1876, he received an urgent request from the Spanish government to transport 25,000 soldiers. Between 1875 and 1877, his company transported 71,000 Spanish military; between 1862 and 1877, he transported 227,174. In 1878, the year when the *Paz of Zanjón* was signed, he was given the title of Marquis of Comillas and in that same year he financed the luxury edition of *l'Atlántida* by Mossèn Cinto Verdaguer, the chaplain on one of his ships. In 1880, he converted the shipping company into an anonymous society and named it the *Transatlántica*. When López died, one of the most important ships in the line that regularly made the Barcelona-Havana run bore his name. His most important monument was erected in the plaza that also bears his name, next to the central edifice of the Barcelona Post Office, near the port. The monument cites the following words by Alfonso XII: "Spain has lost one of the men who lent it its greatest services." Verdaguer dedicated the following verses to him, which are also transcribed on the monument in Barcelona:

Carried by the blessed wings
of your ships, I sought the orange tree
in flower of the Hesperides; but ay!
it is the spoils of the waves that through long ages

conquered it, and I
can only offer you, if it please you, these
leaves from the tree of the golden fruit.
(1876, Steamship *Ciudad Condal*)

The connection between López and Cuba was not limited to the founding of the *Transatlántica*, but also includes the fact that his daughter Isabel married Eusebi Güell i Bacigalupi (1846–1918), protector of Gaudí, the son of Joan Güell I Ferrer (1800–1872), who, in his youth, had obtained the monopoly on commerce to Havana. (See the detailed chapter by Martín Rodrigo, "Iniciativa empresarial i negoci colonial: El primer Marqués de Comillas," in the book catalog compiled by Josep M. Fradera, *Catalunya i Ultramar*.)

11. "El Embarque." The author's translation of the original poem "L'embarch" (p. 18). Note the similarity of this lyric scene with the following verses by Maragall: "I saw ships weigh anchor replete / with sons whom you handed over to death / smiling they went toward their fate / and you sang beside the sea / like a crazy woman."

(The version of the Catalan original of the "Oda a España" by Joachim Molas and Josep M. Castellet in *Ocho siglos de poesía catalana* [Madrid: Alianza, 1969], p. 406. On the theme of Spain in the work of Maragall, the reader may consult the book by Mercedes Vilanova, *España en Maragall*, Barcelona: Península, 1968).

12. This military march was identified with immoderate patriotism. Blasco Ibáñez's phrase is famous: "That odious and boastful Marcha de Cádiz, which Julio Burell used for an article in an anthology titled 'La gran muerta' (*Heraldo*, September 18, 1898), sounds bad to our ears, it is odious, its joy is a cause for pain. It was an electrifying and deranging hymn, and today it is simply a musical source of shame. . . . The Marcha de Cádiz ought not to be the funeral march of men who have been repatriated." Transcribed by Fernando Díaz-Plaja, *1898* (Madrid: Editora Nacional, 1976), pp. 133–34.

13. Situated in the province of Las Villas (Cienfuegos today) on the southern coast of Cuba, bordered on the west by swampy lands into which the Rivers Damují, Salado, and Caunao flow. The city of the same name has a municipal boundary of 1.155 km. It owes its name to José Cienfuegos and Jovellanos (Gijón, 1768–1825), a Spanish general who fought in the War of Independence against Napoleon and was the Captain-General of Cuba in 1825.

14. This term originally referred to the politico-religious tendency that sought to profess an essential Catholicism closely related to conservatism. The term has expanded to describe all religious movements that have as their goal the identification of Church and State and the subjugation of the State to laws based on theocratic authority. Within the strict limits of Spanish political ideas, *integrismo* emerged as a branch of Carlism. In Latin America, it was used to describe certain conservative and hispanicizing movements, and in Cuba, it referred to the agenda to maintain the island under the Spanish crown whatever the cost, and to oppose the solution of autonomy.

15. A city situated on the southern coast of Cuba at the mouth of the Zaza River, in the old province of Santa Clara (later known as Las Villas, divided in turn into various provinces, one of which was Sancti Spíritus). Its port serves the region around the city of Sancti Spíritus.

16. *Rancho* in the text. A term originating in the countryside, used to describe the food served to soldiers.

17. A city founded in 1514 by Diego de Velázquez, situated in the province of Las Villas (today Sancti Spíritus).

18. In contrast to the common and modern meaning of the word *guerrilla*, that name was applied in the armed forces to the formation of experienced combatants, disposed in an open order and meant to protect the rest of the troops. In the conflicts in Cuba, the *guerrilleros* were fundamentally recruited from Cubans to be integrated into these special posts, because of which they were considered traitors and hated by patriotic Cubans.

19. Invented by the German armorer Wilhelm Mauser (1834–1882). A repeating rifle with five cartridges, activated by means of a sliding bolt. Produced in diverse calibers, it was universally adopted by diverse armies, among them the Spanish Army.

20. The river and municipal neighborhood of Sancti Spíritus.

21. Sergeants and corporals.

22. The final destination of the journey was Barcelona and Montblanc.

23. A political formation founded in 1879 as the *Partido Liberal*. Its membership was essentially Cuban. Its ideology was based on liberalism in a general sense, but with the peculiarities dictated by the special circumstances of Cuba in the nineteenth century. For example, the liberals had a tendency to consider themselves favorable to annexation since the model for society that most attracted them was that of the United States, especially the Southern version. When the slave society disappeared as a result of the Civil War, Cuban liberals evolved toward reformism and even incorporated abolitionist concepts. Members of the *Partido Liberal Autonomista* proposed maintaining political ties with Spain, especially during the period from the end of the Ten Years War until 1898. Recommended for the ideological evolution of Cuban liberalism is the *Antología del pensamiento liberal cubano desde fines del siglo XVII hasta fines del siglo XX*. Compiled by Beatriz Bernal with a prologue de Carlos Alberto Montaner (Madrid: Fundación Liberal "José Martí," 1994).

24. Francesc Pi i Margall (Barcelona 1824–Madrid 1901). Son of a textile worker, he attended seminary and later studied law. Resident in Madrid since 1847, he initiated his political activism with manifestos in the revolution of 1854. He presented himself as a deputy but was defeated in the elections by General Prim. Influenced by Hegel, Herder, and Proudhon, he believed in permanent revolution and confrontation with conservative reaction. Founder of the *Partido Federal*, he thought that the future of Spain ought to be based on the federalist pact which he attempted to bring about when the First Republic was proclaimed (February 11, 1873). He was the Minister of the Interior (February–June 1873) and president of the Council of Ministers (June 11–July 18). Among his works, *Las nacionalidades* (1876) and a grand *Historia general de América* (1878) stand out.

25. Founded in 1886, it was dedicated to literature and cultural matters. It was the organ of *El Progreso*, directed by Francisco de J. Rabell.

26. José Miguel Gómez (1858–1921) fought in the separatist wars against Spain, rising to the rank of general. Head of the *Partido Liberal*, he was president of the Republic of Cuba from 1909 to 1913. Under his mandate, the army was reorganized, new railways were built, and the educational system was expanded. He headed a rebellion to protest the election of General Mario García Menocal as president of Cuba, was made prisoner, and forced into exile in the United States, where he died.

27. Signed on February 10, 1878, it put an end to the Ten Years War.

28. The translation by Conangla himself of the original poem in Catalan titled "Fulla d'àlbum" (p. 79).

29. Born in Cabaiguán in 1843, he was a captain in the war, a town councillor and interim mayor of Sancti Spíritus, a member of the Academia de la Historia, and Senator of the Republic in 1920.

30. A name of African origin applied early on to the Cuban insurrectionists. Among related words is the word *mambo*.

31. Material of striped cotton, characteristic of the uniform of Spanish soldiers of that period.

32. The popular name given to barbers after the type created by Pierre Beaumarchais in *El barbero de Sevilla* (1775), *Las bodas de Fígaro* (1784), and *La madre culpable* (1784).

33. Any commander or officer of the Spanish Army could be designated as the examining magistrate in any kind of investigation corresponding to wartime jurisdiction; and these military judges could select anyone among the sergeants and corporals under their orders to serve as secretary of a particular trial.

34. Veteran of the Ten Years War when he took part as the adjutant of Honorato del Castillo y Cancio, commander of the uprising in Sancti Spíritus.

35. Brother of Conangla's mother, María Dolors Fontanilles i Voltas.

36. A decoration in honor of María Cristina de Hapsburgo-Lorena (Gross-Seelowitz 1858–Madrid 1929), Queen of Spain (1879–1885), and Regent (1885–1902), daughter of Archduke Carlos-Fernando of Austria, second wife of Alfonso XII, whom she succeeded as Regent upon his death in 1885, in anticipation of the majority of his posthumous son, the future Alfonso XIII. During this time the Restoration was consolidated by means of the *turno pacífico* ["pacific turn"], agreed upon between the liberal Sagasta and the conservative Cánovas in the Pact of El Pardo, and the last Spanish colonies, Cuba, Puerto Rico, and the Philippines were lost.

37. A religious order founded by Saint Vincent de Paul (born in 1575 in Pouy or Poy, near Dax, France, or in Tamarite de Litera, Huesca, Spain, and died in 1660 in Paris), dedicated to the education of children and care of the ill, the elderly, and the destitute.

38. A daily paper published in Havana.

39. The official publication of the legislative chamber of Cuba.

40. A private publication dedicated to commentary on the political and parliamentary news of the day.

41. Gerardo Machado Morales (Santa Clara 1871–Miami 1939). A general in the War of Independence at the side of Máximo Gómez. He joined the *Partido Liberal* and in 1921 founded the *Partido Popular*. Allied with President Zayas, he succeeded in becoming president of Cuba in 1925. He transformed himself progressively into a dictator with the help of a corrupt and violent regimen that lost favor with the United States. He was overthrown in 1933 and died an exile in Miami.

42. A synonym of civilians and, in this case, of noncombatants.

43. Segovia 1831–Zarauz 1900. He served in Africa (1859–1860) and fought in Catalonia against the Carlists. On September 29, 1874, he proclaimed Alfonso XII the King of Spain. President of the Council of Ministers, he was Captain-General of Cuba twice (1876–1879 and 1895–1896). During his first posting as Captain-General, he signed the *Paz de Zanjón* in 1877.

44. Valeriano Weyler Nicolau (Palma de Mallorca 1838–Madrid 1930) was the

descendent of a Prussian family and early on, in 1863, a volunteer in Cuba. He was Captain-General of Valencia, the Canary Islands, the Balearic Islands, the Philippines, and Catalonia successively, and then went to Cuba in 1896, where he was relieved of his duty in 1897. He was the Minister of War on various occasions and a senator for life. His reputation as a "hard" man above all in Cuba and the Philippines rightly earned him the animosity of his opponents and of fear in Spain. He became famous for his policy of reconcentration, which led the United States to ask for his dismissal because of his excessive cruelty to Cubans. The Conangla archives have preserved this vitriolic sonnet attributed to Don Ricardo de Monte (Cimarrones 1830–1909), writer and Cuban politician:

> A reptile's look, body of a dwarf,
> instinct of a jackal, soul of mud;
> hypocrite, coward, vile and obscene
> as the most revolting quadrumane.
> Once the scourge of Cuba,
> he was devoid of any noble sentiment,
> and today this excrescence of the human race
> makes Satan himself look wholesome.
> Ruin, desolation, hunger and misery
> are the works this horrible pile of vile matter
> dares to execute.
> And Iberia with perfidious intent
> charges such a monster with the government of Cuba
> as the nineteenth century expires!

45. A private institution whose members were predominately members of the Spanish bourgeoisie and well-off Creoles.

46. All these places share a common past since they belong to different periods of the colonization and expansion of the Spanish Empire. Ceuta (like Melilla) has been an enclave under Spanish sovereignty on the northern coast of Morocco. The Chafarinas Islands are three islands adjacent to the Moroccan coast used as a prison at that time. Fernando Poo was the name of an island in the Gulf of Guinea when it was a Spanish colony, now known as Bioko, a part of the Republic of Equatorial Guinea.

47. A Cuban lawyer and politician (Matanzas 1834–Havana 1906), he cooperated with the revolutionary junta during the Ten Years War as one of Céspedes's agents. When he was found out, he was confined to the Isle of Pines. After the *Paz de Zanjón* (1878), he became the founder of the *Partido Autonomista* (1881) under whose terms the government presided until it was dissolved at the end of the War of 1898.

48. Note by Conangla: "The Carta-folleto was published in Havana in 1899 by the *Imprenta Ruiz*, on Obispo 34."

49. An affluent of the Zaza River, whose distant headwaters are on the eastern slope of the Pico del Tuerto, next to the city of Sancti Spíritus.

50. Joan Maragall i Gorina (Barcelona 1860–1911). Journalist, poet, essayist, and translator. See the introduction for his influence on Conangla's work.

51. Manuel de Montoliu i de Togores (Tarragona 1877–Barcelona 1961). Critic, historian of literature, poet, professor in Hamburg, Buenos Aires, and Barcelona.

52. Conangla's translation of his original poem "Soldat d'una nació," p. 32.

53. The word *surgidero* means the "place where ships anchor." A coastal town situated south of the municipality of Batabanó, district of Bejucal, in Havana Province, in the center of what is known as the Gulf of Batabanó.

54. A municipality in the province of Matanzas, on the banks of the bay of the same name, located on the northern coast of Cuba.

55. A municipality situated to the east of the province of Havana.

Chapter 2

1. Municipal, judicial, and fiscal district in the province of Havana, with an area of 518 km^2. Its terrain is varying, flat, and with some hills in the south.

2. This city near Havana originated in a settlement that the Spanish colonial authorities ordered populated by the indigenous inhabitants of the zone in 1556. Early on, in the seventeenth century, it was transformed into the residence of rich families from Havana.

3. A variant of the Catalan language, spoken in the present provinces of Alicante, Valencia, and Castellón, in the old Kingdom of Valencia, especially in the coastal regions.

4. Equivalent to *tú*.

5. A person who writes with skill, well-formed letters, and polish.

6. Upper rows in theaters where the cheapest seats are located.

7. Traditional theater in Barcelona, the oldest theater still operating in the city, named in honor of the Spanish actor and poet Julián Romea (Aldea de San Juan, Murcia 1813–1868).

8. The Castilian name for the Carrer Ample, a street situated parallel to the Paseo de Colón going from the Gobierno Militar, located at the end of La Rambla, to the Post Office building.

9. A sugar plantation situated in San José de las Lajas, to the southwest of Jaruco and west of Aguacate.

10. Conangla's translation of the original "Dintre la nau del temple," p. 39.

11. [Dwellings attributed, like the word itself, to the Taino, the original settlers of Cuba. The houses were constructed of wood, palm fronds, and mud.]

12. This is a translation by Conangla of the original "La missa roja," p. 50. The complete poem was published in the magazine *Joventut* on May 5, 1904 (vol. V, no. 221, p. 292). It cites the date of 1897 in Aguacate and mentions expressly that it belongs to the book in press, *Elegía de la guerra*.

13. [By the time Josep Conangla entered Las Ánimas hospital in Havana, it was already an important site for research on the etiology of yellow fever and its treatment. It was a Cuban often in association with other doctors at Las Ánimas, Carlos J. Finlay, who correctly identified the mosquito (*Aedes aegypti*) as the vector of yellow fever in 1881. His discovery was confirmed in 1900.]

14. Municipal limit of the judicial and fiscal district of Guanabacoa in Havana Province.

15. Dock in the port of Havana, regular place for arriving Spanish ships and, above all, the one identified with the repatriation of troops after the 1898 disaster. See the novel by César Leante, *Muelle de Caballería* (La Habana: UNEAC, 1973).

16. A plain that includes the municipal limit of Jaruco and the greater part of

the western part of Aguacate. A neighborhood within the municipal limit of Jaruco also bears this name.

17. Conangla's translation of the original titled "L'incendi," pp. 42–44. It was not an isolated incident, but rather a constant pattern in the war, intimately related to the politics of the reconcentration, which Weyler himself recognized as the cause of the frequent fires: "Who set the fires? Were they Spanish soldiers? I deny it . . . the insurrectionists were the arsonists, and this caused the reconcentration and the misery . . . when the insurrectionists invaded those towns that they set on fire, the families who resided in them had to flee" (*Diario de las Sesiones del Senado*, May 1, 1898).

Chapter 3

1. A lake in the district of Bauta, in Havana Province.

2. Antonio Maceo Grajales (1845–1896). A mulatto general (hence his title the "Bronze Titan"), who participated in the wars of independence and became famous for his valor and daring actions. He joined the forces for independence in the Ten Years War in which he defeated the Spanish military on numerous occasions, thereby winning the admiration of his adversaries and the discontent of Cuban conservative elements who feared that he would try to found a republic on the Haitian model, governed by negroes. After the *Paz de Zanjón*, he did not lay aside his plans for independence, for he tried to enlist funds and support in New York, but he abandoned his attempts and moved to Costa Rica in 1893, whence José Martí invited him to participate in the new struggle. On December 7, 1896, he fell in combat at Punta Brava, before a column under the command of Commander Cirujeda, after having proceeded to the invasion of the western part of the island.

3. The son of Máximo Gómez, born in the flat scrublands of La Reforma. He died (apparently by his own hand) stretched out over the body of his commander and mentor, Antonio Maceo.

4. María Cristina de Hapsburgo-Lorena (1858–1929). See note 36 in the chapter 1.

5. *Una noche en el bosque* by Apeles Mestres (Barcelona 1854–1936), poet, playwright, and composer. Among his poetic works, *Avant* (1875), *Tradicions catalanes* (1895), and *Montserratines* (1930) stand out, and among his best-known plays, *La nit de Reis* and *La sirena*.

6. Construction of the fortress of San Carlos de la Cabaña, situated next to the canal of the port of Havana, was begun in 1763 after the English conquered Havana.

7. A neighborhood in Havana beside the Almendares River.

Chapter 4

1. All indications are that this is the Catalan journalist Carles Martí i Fernández, who immigrated to Cuba in 1898. He founded *El Comiquito* and *El debate*, wrote for the *Diario de la Marina*, collaborated on the *Revista Bimestre Cubana*, and was the author of a pioneering book on the Catalans in Cuba, *Los catalanes en América: Cuba* (with a prologue by Francesc Cambó) and a monograph titled *Influència d'els catalans en el comerç e industria de Cuba*. He was a special inspector of Public Instruction and secretary of the Asociación de Dependientes de Comercio. He died in 1939. He was the godfather of Conangla's son, Raúl.

2. A street in the center of Havana, parallel to Obispo, that ends in the Plaza de Armas.

3. A street in central Havana named for Alejandro O'Reilly y Casas, a Spanish general (Madrid 1769–1832), commander of rural militias and commander general of the department of the Center of Cuba.

4. A city located between the Almandares and Jaimanitas Rivers in Havana Province, which forms part of the metropolitan area of the capital. Among its most important industries are cement, beer, canned fish and pineapple, construction materials, and rubber products.

5. Today's Avenida Italia.

6. A party that evolved from the *Partido Liberal* founded in 1879.

7. Juana Borrero Pierra (Havana 1877–Key West 1896), writer, author of *Grupo de familia* (1895) and *Rimas* (1895).

8. *Ceiba* is the name of a typical tree of Cuba whose branches and leaves provide dense shade.

9. See the note below on his son Francisco.

10. *The Diario de la Marina* is considered the Cuban presses' most prestigious and important paper. Conservative in its ideology, it was founded in 1844 by Isidoro Araujo de Lira, with capital provided by Ramón Pintó.

11. Born in Cienfuegos in 1900 and deceased in Mexico in 1962, he was the editor of the *Revista de Avance*, a reporter for the *Diario de la Marina*, a delegate to the *Asamblea Constituyente* that wrote the Constitution of 1940, and a representative in the Chamber.

12. The title takes the name of a sauce based on *ají*, a condiment used by the Indians, and the typical Cuban dish composed of pork, eggs, yucca, and carrots, prepared in a pot or big casserole.

13. Pascual Cervera Topete (San Fernando 1839–Puerto Real 1909) was a prestigious naval officer and Minister of the Navy under Sagasta in 1892. With the rank of Rear Admiral, he was in command of the Spanish squadron in the Atlantic during the war with the United States. His fleet was defeated in Santiago de Cuba by the squadron commanded by Admiral Sampson. Taken prisoner and repatriated to Spain, he was judged by a military tribunal, which did not declare him culpable for the naval disaster.

14. Julián del Casal y de la Lastre (Havana 1863–1893) was a Cuban poet whose father was Basque and his mother Cuban. Educated in the Jesuit school in Belén, he collaborated on several Havana magazines such as *La Habana elegante*, *Fígaro*, and *El País* under different pseudonyms. A notable figure in the modernist movement together with figures such as Rubén Darío, he published *Hojas al viento* (1890) and *Nieve* (1892), among other books.

15. Carlos Pío Ulirbach (or Uhrbach) y Campuzano (Matanzas 1822–1897), a colonel in the 1895 war. With his brother Federico, he published books of poetry titled *Gemelas* (1893) and *Oro* (1907).

16. Pedro Antonio de Alarcón (Guadix 1833–Madrid 1891) was a very well known journalist for his *Diario de un testigo de la Guerra de África* (1859) and *De Madrid a Nápoles* (1861). Among his historical narratives, *La Alpujarra* (1874) stands out. As a novelist, he is most known for *El final de Norma* (1855), and above all, for his short narrative *El Sombrero de tres picos* (1874).

17. Havana, 1882, a weekly autonomist paper.

18. He was also the director of *El Hogar*.

19. Havana, 1885, a sports and literary weekly.

20. Havana, 1883, a literary and family-oriented paper.

21. A street in the center of Havana, probably named for Julián de Zulueta, an important businessman of Basque origin.

22. Situated between Old Havana and Central Havana, between the Paseo del Prado (Martí) and Agramonte, there is a statue of José Martí in its center, the work of Juan Villalta de Saavedra.

23. The Centro Asturiano de la Habana was founded in 1886 and was, together with the Centro Gallego, the most important in Cuba. In 1895, it already counted 6,800 members.

24. Constructed between 1774 and 1779, it is situated next to the Calzada de Zapata.

25. Derived from *ñaño*, the name given to an individual who belongs to a secret society composed of blacks. It is also applied to the practitioners of Abakuá, one of the Afro-Cuban religions and to the language used during their rituals.

26. [The volunteers of commerce were so called because they collected their salaries from commercial enterprises. In the Ten Years War, Weyler was asked by commercial interests in Havana to create a battalion of volunteers. Nearly all were paid by commercial enterprises. From the outset, the volunteers were hard to discipline. No documentation was required of them when they joined. Apparently, Conangla refers to this body of volunteers as "that fatal militia" ("*aquella milicia funesta*") because of its illiberal political orientation. From "Milicianos de Valmaseda," www.mgar.net/cuba/cuba_68.htm. Accessed January 4, 2015.]

27. An enterprise in Havana, property of Narcís Gelats i Durell (Lloret de Mar 1846–Havana 1926), founder of the Banco Gelats.

28. An Asturian writer, resident in Argentina, author of diverse works, among them *Cosas del otro mundo* (1889). See below Conangla's note on her true personality.

29. An organ supporting those in favor of the continuation of the colonial regime. Its most outstanding directors were José de Armas y Cárdenas and Paco Díaz.

30. Antonio Cánovas del Castillo (Málaga 1828–Santa Águeda, Guipúzcoa, 1897). After his father died when he was fifteen years old, he moved to Madrid, where he studied law while he also made a name for himself in journalism and published historical novels such as *La campana de Huesca* (1851), and the *Historia de la decadencia de España* (1854). A militant in the Unión Liberal Party, he was Minister of the Interior with Mon in 1864 and Overseas Territories with O'Donnell (1865–1866). During the Restoration, as the leader of the Liberal-Conservative Party, he shared power with the liberal Sagasta in what has been termed the "pacific turn." In his frequent withdrawals from the task of governing, he devoted himself to historical research. Among his works, *Estudios del reinado de Felipe IV* (1888–1889) stands out and his directorship of a *Historia general de España*, published by the Academy of History. During the Cuban War, he replaced the moderate Martínez Campos with the harsh Valeriano Weyler, but he was not a witness to the Disaster, because he was shot by an anarchist named Angiolillo while he was vacationing in the seaside town of Santa Águeda.

31. Miguel Angiolillo (1872–1897), Italian anarchist. Tried and condemned to death, he was executed in Vergara. Apart from the ideological convictions that led him to carry out his attack, it seems that he was in contact with Cuban insurrectionists.

32. Práxedes Mateo Sagasta (Torrecilla en Cameros 1825–Madrid 1903). An engineer, he began his political career as leader of the *Partido Progresista* in Zamora and president of the Junta Revolucionaria in 1854. A deputy to the Cortes Constituyentes in the same year, he directed the newspaper *La Iberia*. In the so-called long parliament (1858–1863), he became famous for his oratory. He participated in the uprising of San Gil (1866) and had to go into exile in France. When the revolution of 1868 took place, he became Minister of Interior in the provisional government, which he exchanged for Minister of State in 1870, and returned that same year to Minister of Interior. He participated in the coalition government of Amadeo I, which was integrated into the *Partido Radical*, and later founded his own *Partido Constitucional*. He presided over his first government in 1871 and won the elections the following year, but a financial scandal obliged him to resign. He returned to power in the interim period after the coup of Pavía and later founded the *Partido Liberal Dinástico* (or "fusionista"). He became president of the government again from 1881 to 1883, and during the regency of María Cristina, he shared power with Cánovas in the "pacific turn." When Cánovas was assassinated, Sagata assumed power at the worst moment of the Cuban War, and resigned the year after the Disaster. He occupied the presidency for the last time in 1901.

33. William McKinley (Niles, Ohio, 1843–Buffalo 1901) was elected as deputy to Congress by the Republican Party (1877–1890). Defeated in his first attempt to become governor of his state in 1890, he won the following year and was reelected in 1893. In 1897 he was elected president of the United States. Inclined to the financial policies of the gold standard and protective tariffs, he initiated the international expansion of the United States with the annexation of Hawaii (1897–1898). After the explosion of the *Maine* in Havana, he decided to intervene in the Spanish-Cuban conflict, with the resulting occupations of Cuba, Puerto Rico, Guam, and the Philippines. He was assassinated by the anarchist L. Czolgosz.

34. Ramón Blanco y Erenas, Marqués de Peña Plata (San Sebastián 1833–Madrid 1906), was Captain-General of Cuba when the United States intervened. He had replaced Weyler near the time of the approval of the decree of autonomy in 1897, and he tried to be conciliatory toward the Cuban insurrectionists. It was not the first time that he was in Cuba since he had been posted there in 1879, and he had put an end to the "Guerra Chiquita" that followed the *Paz de Zanjón* (1878). He was also Captain-General of the Philippines and took part in the military campaign of Santo Domingo in 1861.

35. Segismundo Moret (Cádiz 1838–Madrid 1913). Professor of Public Finance at twenty years of age, he favored free trade because of his connections in England. He was a deputy to Parliament and writer of the Constitution of 1869. He was Overseas Minister under Prim, and later ambassador in London. He founded the *Partido Democrático-Monárquico*, which later fused with Sagasta's *Partido Liberal*, in whose governments he was Minister of State, Public Works and Transport, Interior, and Overseas Possessions when the United States intervened in Cuba. After the war, he was again Minister of Interior (1901 and 1902), and in 1905, he was charged with forming a new government, but the attempt against the life of Alfonso XIII in Morral in 1906 obliged him to resign. He returned to power in 1906, but a censure vote led to his resignation again within forty-eight hours. He had a third opportunity in 1909 after the fall of Maura.

36. Difficult to identify. Although it is unlikely, he may have been a member of

the family of Bartolomé Massó (or Masó) (1830–1907), president of the Chamber of Representatives formed by adherents to Cuban independence in the period from 1895 to 1898, and of the "Republic of Cuba" (1897–1898).

37. This cabinet was a coalition of autonomists and reformers. Eduardo Dolz (1853–1923) was Secretary of Public Works and Communications; Antonio Govin (1849–1915), Secretary of the Interior and Justice; Rafael Montoro (1852–1933), Secretary of Finance; Laureano Rodríguez, Secretary of Agriculture, Industry and Commerce; and Francisco Zayas, Secretary of Public Education.

38. Havana, 1898, a political, polemical weekly, directed by Ricardo Arnautó.

39. Fitzhugh Lee (1834–1905), Consul-General of the United States in Havana. He was the nephew of Robert E. Lee, General of the Confederacy during the North American Civil War, a conflict in which Fitzhugh distinguished himself in the cavalry and was made major general. Later he was governor of Virginia. Cleveland appointed him to the difficult post in Havana. Not very conversant with the reality of the situation in Cuba, he stood out for his support of United States intervention in the war.

Chapter 5

1. A battleship in the United States war fleet. Constructed in 1890 with a displacement of 6,682 tons. It formed part of the North Atlantic squadron, but on October 8, 1897, it received the order to proceed to a port in South Carolina. On December 6, it docked in Key West following the recommendation of North American consular authorities in Cuba that there would be ships in Florida ready for action. On January 5, it sailed for Havana under the command of Captain Charles D. Sigbee.

2. Enrique Dupuy de Lôme (1851–1904). A Spanish diplomat. Minister in Washington from 1892 until the war broke out.

3. José Canalejas Méndez (El Ferrol 1854–Madrid 1912), Minister of Public Works, Grace and Justice in Sagasta's government, who offered him the post of Finance. When the plan for autonomy for Cuba was announced, he broke with the liberal leader.

4. The incident took place at 9:40 p.m. on the night of Tuesday, February 15, and 266 men perished out of a crew of 354.

5. In reality, the *Maine* was in the bay less than a month. It had been anchored to a buoy since January 25.

6. Built in 1884 by the architect Antonio Mayo, it owed its name to General Miguel Tacón. It was the property of the Compañía Anónima del Liceo de La Habana and later on it became part of the headquarters of the Centro Gallego. After the triumph of the Castro revolution, it was renamed the García Lorca Theater.

7. Situated where the Paseo del Prado (today Martí) and San José converge in Old Havana.

8. Constructed in 1884, it owed its name to its founder and owner, Ricardo Irijoa. Early in its history, it was dedicated to representations of zarzuelas and vaudeville shows, and as the venue for public meetings of the *Partido Autonomista*. In 1899, it changed its name to Eden Garden, later it was the seat of the Convención Constituyente, and today it is called the José Martí.

9. A central street in Havana, parallel to the *Paseo del Prado*. Eventually the of-

fices of the Sociedad de Beneficencia de Naturales de Cataluña would be situated in a three-story building.

10. See note 1 of this chapter. According to other North American sources, the explosion took place at 9:40 p.m.

11. Spanish authorities maintained the thesis that the ship sank because of an internal explosion; the North Americans insisted that the damage was caused by external causes, possibly a mine. Some people ventured the thesis that the attack was caused by Cuban insurrectionists, or even that it was an action taken by the United States to accelerate its entry into the war. Since it is impossible to sum up the diverse opinions and sources for this serious incident, it is recommended that the reader consult, among others, the books of the following authors mentioned in the bibliography: Bradford, Blow, Chidsey, Companys, Foner, Friedel, Jones, O'Toole, and Rickover.

12. See especially the books by Companys and Rickover.

13. The Castillo de la Real Fuerza was one of the most important buildings in the Spanish colony, located on the southwestern shore of the canal leading to the port of Havana. It was used by the North American occupation forces, remodeled in 1936 as a national library (until the library was moved in 1957 to the new building in the Plaza Cívica). At present it is a historical museum.

14. This term refers to the post of Colonial Intendant.

15. Stewart Woodford (1835–1913). Minister of the United States in Madrid from 1897 to the outbreak of war.

16. Note by Conangla: "The readers of this *Memoir* who may wish to know or recall more broadly the patriotic terms in which Pi i Margall couched his written and lecture campaigns in favor of an authentic autonomy first, followed later by absolute independence for the Cuban people, can find those unforgettable campaigns presented historically and gathered together in their entirety in my voluminous volume *Cuba y Pi i Margall*, published in 1947 in Havana by the Editorial Lex, with a preamble by the celebrated Cuban intellectual Dr. Enrique J. Varona."

17. For a review of all these details, the books of Companys, Offner, Portell-Vilá, Robles, Serrano, and Trask are recommended.

18. Máximo Gómez Báez (Bani 1836–Havana 1905). A Dominican, he went to Cuba as commander of the Dominican reserve in Santiago de Cuba (1865). He was retired when he joined the Cuban insurrection in 1865 and became head of operations in Oriente Province. In a confrontation with civilians, Céspedes temporarily relieved him of his command. He won decisive victories in Júcaro, Sacra, Paloseco, and Guásimas. When the *Paz de Zanjón* was signed, he had to go into exile, and in collaboration with Martí and Maceo after 1895, he prepared diverse actions—some direct war actions and others involving infiltration. With independence, he did not accept any position and supported the presidency of Estrada Palma.

19. Tomás Estrada Palma (Bayamo 1835–Santiago de Cuba 1908) studied in Havana and Sevilla. When the Ten Years War began, he joined the insurgents and was named "president of the Republic in arms." He was taken prisoner and locked up first in the Castillo del Morro and later deported to Figueres, where he was imprisoned until the *Paz de Zanjón* was signed (1878). Exiled in Paris, Honduras, and New York, he joined José Martí's *Partido Revolucionario*, and when war broke out in 1895, he became the delegate of the insurgents in New York. After independence, he was elected president of the Republic for the term 1902–1906. He fulfilled his man-

date honorably, but accepted the pledge or mortgage imposed by the North Americans through the Platt Amendment (hence the label "Plattista Republic") and the ceding of the naval base in Guantánamo. But when he was fraudulently reelected against José Miguel Gómez in 1906 and experienced social unrest, he solicited more direct intervention on the part of the United States. Roosevelt's representative, Taft, was proclaimed governor and Estrada Palma resigned.

20. Born in Cárdenas, a prestigious historian (his *Historia de Cuba* is especially fundamental), he belonged to a family with Catalan roots. His brothers include Alejandro, a writer, and Juan, founder of the Club Deportivo of Cárdenas, a famous cyclist and basketball champion in Cuba.

21. Nelson Miles (1839–1925), Commander in Chief of the Armed Forces of the United States during the war with Spain.

22. The Castillo de los Tres Reyes del Morro, one of the biggest fortresses in the Caribbean, constructed in 1610 according to a design by the Italian architect, Bautista Antonelli. It dominates the entire bay, the port, and the city of Havana. The lighthouse called El Morro is located at its point.

23. *The Iowa* and the *Indiana* also participated in the blockade of Santiago de Cuba and in the destruction of Cervera's squadron.

24. William T. Sampson (Palmyra, New York 1840–Washington 1902), an admiral, had participated in the War of Secession and he was the head of the department of Naval Artillery (1893–1897). As commander of the United States squadron in the Cuban War, he destroyed Admiral Cervera's squadron, brought about the surrender of the city of Santiago de Cuba, and accepted the surrender of the Spanish troops.

25. A beautiful central boulevard in Havana, now called the Paseo Martí.

26. The Castillo de San Salvador de la Punta, built at the end of the sixteenth century after a plan by Bautista Antonelli. It is situated on the shore opposite El Morro.

27. Caibarién is a municipality in the province of Las Villas (today Santa Clara). An important fishing center, its economy is concentrated on sugar and cattle.

28. Nuevitas is a municipality founded in 1837, situated in the province of Camagüey between the Máximo and Cabreras Rivers, on the northern coast of Cuba in the Bay of Nuevitas. Its economy is centered on cattle, sugar, cement, and shipyards.

29. A reference to Pinar del Río, the westernmost province in Cuba.

30. An important city and port located on the northern coast of Cuba. Its economy is based on sugar cane, tobacco, cattle, fishing, quarries, and the asphalt industry. The city became famous in 1980 when more than 120,000 Cubans left from there, heading for the coasts of Florida in a dramatic exodus that began when a group asked for asylum in the Peruvian embassy in Havana and its example was followed by thousands more. The government reacted by inviting everyone who wanted to leave to do so through the port of Mariel in vessels sent from the United States. Since then, relations between Cuba and the United States have been subject to the threat of a new maritime bridge. Those who immigrated in this way are known as *marielitos*.

31. A reference to the Yumurí River that flows into the city of Matanzas, capital of the province of the same name.

32. Cárdenas is the name of a municipality in the province of Matanzas, situ-

ated on the bay of the same name. Sugar cane, cattle, light machinery, and leather goods constitute the axis of its economy together with tourism at its complex on the beach of Varadero.

33. Santiago de Cuba is the second city of Cuba. Founded by Diego de Velázquez in 1514 and the first capital of Cuba, it is situated on its important bay. At the end of the war, it had more than 45,000 inhabitants. Among its most important historical events were the naval battle of July 3, 1898, which ended the war, and the attack on the Moncada barracks by a group commanded by Fidel Castro on July 26, 1953.

34. See, among others, the books of Alger, Allendesalazar, Bradford, Carter, Chidsey, Feuer, Freidel, Keller, and Portell Vilá.

35. William Rufus Shafter (Galesburg, Michigan 1835–1906), general in the United States Army, commander of troops in Cuba. He disembarked in Daiquiri and seized Santiago de Cuba.

36. Calixto García Iñiguez (1839–1898). Along with Maceo and Máximo Gómez, he was one of the principal military figures in the Cuban insurrections. Commander of the liberation forces in Oriente Province when the United States intervened, he was denied the honor of parading with his troops in Santiago de Cuba after the Spanish surrender.

37. Regla (1856–Havana 1920), lawyer, professor of history, member of the executive committee of the *Partido Autonomista*, deputy to Parliament, and governor of Havana.

38. Havana, 1886, a political and mercantile daily paper.

39. Trotxa would seem to be a Basque or Catalan variant of *trocha* ["trench"], but it could refer to a property of Valentín Trotcha, founder of the Catalan association, the Colla de Sant Mus, in 1887.

40. The *Grito de Yara* of October 10, 1868, began the Ten Years War. This proclamation of independence made by Carlos Manuel de Céspedes was issued from La Demajagua, his plantation near Yara, a town in Oriente Province.

41. José Julián Martí Pérez (Havana 1853–Dos Ríos 1895). The son of Spaniards, he is known as the apostle of Cuban independence. Recognized as one of the great poets and thinkers of America, his life transpired in a series of exiles in Guatemala, New York, Mexico, and Paris, and prison sentences in Cuba and Spain. At the beginning of the definitive war of independence, precisely in the first action of that war, after disembarking in Cuba, he fell in combat.

42. Jules Cambon was the French ambassador in Washington and he assumed the charge of representing Spain after the rupture of diplomatic relations.

Chapter 6

1. Mazantini was also a lawyer. Outside the bullring he had the reputation of being elegant, and he dressed according to the latest fashion.

2. The Calzada de Ayestarán owes its name to Joaquín Ayestarán, of Basque origin, who was an important businessman in the nineteenth century. Luis Ayestarán Moliner (Havana 1846–1870) was a Cuban revolutionary, member of the *Asamblea Constituyente* (1869), who was taken prisoner and tried in the Castillo del Príncipe in 1870.

3. He belonged to the family of Eugenio Sánchez y Fuentes. Born in Barcelona in 1826, he was the director of the *Diario de Barcelona*, and later president of the *Audiencia* [court, tribunal] of Havana in 1867.

4. That project, however, was limited to notes that Conangla had prepared. There is no evidence of a written text.

5. Or Casa Blanca, a maritime neighborhood of Havana, at the foot of the heights of La Cabaña.

6. San Carlos de La Cabaña, the biggest fortress in Cuba, which owes its name to Carlos III. It was built in 1763 according to the design of M. de Vallière and Ricard de Targale.

7. Patricio de Satrústegui was one of the agents of the enterprise Antonio López y Compañía, predecessor of the *Transatlántica*. See Chapter I for the note referring to this enterprise and its founder.

8. The Rif is a mountainous zone in Morocco, bordering the Mediterranean Sea. The Rif War (1919–1926) to which Conangla refers was an uprising of diverse towns and Berber tribes in the region against the Spanish protectorate in Morocco. In the period following the migration of Conangla to Cuba, the conflict in Morocco became one of the most important factors that impelled young Spaniards to avoid military service and immigrate to America, especially to Cuba. By 1996, right on the eve of the anniversary commemorating 1898, seventy-five years had passed since the disaster of Annual, a humiliating defeat in which more than 20,000 Spanish soldiers perished. (See in addition to the copious bibliography, the revision in journalistic style of Manuel Leguineche, *Annual: El desastre de España en el Rif*, Madrid: Alfaguara, 1996.)

Appendix

1. Santiago Rusiñol i Prats (Barcelona 1861–Aranjuez 1931). Catalan painter and playwright. In 1887, he moved to Paris, where in addition to painting, he wrote articles for Barcelona dailies. In 1894, he inaugurated his house-museum in Sitges, the "Cau Ferrat," and there he founded the "festas modernistas," and in Barcelona the group of "Els quatre gats" ("The Four Cats").

2. Havana, 1887. A weekly paper, the organ of the colony of inhabitants from *La Montaña* (the region around Santander).

3. José María de Pereda (Santander 1833–1915). Known for his works focusing on customs and regional life.

4. Narcís Oller i Moraga (Valls 1846–Barcelona 1930). Novelist, considered the father of the modern Catalan novel. His best-known work is *La febre d'or*.

5. Ángel Guimerà i Jorge (Santa Cruz de Tenerife 1845–Barcelona 1924). Catalan poet and playwright, author of *Terra Baixa* and *Mar i cel*.

6. Josep Feliu Codina (Barcelona 1845–Madrid 1879). Playwright, novelist, and journalist.

7. Narciso Sáenz Doez Serra (Madrid 1830–1877). Poet and playwright.

8. Havana, 1895. A newspaper promoting Catalan nationalism.

Selected Bibliography

War of 1895–1898

Aguilar, Luis E. *Prologue to Revolution*. Ithaca: Cornell University Press, 1972.

Alger, Russell Alexander. *The Spanish-American War*. New York: Harper, 1901.

Allendesalazar, José Manuel. *El 98 de los Americanos*. Madrid: Cuadernos para el diálogo, 1974.

Azcárate, Pablo. *La guerra del 98*. Madrid: Alianza, 1968.

Bachrach, Deborah. *The Spanish-American War*. San Diego: Lucent Books, 1991.

Balfour, Sebastian. *The End of the Spanish Empire, 1898–1923*. Oxford: Clarendon Press; New York: Oxford University Press, 1997.

Beck, Henry Houghton. *Cuba's Fight for Freedom and the War with Spain*. Philadelphia: Globe Bible Publishing Co., 1898.

Beede, Benjamin R. *Intervention and Countersurgency: An Annotated Bibliography of the Small Wars of the United States, 1898–1984*. New York: Garland Publishers, 1985.

———. *Military and Strategic Policy: An Annotated Bibliography*. New York: Greenwood Press, 1990.

Benjamin, Jules R. *The United States and Cuba: Hegemony and Dependent Development, 1880–1934*. Pittsburgh: University of Pittsburgh Press, 1977.

———. *The United States and the Origins of the Cuban Revolution: An Empire of Liberty in an Age of National Liberation*. Princeton: Princeton University Press, 1990.

Benton, E. J. *International Law and the Diplomacy of the Spanish American War*. Baltimore: Johns Hopkins University, 1908; New York: Gordon Press, 1997.

Blow, Michael. *A Ship to Remember: The Maine and the Spanish-American War*. New York: Morrow, 1992.

Bradford, James C. (ed.). *Crucible of Empire: The Spanish-American War and Its Aftermath*. Annapolis, MD: Naval Institute Press, 1993.

Carter, Alden R. *The Spanish-American War. Imperial Ambitions*. New York: Franklin Watts Inc., 1993.

Cashin, Herschel V. *Under Fire with the Tenth U.S. Cavalry*. Niwot, CO: University Press of Colorado, 1993.

Cervera y Topete, Pascual. *Escuadra de operaciones de las Antillas*. Madrid: Editorial Naval, 1986.

Chadwick, French Ensor. *The Relations of the United States and Spain: The Spanish-American War*. New York: Russell & Russell, 1968.

Chapman, Charles E. *A History of the Cuban Republic*. New York: Macmillan, 1927.

Chidsey, Donald Barr. *The Spanish-American War*. New York: Crown Publishers, 1971; *La guerra hispano-americana. 1896–1898*. Barcelona: Grijalbo, 1973.

Ciges Aparcio, M. *Del cuartel y de la guerra*. Madrid: Imprenta de Bernardo Rodríguez, n.d.; Alicante: Instituto de Estudios Gil-Albert, 1986.

Collazo, Enrique. *Los americanos en Cuba*. La Habana: Editorial de Ciencias Sociales, Instituto Cubano del Libro, 1972.

Companys Monclús, Julián. *De la explosión del Maine a la ruptura de relaciones dipomáticas entre Estados Unidos y España*. Lleida: Universitat de Lleida, 1989.

Corwin, Arthur. *Spain and the Abolition of Slavery in Cuba, 1817–1885*. Austin: University of Texas Press, 1967.

Cosmas, Graham A. *An Army for Empire: The United States Army in the Spanish-American War*. Shippenburg, PA: White Mane Publishing, 1994.

Crane, Stephen. *The War Dispatches of Stephen Crane*. Edited by R. W. Stallman and E. R. Hagemann. New York: New York University Press, 1964.

De Quesada, Gonzalo, and Henry Davenport Northrop. *War in Cuba or the Struggle for Freedom*. New York: Liberty Publishing, 1896.

Díaz-Plaja, Fernando. *1898*. Madrid: Editora Nacional, 1976.

El Figaro. "La catástrophe del *Maine*: Relación circunstanciada de la terrible explosión ocurrida a bordo del acorazado nortamericano Maine en la noche del 15 de febrero de 1898." La Habana, 1898.

Erice, Francisco. "Patriotismo burgués y patriotismo popular: Los asturianos ante la guerra de Cuba (1895–1898)," in Jorge Uría, *Asturias y Cuba en torno al 98: Sociedad, Economía, Política y Cultura en la crisis de entresiglos*. Barcelona: Labor, 1996, pp. 141–65.

Estévez y Romero, Luis. *Desde el Zanjón hasta Baire*. La Habana: Editorial de Ciencias Sociales, 1974.

Feliciangeli, Alfredo. *La guerra ispano-americana (1898)*. Roma: E. Voghera, 1898.

Fernández, Alfredo Antonio. *La última frontera*. La Habana: Editorial Letras Cubanas, 1985.

Fernández Almagro, Melchor. "Reacción popular ante el desastre," *Arbor*, 1948. A special number dedicated to the fiftieth anniversary of the war in 1898.

Feuer, A. B. *The Santiago Campaign of 1898: A Soldier's View of the Spanish-American War of 1898*. Westport, CT: Praeger, 1993.

———. *The Spanish-American War at Sea: Naval Action in the Atlantic*. Westport, CT: Praeger, 1995.

Flack, Horace E. *Spanish American Diplomatic Relations Preceding the War of 1898*. Baltimore: Johns Hopkins University, 1906.

Foner, Philip S. *Antonio Maceo: The Bronze Titan of Cuba's Struggle for Independence*. New York: Monthly Review Press, 1977.

———. *A History of Cuba and Its Relations with the United States*. New York: International Publishers, Inc., 1962.

———. *The Spanish-Cuban-American War and the Birth of American Imperialism, 1895–1902*. New York: Monthly Review Press, 1972; *La guerra hispano-cubano-norteamericana y el nacimiento del imperialismo norteamericano*. Madrid: Akal, 1972.

Franco, José Luciano. *Antonio Maceo*. La Habana: Editorial de Ciencias Sociales, 1989.

Francos Rodríguez, José. *El año de la derrota*. Madrid: Compañía Ibero-Americana, 1930.

Freidel, Frank. *The Splendid Little War.* Boston: Little, Brown & Co., 1958.
Galindo Herrero, Santiago. *El 98 de los que fueron a la guerra.* Madrid: Editora Nacional, 1952.
García, Carmen. "Nota en torno al nacionalismo historiográfico cubano: Algunos enfoques sobre la intervención norteamericana en la guerra de Independencia de Cuba," in Jorge Uría, *Asturias y Cuba en torno al 98: Sociedad, economía, política y cultura en la crisis de entresiglos.* Barcelona: Labor, 1996, pp. 197–220.
García Barrón, Carlos. *Cancionero del 98.* Madrid: Cuadernos para el Diálogo, 1974.
García del Pino, César. *La acción naval de Santiago de Cuba.* La Habana: Editorial de Ciencias Sociales, 1988.
García Escudero, José María. "El Parlamento ante el desastre," *Arbor*, 1948. Special number.
Gómez Núñez, Severo. *La guerra hispano-americana.* Madrid: Imprenta de Cuerpo de Artillería, 1901.
Gould, Lewis L. *The Presidency of William McKinley.* Lawrence: Regents Press of Kansas, 1980.
———. *Reform and Regulation: American Politics from Roosevelt to Wilson.* New York: Knopf/Random House, 1986.
———. *The Spanish-American War and President McKinley.* Lawrence: University of Kansas, 1982.
Guerra y Sánchez, Ramiro. *La expansión territorial de los Estados Unidos a expensas de España y de los países hispanoamericanos.* La Habana: Cultural, 1935; La Habana: Editorial Ciencias Sociales, 1975.
———, et al. *A History of the Cuban Nation.* 10 vols. La Habana: Historia de la Nación Cubana, 1958.
Hernández, José M. *Cuba and the United States: Intervention and Militarism, 1868–1933.* Austin: University of Texas Press, 1993.
———. *The Role of Military in the Making of the Cuban Republic.* Washington, DC: Georgetown University, 1976.
Jacobsen, Hermann. *Sketches from the Spanish-American War.* Washington, DC: Government Printing Office, 1899.
Jeffers, H. Paul. *Colonel Roosevelt: Theodore Roosevelt Goes to War, 1897–1898.* New York: John Wiley & Sons, 1996.
Jones, S. D. *A Splendid Little War.* Belmont, CA: Fearon Education, 1989.
Keller, Allan. *The Spanish-American War: A Compact History.* New York: Hawthorn Books, 1969.
Kendall, John Smith. *The Day the Spaniards Surrendered Cuba: An Eyewitness Report.* Roanoke, VA: Shady Acre Private Press, 1963.
Langley, Lester D. *The Banana Men: American Mercenaries and Entrepreneurs in Central America, 1880–1930.* Lexington: University Press of Kentucky, 1995.
———. *The Banana Wars: An Inner History of American Empire, 1900–1934.* Lexington: University Press of Kentucky, 1983.
———. *The Cuban Policy of the United States: A Brief History.* New York: John Wiley & Sons, 1968.
Linderman, Gerald F. *The Mirror of War: American Society and the Spanish-American War.* Ann Arbor: University of Michigan Press, 1974.
Lodge, Henry Cabot. *The War with Spain.* New York: Arno Press, 1970.
Martínez Arango, Felipe. *Cronología crítica de la Guerra Hispano-cubano-americana.*

Cuadernos de Historia Habanera, no. 43 (1950); La Habana: Editorial de Ciencias Sociales Instituto Cubano del Libro, 1973.

Mason, Gregory. *Remember the Maine*. New York: H. Holt and Co., 1939.

McIntosh, Burr William. *The Little I Saw of Cuba*. New York: F. T. Neely, 1899.

Méndez Saavedra, Manuel (compiler). *1898: La Guerra hispanoamericana en caricaturas*. San Juan: Gráfica Metropolitana, 1992.

Mesa, Roberto. "Mitologia del 98." Introduction to Carlos García Barrón. *Cancionero del 98*. Madrid: Cuadernos para el Diálogo, 1974, pp. vii–xvi.

Miley, John David. *In Cuba with Shafter*. New York: Charles Scribner's Sons, 1899.

Ministro de Estado. *Libro rojo. Tratado de Paris: Documentos presentados a las Cortes en la legislatura de 1898 por el Ministro de Estado*. 3 vols. San Juan: Editorial de la Universidad de Puerto Rico, 1988.

Morote, Luis. *La moral de la derrota*. Madrid: Imprenta de G. Juste, 1900.

Musgrave, George Clarke. *Under Three Flags in Cuba, a Personal Account of the Cuban Insurrection and Spanish-American War*. Boston: Little, Brown and Co., 1899.

Naranjo Orovio, Consuelo, Miguel Angel Puig-Samper, and Luis Miguel García Mora, (eds.). *La nación soñada: Cuba, Puerto Rico y Filipinas ante el 98*. Actas del Congreso Internacional celebrado en Aranjuez del 24 al 28 de abril de 1995. Aranjuez, Madrid: Doce Calles, 1996.

Navarro Garcia, Luis. *La independencia de Cuba*. Madrid: Mapfre, 1992.

O'Toole, G. J. *The Spanish War: An American Epic, 1898*. New York: W. W. Norton and Co., 1986.

Offner, John L. *An Unwanted War: The Diplomacy of the United States and Spain over Cuba, 1895–1898*. Chapel Hill: University of North Carolina Press, 1992.

Oliver, Miquel Dels Sants. *La literatura del desastre*. Barcelona: Península, 1973.

Otis, James. *Off Santiago with Sampson*. Boston: D. Estes & Co., 1899.

Pabón y Suárez De Urbina, Jesús. *El 98, Acontecimiento Internacional*. Madrid: Ministerio de Asuntos Exteriores Escuala Diplomática, 1952.

Pérez, Louis A. *Army Politics in Cuba, 1898–1958*. Pittsburgh: University of Pittsburgh Press, 1976.

———. *Cuba: An Annotated Bibliography*. New York: Greenwood Press, 1988.

———. *Cuba and the United States: Ties of Singular Intimacy*. Athens: University of Georgia Press, 1990.

———. *Cuba between Empires, 1878–1902*. Pittsburgh: University of Pittsburgh Press, 1983.

———. *Cuba: between Reform and Revolution*. New York: Oxford University Press, 1995.

———. *Cuba under the Platt Amendment, 1902–1934*. Pittsburgh: University of Pittsburgh Press, 1986.

———. *José Martí in the United States: The Florida Experience*. Tempe: ASU Center for Latin American Studies, Arizona State University, 1995.

———. *The Rise and Fall of Army Preeminence in Cuba, 1898–1958*. Albuquerque: University of New Mexico, 1971.

———. *Slaves, Sugar, and Colonial Society: Travel Accounts of Cuba 1801–1899*. Wilmington, DE: Scholarly Resources, 1992.

Pérez Guzmán, F. "La historiografía de las guerras de independencia en veinticinco años de Revolución." *Revisa de la Biblioteca Nacional José Martí*. La Habana, no. 1 (January–April 1985), pp. 41–61.

Portell Vilá, Herminio. *Historia de Cuba en sus relaciones con los Estados Unidos y España*. La Habana, 1938–1941. 4 vols. Miami: Mnenosyne, 1969.

———. *Historia de la Guerra de Cuba y los Estados Unidos contra España. Cuadernos de Historia Habanera*, no. 41, La Habana, 1941.

Portuondo del Prado, F. *Historia de Cuba, 1492–1898*. La Habana: Editorial Pueblo y Educación, 1974.

Pratt, Julius. *Expansionism of 1898*. New York: P. Smith, 1964.

Reid, Whitelaw. *Making Peace with Spain: The Diary of Whitelaw Reid, September–December, 1898*. Edited by H. Wayne Morgan. Austin: University of Texas Press, 1965.

Rickover, Hyman George. *How the Battleship Maine was Destroyed*. Annapolis, MD: Naval Institute Press, 1994; *Cómo fue hundido el acorazado Maine*. Madrid: Editorial Naval, 1985.

Risco, Alberto. *La escuadra del almirante Cervera*. Madrid: Jiménez y Molina, 1920.

Robles Muñoz, Cristóbal. *1898: Diplomacia y opinión*. Madrid: Consejo Superior de Investigaciones Científicas, 1991.

Roig de Leuchsenring, Emilio. *Cuba no debe su independencia a los Estados Unidos*. La Habana: Noveno Congreso Nacional de Historia, 1961.

———. *La Guerra Libertadora de los Treinta Años, 1869–1898. Razón de ser de su victoria*. La Habana: Cincuentenario de la República, 1952.

———. *Los Estados Unidos contra Cuba libre*. Santiago de Cuba: Editorial Oriente, 1959.

Roosevelt, Theodore. *The Rough Riders*. New York: Charles Scribner's Sons, 1899.

Rubio, Javier. *La cuestión de Cuba y las relaciones con los Estados Unidos durate el reinado de Alfonso XII: los orígenes del "desastre" de 1898*. Madrid: Biblioteca Diplomática Española, 1995.

Sáiz Cidoncha, Carlos. *Guerrillas en Cuba y otros países de Iberoamérica*. Madrid: Editora Nacional, 1974.

Santaner Mari, Joan. *General Weyler*. Palma de Mallorca: Ajuntament de Palma, 1985.

Serrano, Carlos. *Final del Imperio. España, 1895–1898*. Madrid: Siglo XXI, 1984.

Smith, Joseph. *The Spanish-American War: Conflict in the Caribbean and the Pacific, 1895–1902*. New York: Longman Publishing Group, 1995.

Spears, John Randolph. *Our Navy in the War with Spain*. New York: Charles Scribner's Sons, 1898.

Suchliki, Jaime. *Cuba: From Columbus to Castro*. New York: Charles Scribner's Sons, 1974.

Thomas, Hugh. *Cuba: The Pursuit of Freedom*. New York: Harper & Row, 1971; Barcelona: Grijalbo, 1973.

Trask, David. *The War with Spain in 1898*. New York: Macmillan Co., 1981.

Trelles, Carlos Manuel. *Bibliografía de la segunda guerra de independencia cubana y de la hispano-yankee*. Publicada en la revista ilustrada "Cuba y América." La Habana, 1902.

Truyol, Miguel G. *Batalla naval de Santiago de Cuba: Guerra Hispano-Americana*. Santo Domingo: Editora Corripio, 1986.

Venzon, Anne Cipriano. *The Spanish-American War: An Annotated Bibliography*. New York: Garland, 1990.

Vivian, Thomas Jondrie. *The Fall of Santiago*. New York: Fenno, 1898.

Watterson, Henry. *History of the Spanish-American War: Embracing a Complete Review of Our Relations with Spain*. Hartford, CT: American Publishing Co., 1898.

Weems, John E. *The Fate of the Maine*. College Station: Texas A&M, 1992.

Weyler, Valeriano. *Mi mando en Cuba (10 febrero 1869 a 31 octubre 1897)*. Madrid, n.d., 5 vols.

Weyler y López de Puga, Valeriano. *En el archivo de mi abuelo*. Madrid: Editorial Gráficas, 1946.

White, Trumbull. *Pictorial History of Our War with Spain for Cuba's Freedom*. Chicago: J. S. Ziegler & Co., 1898.

Wilkerson, Marcus M. *Public Opinion and the Spanish-American War: A Study in War Propaganda*. New York: Russell, 1967.

Wisan, Joseph E. *The Cuban Crisis as Reflected in the New York Press*. New York: Columbia University Press, 1934.

Young, James Rankin. *Reminiscences and Thrilling Stories of the War by Returned Heroes: Containing Vivid Accounts of Personal Experiences by Officers and Men*. Chicago: J. S. Ziegler & Co., 1899.

Relations between Spain and Cuba

Álvarez Acevedo, José María. *La colonia española en la economía cubana*. La Habana: Ucar, 1936.

Bahamonde, Ángel, and José Gregorio Cayuela Fernández. *Hacer la Américas. Las élites coloniales españolas en el siglo XX*. Madrid: Alianza, 1992.

Carrera y Justiz, Francisco. *El municipio y los extranjeros: Los españoles en Cuba*. La Habana: La Moderna Poesia, 1904.

Cayuela Fernández, José Gregorio. *Bahía de Ultramar: España y Cuba en el siglo XIX. El control de las relaciones coloniales*. Madrid: Siglo XXI, 1993.

Cimadevilla Alonso, Francisco. *La labor de los españoles en Cuba*. Madrid: Imprenta Juan Pueyo, 1921.

de la Iglesia, Álvaro. *Cosas de antaño*. La Habana: Imprenta de Maza y Cía., 1917.

———. *Tradiciones cubanas*. La Habana: Instituto del Libro, 1969.

Díaz Ayala, Cristóbal. *Música cubana del Areyto a la Nueva Trova*. San Juan, Puerto Rico: Cubanacán, 1981.

Dihigo, Juan Miguel. *Pi y Margall y la Revolución Cubana*. La Habana: El Siglo XX, 1928.

Dollero, Adolfo. *Cultura Cubana*. La Habana: El Siglo XX, 1916.

Eiras Roel, Antonio (ed.). *Emigración española portuguesa a América* (Actas del II Congreso de la Asociación de Demografía Histórica), Vol. 1. Madrid: Instituto de Cultura Juan Gil Albert, April 1990, pp. 9–31.

Estévez y Romero, Luis. *Desde el Zanjón hasta Baire*. La Habana: Ed. Ciencias Sociales, 1974.

Fernández, A. M. *España y Cuba. 1868–1898*. La Habana: Editorial Ciencias Sociales, 1988.

Franco, José Luciano. *Comercio clandestino de esclavos*. La Habana: Editorial de Ciencias Sociales, 1980.

García López, J. R. *Las remesas de los emigrantes españoles en América. Siglos XIX y XX*. Colombres, Asturias: Júcar, 1992.

Hennessy, Alistair. "Spain and Cuba: An Enduring Relationship" in Howard J.

Wiarda (ed.), *The Iberian-Latin American Connection: Implications for the U.S. Foreign Policy*. Boulder, CO: Westview Press; Washington, DC: American Enterprise Institute, 1986, pp. 360–74.

Hernández Sandoica, Elena. *El pensamiento burgués y problemas coloniales en la España de la Restauración*. Madrid: Universidad Complutense, 1982.

Iglesias, Fe. "Características de la inmigración española en Cuba," in Sánchez-Albornoz, Nicolás (ed.), *Españoles hacia América: La emigración en masa, 1830–1930*. Madrid: Alianza, 1988, 1995, pp. 27–297.

Luzón, José Luis. "Cuba, país de inmigración," *Ideas '92*, vol. 1, no. 2, Spring 1988, pp. 73–80.

———. *Economía, población y territorio en Cuba (1899–1983)*. Madrid: Instituto de Cooperación Iberoamericana, 1987.

Macías Hernández, Antonio M. *La migracíon canaria, 1500–1980*. Madrid: Júcar, 1992.

Mainer, J. C. "Un capítulo regeneracionista: el hispanoamericanismo (1892–1923)," in *De la crisis del Antiguo Régimen al franquismo*. Madrid: VII Coloquio de Pau, Edicusa, 1977, pp. 149–203.

Maluquer de Motes, Jordi. *Nacíon e inmigración: Los españoles en Cuba (ss. XIX y XX)*. Madrid: Júcar, 1992.

Márquez Sterling, Carlos. *Historia de la isla de Cuba*. New York: Las Américas, 1963.

Marrero, Leví. *Cuba: Economía y sociedad*. 12 vols. Madrid: Playor, 1980–85.

Martín Montalvo, Casilda, María Rosa Martín de Vega, and María Teresa Solano Sobrado. "El hispanoamericanismo, 1880–1930." *Quinto Centenario*, no. 8 (1985).

Mesa, Roberto. *La idea colonial en España*. Valencia: Fernando Torres, 1976.

Moreno Fraginals, M. R., and J. J. Moreno Masó. *Guerra, migración y muerte: El ejército español en Cuba como vía migratoria*. Colombres, Asturias: Júcar, 1992.

Moreno Fraginals, Manuel. *El ingenio. Complejo económico social cubano del azúcar*. La Habana: Editorial de Ciencias Sociales, 1974, 1986.

Moro Barreñeda, José María. "El servicio militar en Asturias y la guerra de Cuba," in Jorge Uría, *Asturias y Cuba en torno al 98: Sociedad, economía, política y cultura en la crisis de entresiglos*. Barcelona: Labor, 1996, pp. 99–122.

Naranjo Orovio, Consuelo. "El sueño cubano. Una tradición mantenida en el siglo XX," in Antonio Eiras Roel (ed.), *Emigración española y portuguesa a América* (Actas del II Congreso de la Asociación de Demografía Histórica), Vol. 1. Madrid: Instituto de Cultura Juan Gil Albert, April 1990, pp. 117–25.

Ortí, Alfonso. "Regeneracionismo e historiografía: El mito del carácter nacional en la obra de Rafael Altamira," in Armando Alberola (ed.), *Estudios sobre Rafael Altamira*. Alicante: Instituto de Estudios Juan Gil-Albert y Caja de Ahorros Provincial de Alicante, 1987, pp. 275–351.

Ortiz, Fernando. *Contrapunteo cubano del tabaco y el azúcar*. Las Villas: Universidad Central, 1963; *Cuba Counterpoint: Tobacco and Sugar*. New York: Knopf, 1947.

———. *La música afrocubana*. Madrid: Júcar, 1975.

Palazón, Salvador. *Capital humano español y desarrollo económico latinoamericano. Evolución, causas y caracteristicas del flujo migratorio (1882–1990)*. Alicante: Institut de Cultura Juan Gil-Albert, 1995.

———. *Los españoles en América Latina, 1850–1990*. Madrid: Cedeal, 1995

Pardos, Gerardo. *Libro de oro hispano-americano: Cuba*. Vol. I. París-Madrid: Editorial Hispanoamericana, 1917.

Portell Vilá, Herminio. *Nueva historia de la República de Cuba*. Miami: La Moderna Poesía, 1986.

Reverter Delmas, Emilio. *Cuba española: Reseña historíca de la insurrección cubana en 1895*. 6 vols. Barcelona: A. Martin, 1897–1899.

Roy, Joaquín. "Cuba: Des inconnues pour l'avenir." *L'Espagne et l'Amérique Latine, Documentation Française*, París, no. 595 (Nov. 11, 1988), pp. 24–28.

———. "A Cuba Postscript," in *The Ibero-American Space*, Joaquín Roy and Albert Galinsoga (eds.), Miami/Lleida: Iberian Studies Institute/Jean Monnet Chair, 1997, pp. 205–66.

———. *Cuba y España: Percepciones y relaciones*. Madrid: Biblioteca Cubana Contemporánea, 1988.

———. "España, la Unión Europea y Cuba: La evolución de una relación especial a una política de gestos y de presión." Occasional Paper Series, vol. 1, no. 2 (September 1996). Miami: University of Miami, Cuban Studies Association.

———. "España y Cuba: Una relación muy especial." *Afers Internacionals*, no. 31 (1996).

———. "España y Cuba: ¿Una relación *muy* especial?" in Joaquín Roy (ed.), *El espacio iberoamericano*. Barcelona/Miami: Centro de Estudios Internacionales/Instituto de Estudios Ibéricos, University of Miami, 1996, pp. 185–224.

———. "Las relaciones actuales entre Cuba y España." *Política Exterior*, vol. I, no. 3 (Summer 1987), pp. 282–86.

———. "Las relaciones actuales entre Cuba y España" (rev. vers.). *Afers Internacionals*, Barcelona, nos. 12–13 (1988), pp. 5–19.

———. "Las relaciones Madrid–La Habana." *Política Exterior*, vol. II, no. 6 (Spring 1988), pp. 275–79.

———. "Relaciones y percepciones entre España y Cuba: Trasfondo de la 'Crisis de las embajadas.'" *Cuba 1990: Realidad y futuro*, Carlos Robles Piquer (ed.), Santiago de Compostela: Fundación Alfredo Brañas, 1991, pp. 27–47.

———. "Spain and Cuba: A Very Special Relationship?" in *The Ibero-American Space*, Joaquin Roy and Albert Galinsoga (eds.), Miami/Lleida: Iberian Studies Institute/Jean Monnet Chair, 1997, pp. 187–204.

Sánchez-Albornoz, Nicholás (ed.), *Españoles hacia Améрca: La emigración en masa 1830–1930*. Madrid: Alianza, 1988, 1995.

Santa Cruz y Mallen, Xavier de. *Historia de familias cubanas*. 10 vols. Miami: Ed. Universal, 1985.

Tuñon de Lara. *Costa y Unamuno en la crisis de fin de siglo*. Madrid: 1974.

Uría González, Jorge. *Asturias y Cuba en torno al 98: Sociedad, economía, política y cultura en la crisis de entresiglos*. Barcelona: Labor, 1996.

Relations between Catalonia and Cuba

Ardevol, José. *Introducción a Cuba: La música*. La Habana: Instituto del Libro, 1969.

Bau, Calasanz. *Historia de las Escuelas Pías en Cuba*. La Habana: Escuelas Pías, 1957.

Bernades, J. M. *Els catalans a les Indies (1493–1830): Burócrates, clergues, profesionals liberals*. 3 vols. Barcelona: Generalitat de Catalunya, 1991.

Carpentier, Alejo. *La música en Cuba*. México: Fondo de Cultura Económica, 1946.

Castells, Víctor. *Catalans d'América per la indepéndencia*. Barcelona: Pòrtic, 1985.

Centre Catalá. *Memòria de les activitats socials del Centre Catalá*. La Habana: Imprenta Salud, 1926.

Cepeda Adán, J. "José Xifré Casas: El indiano catalán que simboliza la transformación económica," in *Forjadores del Mundo Moderno*. Barcelona, 1950, pp. 327–40.

Codina, Juan Ignacio, J. Ferrer, and M. Gómez. "América com a fugida: Servei militar i emigració ultramarina al Prat al segle XIX," *3as. Jornades d'Estudis Catalano-Americans*. Barcelona: Generalitat de Catalunya, pp. 61–73.

Colla de Sant Mus. *Reglamento*. La Habana: La Universal, 1885.

Comissió Catalana del Cinqué Centenari del Descobriment d'Amèrica. I. Jornades d'Estudis Catalano-Americans. Barcelona: Generalitat de Catalunya/Comissió Catalana del Cinqué Centenari del Descobriment d'Amèrica, 1985.

———. *II. Jornades d'Estudis Catalano-Americans*. Barcelona: Generalitat de Catalunya, 1987.

———. *III. Jornades d'Estudis Catalano-Americans*. Barcelona: Generalitat de Catalunya, 1990.

Chávez Alvarez, Ernesto. *La fiesta catalana: presencia hispánica en la cultura cubana*. La Habana: Editorial de Ciencias Sociales, 1989.

Delgado Ribas, Josep Maria. "Els comerciants catalans en la cursa de les indies durant el segle XVIII," III. *Jornades d'Estudis Catalano-Americans. Barcelona: Generalitat de Catalunya*, 1990, pp. 75–88.

———. "La emigración española a América latina durante la época del comercio libre (1765–1820): El ejemplo catalán." *Boletín Americanista*, 1982, no. 32, pp. 115–37.

Fabregat i Arrufat, Ramón. *Maciá. La seva actuació a l'estranger*. Mèxic: Edicions Catalanes a Mèxic, 1952.

Fradera, Josep María. *Catalunya i Ultramar. Poder i negoci a les colònies espanyoles (1750–1914)*. Barcelona: Museu Marítim-Àmbit, 1995.

———. *Crisi colonial i mercat interior, 1814–1837: Les bases comercials de la indústria moderna*. Tesis doctoral presentada en la Universidad de Barcelona en 1983.

———. "La importància de tenir colònies: El marc històric de la participació catalana en el complex espanyol d'Ultramar," in J. M. Fradera, César Yáñez, and A. García. *Catalunya i Ultramar: Poder i negoci a les colònies espanyoles (1750–1914)*. Barcelona: Museu Marítim-Ambit, 1995, pp. 21–52.

———. "Miquel Biada i l'esclavitud a Cuba." *Fulls del Museo Arxiu de Santa Maria de Mataró*, 1982, p. 15.

———. "La participació catalana en el tráfic d'esclaus, 1789–1845." *Recerques*, no. 16 (1984), pp. 119–34.

Franco, J. L. *El comercio clandestino de esclavos*. La Habana: Editorial de Ciencias Sociales, 1980.

Giralt, J. R. *El progreso catalán en América: Cuba*. Santiago de Chile: Blaye y Giralt, 1927.

Jou i Andreu, D. "Els sitgetans a América: Un intent de valoració cuantitativa." *3ras. Jornades d'Estudis Catalano-Americans*. Barcelona: Generalitat de Catalunya, pp. 109–22.

L'Avenç. Dossier. "Els catalans en el tràfic de negres. Catalunya i Cuba en el segle XIX: El comers d'esclaus," no. 75 (October 1984), pp. 42–72. Articles by Josep María Fradera, J. Rovira Fors, Marius Armengol, Manuel Moreno Fraginals, and Rebecca J. Scott.

Maluquer de Motes, Jordi. "La burgesia catala i l'esclavitud colonial: Modes de producció i pràtica política," *Recerques*, vol. 3 (1974), pp. 83–36.

———. "Los catalanes en América (c. 1760–1868): La mirada de los contemporáneos," *Historia y Sociedad*, vol. III (1990), pp. 9–35.

———. "L'emigració catalana a América durant la primera meitat del segle XIX: Una visió global," *3as Jornades d'Estudis Catalano-Americans*. Barcelona: Generalitat de Catalunya, 1990, pp. 161–70.

———. "La formación del mercado interior en condiciones coloniales: La inmigración y el comercio catalán en las Antillas españolas durante el siglo XIX." *Santiago*, vol. 69 (1988), pp. 89–112.

———. "El problema de la esclavitud y la revolución de 1868," *Hispania*, vol. 117 (1971), pp. 55–75.

Martí, Charles. *Los catalanes en América: Cuba*. La Habana: Hernández, 1920; Barcelona: Minerva, 1921. Preceded by a letter/prologue by Francesc Cambó y de Mario Garcia Kolly.

———. "Influència dels catalans en el comerç i indústria de Cuba." La Habana, 1923.

Martínez Shaw, Carlos. *Cataluña en la carrera de Indias (1680–1756)*. Barcelona: Crítica, 1981.

———. "L' emigració catalana a América (1492–1824). Un balanç provisional." *3as Jornades d'Estudis Catalano-Americans*. Barcelona: Generalitat de Catalunya, 1990, pp. 15–22.

Moreno Fraginals, Manuel. "Cuba al segle XIX. ¿Colònia espanyola?" in Fradera et al., *El comerç entre Catalunya i América, segles XVIII i XIX*. Barcelona: L'Avenç, 1986.

———. "Inmigració lleves i guerres colonials. El cas cubá: 1834–1878." *3as Jornades d'Estudis Catalano-Americans*. Barcelona: Generalitat de Catalunya, 1990, pp. 23–37.

Navarro Serra, Vicente. "El general Juan Puñet Mayench, héroe de la Guerra de Cuba." *Historia y Vida*, 243, año XXI (June 1988), pp. 110–19.

Nova Catalunya. La Publicada en La Habana entre 1908 y 1932, y continuada entre 1942 y 1959. Founded by Claudi Mimó; outstanding directors Josep Murillo (who underwrote it for many years) and Josep Conangla.

Oliva Melgar, José María. *Cataluña y el comercio privilegiado con América en el siglo XVIII: La Real Compañia de Comercio de Barcelona a Indias*. Barcelona: Universidad de Barcelona, 1987.

———. "El fracàs del comerç privilegiat," in Fradera, *El comerç entre Catalunya i Amèrica*, pp. 37–63.

Olivé Serret, Enric, and Teresa Abelló Güell. "Actitud d'anarquistes i catalanistes front a la independéncia de Cuba (1895–1898)." *I. Jornades d'Estudis Catalano-Americans*. Barcelona: Generalitat de Catalunya, 1985, pp. 257–81.

Ramírez, Serafín. *La Habana artística: Apuntes históricos*. La Habana: Imprenta del E. M. de la Capitanía General, 1891.

Rocamora, Joan. *Libro Blanco. Cataluña*. Buenos Aires: Ediciones de la Revista Catalunya, 1956.

Roy, Joaquín. *Catalunya a Cuba*. Barcelona: Editorial Barcino/Fundació Jaume I, 1988.

———. *Catalunya a Cuba*. Barcelona: Barcino, 1991.

———. "Catalunya a Cuba: La Societat de Beneficència de Naturals de Catalunya." *I. Jornades d'Estudis Catalano-Americans*. Barcelona: Generalitat de Catalunya/ Comissó Catalana del Cinque Centenari del Descobriment d'América, 1985, pp. 313–23.

———. "Los catalanes en Cuba. Sus protagonistas y sus instituciones: La Sociedad de Beneficencia de Naturales de Cataluña," *Ideas '92*, 9 (Fall 1991), pp. 73–85.

———. Josep Conangla i Fontanilles, *La Constitució de L'Havana i altres escrits*. Edited by Joaquín Roy. Barcelona: Edicions de la Magrana/Diputació de Barcelona, 1986.

———. "L'origen commercial i geogràfic dels dirigents de la Societat de Beneficència de Naturals de Catalunya de L'Havana." *II. Jornades d'Estudis Catalano-Americans*. Barcelona: Generalitat Catalunya/Comissió Catalana del Cinque Centenari del Descobriment d'América, 1985, pp. 397–420.

———. "Poesia de Josep Conangla sobre la guerra de Cuba." *Revista de Catalunya*, no. 19 (May 1988), pp. 151–63; extended version in *Actes del Colloqui d'estudis Catalans a Nordamérica*. Barcelona: North American Catalan Society/Publicacions de l'Abadia de Montserrat, 1988, pp. 201–8.

———. "Poesia i memòries de Josep Conangla sobre la guerra de Cuba." *III. Jornades d'Estudis Catalano-Americans*. Barcelona: Generalitat de Catalunya, 1990, pp. 197–208.

———. "Poesía y memorias de Josep Conangla i Fontanilles sobre la Guerra de Cuba." *Revista Iberoamericana*, vol. 8, nos. 146–47 (January–June 1989), pp. 129–59.

———. "Present i futur dels centres catalans a Amèrica." *Revista de Catalunya*, no. 17 (March 1988), pp. 79–84.

Sauret, Joan. *L'exili polític català*. Barcelona: Aymà, 1979.

Sociedad de Beneficencia de Naturales de Cataluña. Reglamento. La Habana: Imprenta M. Soler, 1851.

———. *Llibre d'Or*. L'Havana, 1940. Published in honor of the Centenary of the Sociedad. Written by Josep Maria Poblet. There is another version in Castilian.

———. *Libro de Oro, 1941–1990*. Edited by Ernesto Chávez Alvarez. Prologue by Pere Pi Sunyer. Barcelona: Commissió Catalunya-América, 1992.

———. *Memoria*. La Habana, 1954.

Sonesson, Birgit. *Catalanes en las Antillas: Un estudio de casos*. Gijón: Archivo de Indianos, 1995.

"Vida Catalana." Publication founded in 1914, dedicated to the social activities of the Catalan colony in Havana.

Vinymata, Eduard. "Josep Miró i Argenter: De nacionalista catalá a heroi de la independencia de Cuba." *Revista de Catalunya*, vol. 52 (May 1991), pp. 33–43.

Virella i Bloda, Albert. *L'aventura ultramarina de la gent de Vilanova i la Geltrú i la missaga dels Samá*. Vilafranca del Penedés, 1990.

Yáñez Gallardo, César. "Cataluña: Un caso de emigración temprana," in Nicolás Sánchez-Albornoz (ed.), *Españoles hacia América: La emigración en masa, 1830–1930*. Madrid: Alianza, 1988, 1995, pp. 123–42.

———. "La emigración catalana a América : Una visión de largo plazo," in A. Eiras Roel (ed.), *La emigración ultramarina 1492–1914*. Madrid: Tabapress, 1991, pp. 173–88.

———. *Saltar con red: La temprana emigración catalana a América (1830–1870)*. Madrid: Alianza, 1996.

———. *Sortir de casa per anar a casa: Comerç, navegació i estratègies familiars en l'emigració de Sant Feliu a Amèrica en el segle XIX*. Sant Feliu de Guixols, 1992.

Index

www.ingramcontent.com/pod-product-compliance
Lightning Source LLC
LaVergne TN
LVHW050603110926
847619LV00018B/139